KU-415-407

PRINCESS
STEPPING OUT OF
THE SHADOWS

JEAN SASSON

BANTAM BOOKS

TRANSWORLD PUBLISHERS
61–63 Uxbridge Road, London W5 5SA
www.penguin.co.uk

Transworld is part of the Penguin Random House group of companies
whose addresses can be found at global.penguinrandomhouse.com

Penguin
Random House
UK

First published in Great Britain in 2018 by Bantam Press
an imprint of Transworld Publishers
Bantam edition published 2019

Copyright © The Sasson Corporation 2018, 2019

Jean Sasson has asserted her right under the Copyright,
Designs and Patents Act 1988 to be identified as the author of this work.

This book is a work of non-fiction. In some cases names have
been changed to protect the privacy of others.

Every effort has been made to obtain the necessary permissions with
reference to copyright material, both illustrative and quoted. We
apologize for any omissions in this respect and will be pleased to make the
appropriate acknowledgements in any future edition.

A CIP catalogue record for this book
is available from the British Library.

ISBN
9780857504180

Typeset in 10/12.5 pt Sabon by Integra Software Services Pvt. Ltd, Pondicherry
Printed and bound in Great Britain by Clays Ltd, Elcograf S.p.A.

Penguin Random House is committed to a sustainable
future for our business, our readers and our planet. This book
is made from Forest Stewardship Council® certified paper.

1 3 5 7 9 10 8 6 4 2

CUMBRIA LIBRARIES

3 8003 04559 7317

Princess
'Anyone with the slightest interest in human rights will find this

personal story . . .

Betty Mahmoody, bestselling author of *Not Without My Daughter*

Daughters of Arabia
'Women with everything but freedom . . . gripping revelations'
Daily Mail

Desert Royal
'Unforgettable in content, fascinating in detail . . . a
book to move you to tears'
Fay Weldon, author, essayist and playwright

Mayada
'An astonishing read'
Woman's Own

Love in a Torn Land
'A very human look at the struggle of the
Kurds in Iraq and one woman's heroism'
Booklist

For the Love of a Son
'[Thank you] for sharing your extraordinary
and heart-breaking story with the world'
Hillary Rodham Clinton, former US Secretary of State

Princess: More Tears to Cry
'In her new book Princess Sultana vividly describes life
inside one of the richest, most conservative kingdoms in the
world . . . [She] leads a privileged life [but] even she must work
in secret to record these stories of women who have
been beaten, scorned and even hanged'
Goodreads

www.penguin.co.uk

Also by Jean Sasson

Non-fiction:

*The Rape of Kuwait: The True Story of the Iraqi Atrocities
Against a Civilian Population*

Princess: A True Story of Life Behind the Veil in Saudi Arabia

Daughters of Arabia (Princess Sultana's Daughters in US)

Desert Royal (Princess Sultana's Circle in US)

*Mayada, Daughter of Iraq: One Woman's Survival
Under Saddam Hussein*

Love in a Torn Land: One Woman's Daring Escape from Iraq

*Growing up bin Laden: Osama's Wife and Son Take Us
Inside Their Secret World*

*For the Love of a Son: One Afghan Woman's Quest
for Her Stolen Child*

American Chick in Saudi Arabia

*Yasmeena's Choice: A True Story of War, Rape,
Courage and Survival*

Princess: More Tears to Cry

Princess: Secrets to Share

Historical Fiction:

Ester's Child

For additional information about Jean Sasson
and her books, please visit:

http://www.JeanSasson.com
Blog: http://jeansasson.wordpress.com/
Facebook: http://www.facebook.com/AuthorJeanSasson
Twitter: http://twitter.com/jeansasson
ASK: http://ask.fm/jeansasson

To the girls and women of Saudi Arabia who have suffered and died under the archaic guardianship laws of our country, we will remember you.
And to those suffering still, help is on the way.

All that is written here is real.
Some of the stories are very happy while some are tragically sad.
But all are true.
A few names have been changed to protect those who would come to great harm should their true identity be known. But the names of many others have been revealed.

– *Jean Sasson and Princess Sultana al-Sa'ud*

Contents

A Note from Jean Sasson ix

Introduction by Princess Sultana al-Sa'ud 1

Chapter One: Let Them Know You Are Coming 7

Chapter Two: The Joys and Torments of Family 38

Chapter Three: The Mystery of the Ninja Girl 72

Chapter Four: The Heart of Evil 98

Chapter Five: Kareem: A Kitten's Kiss 122

Chapter Six: Doctor, Doctor 144

Chapter Seven: Destroy the Guardianship Law 163

Chapter Eight: A Sprinkling of Stars 184

Chapter Nine: Before I Go 207

Chapter Ten: Once Upon a Time 231

A Closing Note from Jean Sasson 256

Epilogue: Final thoughts from
Princess Sultana al-Sa'ud 269

Appendices 275

All About Jean Sasson 349

A Note from Jean Sasson

As of January 2018, there have been five books written and published about the extraordinary Princess Sultana, a high-ranking member of the House of al-Sa'ud. These books share details of her personal life, and they reveal her tremendous courage and resourcefulness as she battles on behalf of women's rights in Saudi Arabia and around the world, for there is discrimination against women in nearly every country.

The books I have written about Princess Sultana have been embraced by women – and men – in eighty editions of the first book, *Princess*, distributed worldwide in approximately forty countries. The books about this remarkable woman made the bestseller list in every country where they were published. Astonishingly, they have never gone out of print in a publishing world where most non-fiction books fade away from public attention within a few years.

Now, after twenty-six years, interest in Princess Sultana's life has not diminished, rather it has flourished. This makes the *Princess* series (now a collection of six books) a phenomenon in the world of non-fiction publishing. No other book in this genre has ever kept the interest of readers in this fashion.

Why has this happened?

The answer is simple. The generation of girls and women who first embraced the captivating story of a Saudi princess guided their daughters to the princess, and now the granddaughters of the original readers are also following the life of Princess Sultana. Furthermore, mothers, wives, daughters and sisters are steering the men in their lives to read the books, expanding curiosity about a princess born in the desert of Saudi Arabia. This word-of-mouth from mother to daughter, from aunt to niece, from grandmother to granddaughter, from neighbour to neighbour, and from wife to husband, has resulted in many thousands of new readers eagerly anticipating further stories from deep within a mysterious kingdom – one on the threshold of change.

During the late summer of 2017 and early 2018, electrifying announcements came from the king's palace regarding the rights of women. After years of struggle, hope and anticipation, positive changes for Saudi Arabian women were suddenly being discussed publicly. These changes, which have the potential to affect all Saudi women, are now on the verge of becoming a reality. Princess Sultana and I concurred that such exciting events make it imperative to keep readers informed.

The princess and I are delighted to report on the marvellous reforms coming to the country she loves. We shall continue to write about how the women of Saudi Arabia are affected, as well as the ongoing battles for and against women in other lands where millions continue the struggle to live in peace and with freedom. This includes those who were born and raised in the United States and Europe who have also faced discrimination.

Thus, with book six, *Princess, Stepping Out of the Shadows*, we hope to inform, inspire and celebrate the coming changes that will ensure every female will have the right to live in dignity, regardless of her country, race, religion or culture. Perhaps Saudi Arabia will surprise the world and become a guide-post for all countries that continue to face the intricate problems of female inequality.

SAUDI ARABIA

Introduction by Princess Sultana al-Sa'ud

To readers who may be questioning if anything is new with the women of Saudi Arabia, my response is swift. Yes! A wind of change is blowing through this kingdom – a wind that is bringing optimism and hope to its people.

Yet, before we revel in joy, our optimism must be tempered, for one major obstacle stands between Saudi women and true freedom, and it relates to the guardianship law in our land, which threatens to dilute any promises made to women. For those unfamiliar with this archaic practice, they should know that every female born in Saudi Arabia is shackled by a law that bequeaths men the automatic right of absolute control over the women in their family. This burdensome law remains intact even as our future king proclaims his plans to allow Saudi women the joy of full personal freedom.

But let me look to all that is positive, and begin to explain how and why I am hopeful that we are on the threshold of change.

The first question that will come to most minds is this: What or who has brought about this sudden and startling reversal regarding the status of women in the desert kingdom?

All who study civilization know that social change is seldom simple, and this is doubly true for Saudi Arabia. Why? Because it is the land best known around the world for harsh, rigid rules that are hostile to half the nation's citizens – its women.

Through my intimate knowledge of Saudi Arabia and its royal family, readers will learn that two forces are behind this much-desired and needed reform.

The first is time – the history of civilization tells us that time alters all things.

The second is a lone man. Unrivalled in our modern life when it comes to boldness and courage, he is set on a path to transform an entire nation. This is the man who is spawning the ideas of freedom so long lodged in the hearts of many Saudi women and some Saudi men. *This is the man who will be king.*

Muhammad bin Salman bin Abdul Aziz al-Sa'ud is the son of the present king, Salman, and the grandson of the first king, Abdul Aziz. He was always an exhausting force to those around him. Even from the time he was a toddler, little Muhammad never stopped moving forward. This is according to his own mother, who is one of my royal cousins. The young Muhammad was an unusual boy; he had such an optimistic nature that he constantly exhibited a broad smile. His dashing personality could not hide his fondness for fairness. Despite his cheerful attitude, he was applauded for his quick and deep intellect. Educated as a lawyer, this serious-minded student was second in his class.

None in our immediate royal family were surprised by his accomplishments, for the unique boy grew into an exceptional man, yet I will admit that some were astonished when he was elevated over other royal cousins, older and with more experience in government. While many royals predicted that Prince Muhammad bin Salman would *one day* be king, few royals expected Muhammad to be the *next* king.

In Saudi Arabia, every king upon his death is succeeded by the current Crown Prince. When the new king assumes power, he appoints the next Crown Prince, who will succeed him upon his death. Thus every king has the power to appoint his successor. Historically, the transitions have generally been smooth, although there have been tensions.

The current Crown Prince is only the second of the original king's grandsons to hold the position of Crown Prince. Previous to Crown Prince Muhammad bin Salman, Prince Mohammed bin Naif was the chosen successor, but on 21 June 2017 King Salman chose to depose Naif as the Crown Prince and replace his deceased brother's son with his own.

There is an Allegiance Council (created in 2006 by King Abdullah) that was supposedly given the authority to facilitate the Saudi royal transfer of power, but thus far the Council has not opposed appointments made by the king.

Prince Muhammad bin Salman bin Abdul Aziz al-Sa'ud's path now is set, and king he will be. And for that I say, *Alhamdulillah* or Praise God!

Truthfully, I believe that my cousin Muhammad will follow the legacy of our greatly acclaimed grandfather, Abdul Aziz, the founder and first king of Saudi Arabia.

For those of you not familiar with the creator of Saudi Arabia, he was a bold and cunning man who accomplished the impossible when he bound together the warring tribes of Arabia, numbering at least twenty-five, into a nation. His astounding triumphs will be briefly narrated in the pages to follow.

I am disappointed to tell you that a few disgruntled characters in the royal family have expressed displeasure at Crown Prince Muhammad's remarkable rise to power, for there is jealousy lurking in the hearts and minds of many people of this world. Yet many members of the royal family support him. Most importantly, the Saudi youth love him, poring over his decisions and applauding his vision of a new world on the horizon, one where women are not kept in purdah and the youth can expect jobs to follow education. With 58.5 per cent of the Saudi population under thirty, an age where most humans experience an awakening of dissatisfaction and censure of their leaders, it is unusual and significant that the youth of any land wholly support their king or president. Yet this is the remarkable state of affairs in Saudi Arabia.

No one can deny that a widening stream of events is now occurring in the kingdom, bringing many citizens closer to the goals they aspire to: to live as free men and women in a country where they can pursue their dreams without fear of societal condemnation.

Even as I celebrate, I must continue to expose the stories of women who are still suffering from the cruelty and brutality of the men who are their guardians. Not every man in Saudi Arabia has the insight and vision of the king-to-be; they do not understand the importance of welcoming half the nation's citizens into a partnership or how vital it is for women to stand side by side with our men in support of our Crown Prince as he attempts to lead this kingdom into a new, modern era of greatness.

There is only one certainty as to the emotions this book will bring. Readers will rejoice, and readers will mourn, for *nothing* is simple in Saudi Arabia.

Chapter One

Let Them Know You Are Coming

I AM A PRINCESS IN the House of al-Sa'ud in the Kingdom of Saudi Arabia. In the land of my birth, a princess is for ever. A princess is born a princess and dies a princess. This is because the princesses of Saudi Arabia have never known the pleasure of exerting influence; therefore, no men in power felt the need to pull the crowns off our heads. This indubitable position means that princess power lurks under the obscurities of royal lives, although any power felt by a princess in Saudi Arabia is destined to remain hidden in shadows.

But the power of Saudi women is changing. As of the Islamic year 1439 (2018), I, along with many other women in the Kingdom of Saudi Arabia, will be stepping out of the darkness to embrace long-sought and greatly desired changes in our personal liberties.

The journey of Saudi females groping in darkness down the worn path of oppression is known to many. They have learned of our imperfect lives through various sources, including news reports, government studies, personal cries for help and the books written about my life, as well as the lives of my family, friends, and other women and men in Saudi Arabia. To my astonishment and great happiness, our battles for justice were recognized and our pleas for help were heard by many the world over.

I know for certain that this is the case, for I have seen letters from readers and so understand that my personal story has touched the hearts and minds of people in every country on earth. Many of these readers express true affection for me and for my country. But certain members of my family do not always agree that my story has produced positive feelings for me, and for Saudi Arabia.

I remember not so long ago when my brother Ali created a scene in my home after discovering the fifth book about my life in a bookstore in London. He burst past our doorman and into our home without the usual formalities courteous people reserve for visiting. Instead, a very angry Ali was holding the book *Princess, Secrets to Share* in his hand, shaking it above his head as though it were an objectionable tambourine.

Since the time we were children, no one could exceed my brother in creating dramatic scenes. While every other man I know in the Saudi royal family tends to react in a calm, mature and measured manner when difficult situations develop, my brother behaves like a petulant child.

I stood and stared as my brother made a spectacle of himself. Ali was stumbling, for his gait was faster than his bulk could support, his face was red, and his voice was at such a high volume that the servants came running to see for themselves if the world was coming to an end.

Ali was shaking in anger, his tone accusatory. *'Sultana! Will you never stop?'* He tossed the book to the floor and kicked it, the force of his punts knocking one of his sandals from his foot. His assault ripped the pages from the book's spine. 'Sultana, these books do nothing but create negative feelings about you!' My brother actually emitted a growling noise, as he kicked the book a final time. 'And our family!' Ali pursed his lips and glared with a laser-like glower so piercing that there was no doubt that he was on the verge of saying very spiteful words.

I shook my head slowly in reaction to his angry declarations. I knew my brother was wrong about my books creating animosity towards me, my family and my country, and I refused to match his antagonism. I have learned with the passing years to restrain my emotions, if possible, and most particularly in disagreements on family matters.

Besides, on that morning I was feeling serene, for I had just enjoyed a lengthy and most enjoyable conversation with my son, Abdullah, who had taken his wife and two children to Europe for a holiday. Our talk had been so pleasurable that it was now difficult for anyone to trigger my temper, which I generally control but, admittedly, on occasion can be as volatile as my brother's. I said nothing as I watched his ridiculous reaction. All in my immediate family know that only the silence of my grave will cease my fight for the rights of women. Most importantly, I did not react to Ali's rantings because I knew that he was wrong!

I looked around to see our servants watching my brother carefully. Ali was known to insult them *if* he noticed their presence. But they remained since all knew that Ali rarely notices those who serve him. I said nothing, for those who work in our homes are trust-worthy and discreet, accustomed to seeing and hearing most of our family dramas. They had little concern as to the source of Ali's distress and were merely enjoying a break in their routine. Some, perhaps, were concerned that my brother might become violent, for in the past he had shoved those who were the source of his anger.

The truth is that the books about my life, my family, my friends and other women from the region have not created negative feelings about anyone who is innocent of brutal acts against females. And I believe that any Saudi citizen, or for that matter any person, regardless of nationality, would feel that those guilty of inten-tional cruelty should be punished and rejected by all. Certainly, as I have said, the books about my life have not brought ill will to my country, but instead have opened a window on to our world. Our lives have always been so secretive and our culture unfamiliar to other nationalities, who know little of any significance about us. Prior to the stories about my life, most people thought of Saudi Arabians as people who are oil-rich and lazy – people who contribute little to the world and care only for themselves. We are seen as selfish, sitting atop vast reserves of black gold. But the stories I have shared, documenting my life, have unexpectedly cre-ated an understanding that has brought affection to those in our country who push for change. Readers whose minds have been opened as to the truth of our lives write to tell me how they have come to know that Saudi Arabians are like most others in the world; we are a nation made up of good and bad people, and many make valid and important contributions to society and to the world.

I am told through the communications I receive that readers feel they have come to know the women, and the men, of my family. There are many who say they had no knowledge that Saudi men could be so understanding and sensitive about the issues of life until they read about my husband, my son, my sister Sara's husband and other exceptional men in the royal family.

Nothing is more important than creating understanding and sharing knowledge amongst different nations and cultures, and this is what the books about my life have accomplished. Consequently Ali's empty words could not convince me otherwise.

After Ali understood that I was not going to be drawn into a verbal battle with him, he gathered his senses, picked up the book and, realizing he had an audience, glanced caustically at the servants, exclaiming, 'Have you no work? Does my sister pay you to gawk?'

The servants quickly scattered.

With their exit, Ali's tirade ended, although he looked at me with disappointment flashing in his eyes.

'You know, Sultana, if anyone outside our immediate family discovers you to be this princess, your children will be the ones to suffer for your folly.'

I felt stricken by his threatening words but did not respond, intentionally keeping my face expressionless, for what could I say? His words held an important truth which often makes me uncomfortable. If my identity as Princess Sultana becomes popular knowledge within the Saudi royal family, my children will indeed suffer, for they will be scorned by many they now consider friends.

All who know me understand that my children and grandchildren are the most important people in my life and are the true reason I have never come forward to reveal my face and identity to the world. I must protect my children from being rejected or ridiculed by their relatives and friends. Most children in Saudi Arabia would feel shame to have a mother whose life is publicized to the world, for most women in our isolated world still live very private lives. Despite the fact that my stories are told in order to promote understanding of my world, most would not appreciate the reasons behind the revelations. They would not know of my passion to fight for equal rights for women.

In Saudi Arabia, the entire family is held to blame if any member acts or reacts in a manner considered unacceptable. My children are happy and well adjusted, and any harm to them brought by my actions would render me weak from sorrow.

Once Ali realized that he could say nothing to provoke me to retort in wrath, he abandoned his anger and behaved normally, as if nothing had happened and he had not stormed into my home with strident and insulting words.

'Sultana,' he said with a smile, 'are you going to offer me a coffee?'

I laughed.

My brother laughed.

Did we finally understand one another? We had been sparring since the time we were children only because Ali was a natural-born bully. Did he comprehend that he could no longer control his adult sister? Had I reached a position of harmony with my brother's need to control all women in his sphere of influence? Only time would tell, so I lightly shrugged my shoulders and issued the invitation he expected.

'Of course! Come with me to the sitting room, and we'll have a coffee and a sweet.'

And so the morning ended without further commotion, as Ali disclosed the most recent news of his new wife and their toddler son, who was spoiled by his father and whom Ali claimed to look and behave exactly as he had as a child.

'Is that so?' I replied, a smile lurking under my words, recalling how Ali had tormented his sisters in his youth with his demanding ways and aggressive conduct. Secretly I hoped that his son was nothing like his father, when it came to selfishness and lack of compassion.

I felt relieved when Ali left within the hour to tend to business affairs, but admittedly I was glad that we had parted amiably, something rare in our long and quarrelsome relationship.

*   *   *

I had no indication that day of the surprises that were about to be revealed in my country. My happiness was soon rising, for it was not so long after my brother's visit that an unexpected announcement came from the men who rule Saudi Arabia, a revelation that promised a better future for all Saudis – women and men. Our world was about to be enriched to an extent that most could only imagine. Indeed, none of us has ever believed that we might live long enough to witness such progressive changes.

Only a few short months later, many of us would be celebrating the fact that we were fortunate that one of the highest-ranking people in the kingdom had determined to bring the best transformations to our nation and to make our country great in the eyes of the world.

As I mentioned earlier, this unexpected social revolution is being spearheaded by a young male royal named Muhammad bin Salman bin Abdul Aziz al-Sa'ud, who has appeared to us as a miracle; a bold man who is pushing away the darkness cloaking all females in his country.

I am proud to say that this young cousin is of my father's family. Although I cannot claim to visit with the Crown Prince personally, I spent time with him when he was only a child. Such visits automatically ceased when he grew into male maturity. However, the men of my family have had many occasions to be in his company and have spoken well of him. Now that he has stepped to the front of the world's attention, memories of his babyhood, his toddler years and childhood are returning to me. Furthermore, past conversations with my husband Kareem, my son Abdullah and other male members of my immediate family pertaining to visits once the child became a man are reappearing in my mind. The men of my family have long praised this cousin and maintained that he is a man who speaks for all Saudis, not just for the royals who have held fast to power since 1953.

Looking back to our history, that was the moment the founder of the kingdom, our grandfather King Abdul Aziz, drew his last breath in the mountain city of Taif on the 2 Rabie al awal 1373 (9 November 1953) in the palace of his son, Faisal. Although he died in Taif, and the funeral prayer was conducted in that city, Grandfather was returned to Riyadh to be buried at the Al Oud Cemetery. While I know the location of the Al Oud Cemetery, I have no idea where his grave is located within it. Since Saudis do not visit and mourn at the grave, I have been told that none of his sons visit that site and all who attended his funeral can no longer identify it, which is an enormous disappointment to me, his granddaughter. How I wish I knew the exact spot my grandfather was buried. If so, no one could keep me from visiting, just to feel his presence.

Uncle Faisal grew to be a fine man, highly respected by his father, and would follow his older brother, Saud, in ascending the royal orbit to assume the rank of king only a few years after his father's death.

Although I was not yet born to my mother when my grandfather passed from this earth, I have heard endless stories of his life, his exploits, his courage and his multiple triumphs – on the battlefield, and in administrative and diplomatic encounters with aggressive Saudi tribesmen, as well as prominent statesmen from all over the world, from the beginning of his struggles until the time of his rise to great power. He was, as Kareem is fond of telling our children, 'a man who would let you know he was coming'. Since his death, in fact, our family has impatiently waited for one of his sons, or grandsons, to let us know he is coming! And now it seems this day is upon us. We believe that Crown Prince Muhammad is demonstrating the same astonishing qualities as the man who was responsible for the formation of Saudi Arabia and for the fate of the family who now rules. All who know our Crown Prince personally say that he is a formidable character who possesses extraordinary leadership skills and has a powerful intellect, not unlike our grandfather.

My country and our people need such a man. Just considering what I have heard of his plans, as I consider what is coming our way, I feel breathless with excitement. I believe that nothing less than a miracle is roaring across the entire country, a phenomenon that will bring a positive kind of disturbance that will shake the hearts of all. Some hearts will be moved by joy, others by sorrow.

Never did I believe that I would be so fortunate to live a life long enough to see the moment when absolute male power over women in Saudi Arabia will come to an end, but I believe that now I shall.

Now I long for those who care about me and my country to turn the pages of this book with the same anticipation and joy as I feel when revealing how this miracle developed and grew, and how finally, after many years of all-embracing male domination, freedom will become a reality for many of the ten million or so Saudi women living today. Know that in this book you will hear from women who never believed that their dreams of true freedom would be realized, as well as

16

from women whose dreams are still tightly suppressed by the male guardians who cling to ancient customs and traditions in order to maintain complete control.

I cannot contain my joy each time I consider the anger and hostility springing from the hearts and minds of those immovable and dominating men of my country, men who believe it is their rightful privilege to rule over women, men who are seething like dangerous volcanoes because a bold, intelligent and fair-minded prince is coming to power. When this occurs, their brutish behaviour will be curbed. These angry men are of all ages and come from many social circles, including the proud Bedouin, the city poor, the professional and business classes, even the royal family. Since the day they came to an age of understanding, these men have held tightly and unfairly to absolute control of Saudi women.

But no more. No more . . .

*   *   *

The story you are about to read will be told with the highest hope and greatest enthusiasm.

I extend my hand to you in invitation. Come with me on a brief journey into Arabia, my desert kingdom, to feel with me the distinctive magic hovering over the darkness of human cruelty. Together we shall cross centuries to travel back in time to the very beginning, for only then is it possible to appreciate how the Saudi Arabians of today continue to live with archaic customs and how urgent is the need for social transformation – brought about by our king-in-waiting.

I cloak my thoughts to the modern world I know so well, opening my mind to concentrate on a time long ago and far away from the life I now live as a Saudi princess in the House of al-Sa'ud. After a few moments of deep breathing and intense mental concentration, I find myself gradually drifting back in time to pre-Islamic Arabia to view the land and ancestors I love, as seen through the eyes of my predecessors many hundreds of years before I was born.

An ancient setting comes to life for me, in multi-coloured scenes. There is a vast plateau, rising loftily to nearly 12,000 feet. Blue skies sparkle above. The hue of dark golden sand stretches in every direction. The green of lush oases and palm-studded villages occasionally breaks the rolling visage of the swirling peaks of sand. Water is unseen to my eyes and most would claim that in the arid waste of Arabia water cannot exist, but I know otherwise, and if I had the ability to drop to the sands to explore the wadi I know that drinkable waters exist in shallow wells.

But that I cannot do.

I see a small, mud-coloured village. People scurry under stunted palms, wearing long garments and head coverings to guard their skin and hair from a searing desert sun capable of burning the flesh off their bodies. These people are short and thin but strong because survivors of desert life must be physically sturdy to combat the harsh environment, toiling day after day in a struggle to find or produce food.

These people belong to a structure of families united in tribes. Before Prophet Mohammed, Arabia was not a country ruled by one political component. Indeed, occupants of Arabia felt duty and loyalty *only* to their tribe. Each was ruled over by the sheik chosen by leaders of the clan. The sheik would come from a prominent family considered wise in matters of conflict, whether war with other tribes or discord within the tribe.

Most living in Arabia during the ancient days were nomad Bedouins, people who followed the seasonal rains as they moved their scarce and skinny flocks from one pastureland to another. The desert belonged to the territorial Bedouin and no one could cross the sands without permission – and, in most cases, monetary payment for the privilege of using the ancient paths. Route charging was one of the few methods of generating revenue for the Arabian Bedouins.

But during those ancient times there were others besides the Bedouins living in Arabia. There were townspeople who settled to live in villages near the wadis, such as those I am now watching, and people such as my own al-Sa'ud family. Where the soil permitted, men and women strained to coax vegetables and grains from the earth. Others cultivated orchards, while a few grew aromatic plants such as frankincense or cupped trees to extract myrrh from the trunks.

Suddenly, in my mind's eye, I see a small herd of camels and a few prancing horses. Arabs love horses above all belongings, but the camel has always been the desert dweller's best friend. The camel provides reliable transportation, milk for nourishment, urine for health and beauty treatments, dung to burn for fuel, meat for meals, and hide to make clothing and tents. Without the camel, it is doubtful that human life could have existed in the bleakness of the sands.

Suddenly I realize that these townspeople are assembling at a fair, which was a common way of bringing together farmers, merchants and poets. At such fairs they sold their wares and occasionally enjoyed being entertained.

It is as though the scenes spread before me are led by my own thoughts, for at that moment my eyes see entertainers and my ears hear artists singing their creations to musical accompaniment. These men are poets who favour certain musical instruments, such as reed pipes, flutes and tambourines. There are girls dressed in ordinary clothing of the time performing in a carefree manner, actions rarely seen in modern-day Arabia. They are participating in the amusement by dancing, which is a bit of a shock, until I remind myself that during the days of ignorance, which was the time before Islam, the people of the Arabian desert lived much as they pleased without any regulatory practices regarding the mixing of men and women. In those early years, it was not considered indecent for women to dance with unbridled joy while men who did not know them personally savoured the sight.

I notice a few women who are not moving to the beat of the music but are watching the poets and the dancers from the background. I wonder who they are. Are they the wives of the poets? Are they interested observers? Either could be the case, for all Arabs – men, women and children – love poetry.

Poets were, and are still, held in high esteem in Saudi Arabia – adored by their fans, a little like rock stars today. Since the beginning of civilization in Arabia, poetry and the fullness of language has been a source of great pride in our culture. The art of words in the desert is part of an oral tradition, with stories heard, remembered and then passed down through the generations.

Nothing has changed from that day until now when the topic is the Arab love of poetry. Then, as now, we are poets at heart, for the Arab temperament is disposed to intense feelings. Poems are written as rhymes, with endless verses quoted to honour warriors, kings and the incomparable beauty of Arab women. I know that in ancient times tribes often competed against each other and the winning poetry was named 'the Golden Songs' and protected like treasures in the coffers of kings or leaders by other titles. Perhaps I am watching such a poetry contest as I hover over ancient Arabia.

There are no veiled women in attendance but that does not surprise me – I know from my life's work of studying the status of women from ancient to modern times that few women were veiled during the time before Islam. However, a limited number of women (those from the wealthy classes) would wear the veil in order to elevate themselves to a status of high desirability, as no man would be able to keep his senses if he were to view her beauty. When these veiled, heavily cloaked and perfumed women passed through the streets, all would stand in awe and wonder, believing that the most beautiful creature was within reach. Those covered figures created endless dreams of desire for the men, who savoured the thought that one day they too would win a woman so beautiful that she must hide her beauty or chance creating a human stampede.

Additionally, some upper-class women wed to chieftains or rulers would veil to distinguish themselves from the common people.

Suddenly my eyes are drawn to a single figure. It is a man whose appearance startles me because even from a distance he holds a remarkable resemblance to my handsome husband, Kareem. He has the same golden-brown skin, black eyes, chiselled jaw and open smile. I am entranced, for I am a woman who greatly loves her husband, even after years of marriage and the challenge of birthing and nurturing three children.

My concentration stays with this man as he abandons the fair to walk a short distance down a narrow, winding walkway between stucco houses that are rectangles of sun-dried brick cemented with mud. The roofs are mixtures of mud and palm leaves. The shabby construction of private homes proves that this is a poor village, for even in those days the wealthy constructed homes with interior courts, creating shelters for their families that were citadels of privacy.

The man who physically resembles Kareem walks on a street that is floored with hard sand. He moves past four or five homes until he reaches a modest dwelling comparable to all others. To my eyes, it is as though the home has no roof and I can watch his movements and actions. The humble dwelling has only four rooms; the floor, as the street, is hard-packed dirt. The handsome man passes through the main sitting room to enter a second chamber, which is a sleeping area with two cots. He boldly approaches a woman who is tenderly focusing on an infant. Believing I am going to see an affectionate scene, out of modesty I start to take my mind elsewhere. But then I catch sight of an incident that causes me to cringe in shock. The handsome man physically strikes the woman with his hand. She screams, then grabs and shields her baby. Her husband bellows in fury, striking her again and again. The face I found handsome is no longer appealing, as he blushes red with rage. His disagreeable character shows on his face, as he grimaces in heated irritation at his wife and child.

I gasp when the baby cries pitifully. I then understand that her father is incensed because the tiny one is a female. This is no surprise since until Islam in Arabia female babies were typically undesirable, not only to the fathers but often to the mothers and even the community. But it is clear to me that this mother loves her baby. She cups her hand over the infant's mouth to silence the child, for the infant's loud sobs are making the man even more furious. I stare in horrified disbelief when the man roughly tugs the infant from the mother's arms and rushes out of their home and away from the small village to carry the crying baby to a sandy area.

After the child is taken, the young mother collapses to the floor and remains there, unmoving, as stiff as a long-dead corpse.

My eyes return to the father. He tosses the helpless baby to the ground and begins feverishly to dig a hole. The sand seems to be fighting against his brutish plan, for as he hollows out what will become the grave the sand slides back into the cavity.

I am aghast as I watch the grisly scene, but remember that the pages of time have been turned back and

I am not an actual witness to the murder about to be committed. Tears well in my eyes, as I feel I am a spectator to a terrified baby who is sensing the horror fast becoming her reality. With eyes tightly closed, she is shrieking and flailing her little arms.

Her father's heart is unmoved. He quickly prepares the burial place and cruelly pushes his kicking infant into the small hole, shoving and kicking the sand until the grave is fully covered.

I see movement under the sand! A baby girl buried alive!

The horror! The terror!

I become paralysed by the revulsion of the moment, for I know that in the time before Islam society was addicted to female infanticide. Unwanted infant daughters were often slain by live burials, repeated thousands of times during that age of ignorance. Although I know the barbarity I have witnessed happened centuries before, the scene feels as real to me as if it were occurring at that moment.

In anger and sorrow, I watch as the murderer strolls back into his village, seemingly without concern for the agony he has wrought. The moment his terrified child was covered in sand, choking to death, he thought of her no more. He speaks with a few men along the way, who appear to congratulate him on ridding his family of a daughter who, in their eyes, will only create endless problems.

Men celebrate with their kinsmen and friends while infant daughters inhale sand until death claims their sweet, innocent little lives and mourning mothers weep in sorrow.

My wanderings fail to bring me the happiness I desire; instead, I reel from extreme misery. From my studies of Islam and of the enhancements brought to female lives, I have always known that the days of ignorance were the most dangerous time in human history to be a female, whether an infant, a girl or an adult woman. There was no punishment for murdering females; rather, there were congratulations and celebration! For fathers, grand-fathers and uncles a baby girl was considered the greatest curse. Those who were born ignorant, and died ignor-ant, truly presumed that females would bring nothing more than unnecessary expense and humiliation to their family name. Male children consumed all monies avail-able in family life, and their every action, whether impacting the family negatively or positively, was con-sidered a cause for merriment.

Truthfully, history tells us that happiness eluded the majority of those born female. Even if a baby daughter was spared a sandy grave, she would endure a lifetime of desperate neglect and drudgery.

Girls would be married while still young children.

Females would never be companions or friends of their husbands, always servants.

A wife's duty would be to tend to her husband's needs.

A wife's duty would be to produce many sons, who would grow to be warriors.

A wife could be divorced at any time and for any reason.

A mother's children could be taken from her.

Females could be passed from man to man like an object, losing their identity, their pride and any sense of decency.

A woman, once abandoned by her husband, lived in fear of poverty and starvation. Without her man to provide for her, no one would offer food or shelter.

During that dark time in Arabia, this was the life experienced by most women. There was nothing to curb the cruelty of men – no laws, no social condemnation, and certainly no religion.

In pre-Islamic Arabia, the desert tribes did not practise an official, organized religion but instead had a primitive fear of deities in stars or in the centre of the earth, which they observed by performing various rituals for protection from these mysteries of life. No one knows for certain if people at that time believed in the afterlife, but ancient narratives describing the securing of camels foodless to the owner's grave indicate that the deceased believed he would need a method of transport wherever it was he was going.

Their religion, if that is what we choose to call it, was primitive and lives were similarly archaic.

*　　*　　*

Everything changed in Arabia when the most important figure in medieval history was born in the city of Mecca. All that I learned about this important man was taught to me by my mother, a woman who lived the most virtuous life of anyone I have ever known. Every question in her life was solved by reading the pages of the Koran. Every action of her life was intricately bound with Islam.

Mother told me, 'Sultana, you are a child of God. To live the good and pure life of a Muslim, you must know every aspect of Islam.'

How I wanted to be an image of my mother, but I was never able to attain her purity of spirit. I have been told by my sisters that I was born with what they describe as a double naughty gene! Despite my obvious shortcomings, I was fortunate to learn from Mother about the Prophet of God, who was responsible for bringing Islam to Arabia.

Mother told me in simple terms that this important individual was the child born to a man named Abdallah and a woman named Amina, who married in the year 568. Abdallah was with his bride for only three days before embarking on a mercantile expedition, dying at Medina on his return trip to Mecca. In 570, two months after Abdallah's death, his wife, Amina, gave birth to a male child named Mohammed, meaning 'highly praised'.

The child Mohammed's ancestry was distinguished. His father's uncle, Hashim, was a wealthy merchant, philanthropist and one of Mecca's important chiefs. At Hashim's death, his prestigious position was assumed by his younger brother, who was the father of Abdallah.

Despite the elevated position of the family, Mohammed's patrimony was modest. His father had left him an unpretentious house, a flock of goats and five camels. There was also a slave who nursed Mohammed in his infancy.

When Amina died six years later Mohammed's grandfather, an elderly man of seventy-six years, took over his care. At the grandfather's death, Mohammed's uncle Abu Talib assumed the obligation.

The men responsible for the child Mohammed treated him with enormous care and great affection, and despite his lack of formal education the man Mohammed would one day write what would become the most famous and eloquent book in the Arabic language.

The child Mohammed grew into a man of strength and dignity. As he aged, he became more and more absorbed in thoughts of religion, withdrawing alone or with his family to Mount Hira, three miles from Mecca. There he spent many nights and days in a cave, praying, meditating and fasting. It was in the year 610, while he was sleeping there alone, that Mohammed was approached by the angel Gabriel, ordering Mohammed, 'Read!'

Mohammed replied, 'I do not read.'

Gabriel pressed against Mohammed so tightly that he thought he would die. Gabriel ordered once more: 'Read!'

Mohammed began to read loudly, and the angel Gabriel loosened his grip and disappeared from Mohammed's dream. When Mohammed awoke the following morning, he said that the words he had read were written in his heart, never to be forgotten. When he left the mountain, he heard a voice from heaven. 'O Mohammed, thou art the messenger of Allah, and I am Gabriel.'

Mohammed raised his head towards heaven to see Gabriel in the form of a man.

Gabriel repeated the words: 'O Mohammed, thou art the messenger of Allah, and I am Gabriel.'

The newly defined Prophet Mohammed returned to Mecca in a flash, where he told his wife Khadija of his astonishing visions. Khadija accepted them as a true revelation from heaven, encouraging her husband to announce his mission for God.

After Prophet Mohammed endured many struggles and fought many battles, the creation of a new religion called Islam was a great triumph. The subsequent explosion of the Islamic Arab armies in invading, occupying and converting half of the Mediterranean world to Islam is the most extraordinary phenomenon in medieval history.

Many social changes took place across the Arab peninsula under Islam, including security for all, but most importantly the lives of girls and women profoundly improved.

Prophet Mohammed condemned formerly common and brutish practices such as female infanticide. Appalled to observe that Arabians prior to Islam were fixated on murdering their daughters, he spoke out against the heinous practice on many occasions until the monstrous custom was finally discarded by most. It's such a shocking concept that most women who know of the tradition carry a secret fear of the prospect.

Even I once felt panic and alarm at being buried alive.

This happened after my brother Ali and I had engaged in a physical spat over a toy, a mechanical horse given to me by one of my uncles. I was the victor, keeping what was mine. My brother was furious because he was accustomed to winning due to his larger size, but my cunning powers had overtaken my brother while we were still children. I had easily succeeded in convincing him that I would relinquish my little horse.

With a smug smile, he relaxed to walk with his hand outstretched to claim what was not his, but I looked over his back to call out, 'Mother!' He froze for an important moment, believing that our mother was a witness to his wicked behaviour, and that's when I moved as fast as the swirling winds in a sandstorm to conceal my little horse in a top-secret cupboard in my bedroom.

My bewildered brother was unable to find my hiding place and he was so upset that he sputtered in anger before rushing into the back garden. I followed to see him seize one of the gardener's digging tools to hollow a pit in the flower bed where the sand was soft and malleable.

Bragging about my triumph, I ridiculed him, laughing, 'No, my brother, I did not hide the horsey in the flower bed!'

Ali grabbed a handful of sand and threw it at me, screaming, 'Eat this.'

My mouth was still open due to my laughter, thus grains of gritty sand landed on my tongue.

'Taste it!' my brother ordered. I well knew his implication even before he shouted, 'You should have been buried alive at birth, Sultana!'

I tried to spit out the sand and stepped back, ready to make a run for my life should my brother try to force me into a hole in the ground. There were times that my brother truly frightened me. I had once heard my older sisters whispering about the ancient habit of burying baby girls alive in the desert. Given the chance, would my brother really do me the ultimate harm? For sure, I could easily see that he so hated me that he wanted me out of our family, perhaps buried in the big sands surrounding Riyadh.

I was young enough to still cry out for my mother and so I ran looking for the safety of her arms, telling her between tears, 'Ali wants to bury me in the garden! He tried to make me eat sand!' I opened my mouth as wide as possible, pulling my tongue out with my fingers. 'See! See the sand!' Mother looked but could see nothing because during the excitement I had indeed swallowed it.

'Darling Sultana, your brother did not mean the words he uttered,' my mother reassured me. 'He is a young boy, foolish at times, and he will regret those words when I speak with him.'

I remember her soft but steady voice as if it were yesterday, as she continued soothing her youngest child. 'Sultana, hush, child. You will not be buried in the sands. Prophet Mohammed forbade such a thing. It is now a serious crime with punishment.'

I memorized the words she spoke, for I wanted to be ready to teach my brother Ali lessons that he should know.

'These words were spoken by the greatest man to ever live, the man who was given the wisdom of God directly through angels.'

I felt a rush of excitement because I did not know what this wisdom was but surely longed to learn so I could use such knowledge against my brother when he and I engaged in physical disagreements.

'Sultana, the Prophet valued his own daughters dearly, and he said these words: anyone who brings up two daughters properly will be very close to me on the Day of Judgement.'

31

My mother smiled sweetly, kissing my head and my cheeks before resuming the messages she wanted me to know.

'There is a lovely story relating how the Prophet reprimanded a man once for showing favour to his son over his daughter. This man, in the presence of Prophet Mohammed, kissed his son and put him on his lap but did not do the same for his daughter, who was also by his side. The Prophet objected, telling the man that he was an unjust father and that he should have also kissed his daughter and placed her on the other side of his lap.'

I nodded my small head, comprehending that the revered Prophet had taken up for girls in an important manner.

'Sultana, there will be no babies buried alive ever again. Let your heart be happy, daughter, and know that in the eyes of God you are as important as your brother.'

My mother sighed as once more she tenderly pulled me close. 'And, Sultana, your mother prays to God with thanks that I am of this time in Arabia, for my heart would have stopped beating had any daughters of mine been taken to the sands to die.'

It was on that day that I learned from my mother that the Koran makes no distinction between the sexes, considering the birth of the female as a gift and blessing from God, the same as a male child. The verses my mother shared helped to cool my heated heart. But, despite the fact, as I was being pacified I was plotting revenge on my spoiled and brutish brother.

*　　*　　*

My wandering mind abruptly diverges from my personal memories to return to the electrifying past of Arabia. I am floating above vistas of the central region of the peninsula, where I pass over a mud-walled village situated on a plateau in the middle of the desert in the region known as Najd. The population is larger than most, with nearly 10,000 residents. Instinctively, I know this is Riyadh in the late 1800s, a time when the power of my family, the al-Sa'ud, had declined.

For more than a hundred years, from the mid-1700s, we had been a main power in the region, but in 1890 all was lost when our key regional rivals, the al-Rashid tribe, conquered and occupied Riyadh and the surrounding area.

My wandering eye does not linger in Riyadh, for in a blink my ancestors fell from the high perch of sovereignty to the level of powerless and homeless paupers. Their only possessions were what they could carry. After fleeing Riyadh, they temporarily found refuge with the al-Murrah, a Bedouin tribe located in the southern desert of Arabia.

The al-Murrah had accompanied the al-Sa'ud on tribal raids, so they were an approachable tribe in times of trouble.

From overhead I can see a lonely figure pacing amid the thorn trees in the flat desert sands on the peripheries of the al-Murrah's black-haired tents. This man is of a towering stature and I automatically know that I am looking at my grandfather, Abdul Aziz, when he was only a teenager. He looks just as I have so often heard him described by my own father, who was one of the younger sons born to my grandfather – born too late to fight beside his father during the momentous period of making a nation, but old enough to accompany his father on camel rides in the desert after Saudi Arabia was formally named a nation.

I am open-mouthed in wonder, gazing at a man who appears physically to be perfectly formed. My grandfather is massive, with a broad chest and shoulders. His back is ram-rod straight. His head is large, befitting his body size. He has a broad face, dark brown eyes and a large nose, with a thick moustache and light beard. He was famous for saying, 'I am nothing but a simple Bedouin,' but truthfully he looks like the king he became.

My grandfather is obviously deep in thought, for he appears to be quivering with suppressed excitement. Perhaps he is already plotting revenge against the al-Rashid tribe, for I know that his troubles were many after his family was routed from their home in Riyadh to live in shameful exile.

He remains alone and thoughtful until the sun fades and disappears into a moonless dark night, pausing only for times of prayer. I am not surprised at this scene, for my father once told me that his father had never missed a prayer. Even when he was fighting a battle he would make certain to cease momentarily to place his prayer rug on the sands and face Mecca.

The desert night is cool and he lights a fire from the palm ribs, then sits staring into the fire without eating or drinking. Finally he rises from the sand, brushing off his clothes with his huge hands before making the dawn prayer and returning to a black-haired tent where his father is sleeping. But my grandfather does not sleep. He stares into nothing until the sun rises full and yellow on a new day. I know in my own heart that his thoughts rest on the Najd, the only home he had ever known, and the home he cannot forget.

My family's exile kept them for nearly two years with the al-Murrah. That time of banishment was not wasted. Grandfather told his sons many stories of how he trailed the men of the al-Murrah and absorbed their desert skills, abilities that would help him when he fought to form a nation, for Arabia was a land of tribes. My grandfather acquired crucial familiarity with the Bedouin life, knowledge that he could have never known without the al-Murrah. The village Arab became an expert in tracking and raiding, and his heightened skills enhanced future negotiations with the numerous tribes of Arabia when he fought and bargained to bring them all together.

After two years of Bedouin life the al-Sa'ud sought and gained refuge in Kuwait. Once again the young Abdul Aziz prudently observed and developed skills he could never have attained had he remained in the Najd, a region of Arabia too harsh to invite intruders. However, a few world powers such as England, Germany and the Ottoman Empire had a great interest in Kuwait, for it was a coastal land with much promise. Due to their pearl diving and shipping of merchandise all over the region, Kuwaiti rulers were accustomed to travelling the world, thus becoming familiar with lands and peoples outside the desert region.

My grandfather's father was often at the Kuwaiti Emir's court and took his son, my grandfather, with him. The Kuwaitis, led by their Emir, who was so cunning that he was called Mubarak the Great, were expert dealers, trading wares with the English, the Turks, and other regional and European powers. It was there, in Kuwait, that my grandfather acquired a host of invaluable skills in negotiating with foreign powers.

Thus, in his young manhood, Grandfather acquired multiple talents of how to successfully negotiate with Bedouin tribes and with Western statesmen. None could obstruct him at the bargaining table, whether the talks were inside a black-haired tent with uneducated but clever Bedouin or in an opulent structure encountering the most educated men of Europe and America.

My grandfather confronted defeat with determination and defiance, and when he heard that the al-Rashid were plotting to attack our family's Kuwaiti hosts, Grandfather convinced his father and the Emir of Kuwait that he should return to Riyadh to displace the al-Rashid.

His verbal skills did not fail him. Although he was provided with little assistance, he did have permission to make the attempt to recover Riyadh and the surrounding region of Najd when he travelled with a small band of fighters to overthrow the al-Rashid.

Those familiar with the history of Saudi Arabia know that one man changed the future of the entire region, and that one man was my grandfather.

Against overwhelming odds, he defeated and retook the Najd. But his dreams did not fade and end with its occupation. During those years of exile, he had dreamed of luring all the tribes to the idea of a nation, making Arabia into one country recognized by the world. If Arabia did not become an established nation, he knew that our land would one day be occupied by foreign powers, like all the Middle Eastern countries bordering Saudi Arabia. This idea he could not bear.

Grandfather's dreams became a reality after fighting for two decades, using his military and diplomatic skills to defeat all who stood in his way. Without my grandfather, there would be no Saudi Arabia today. Arabia would still be a vast desert land filled with warring tribes, perhaps ruled by a foreign nation.

One man.

Many tribes.

One country.

My eyes have taken me on this wonderful journey to see my grandfather in his prime. He was all I had hoped for and more.

Now, sixty-five years after my grandfather's death, I take joy in closely watching Saudi Arabia's tall, handsome and intelligent Crown Prince. When he boldly makes announcements of the changes he will bring to our country and declares that he will make Saudi Arabia great again, I smile and look at Kareem.

'My husband,' I say, 'he is no longer coming. He has come.'

Chapter Two

The Joys and Torments of Family

THE WORLD HAS TURNED MANY times since I lost my mother, but with each turn I love her more.

From my own readings of the advancement of civilization, I know that the world has grown old discussing a mother's love for a child and a child's love for their mother. My darling mother was the embodiment of the richest love for her eleven children, but most especially for me, her youngest and most challenging daughter. I was the perpetrator of many naughty deeds, but despite my conduct, or my latest transgression creating upheaval in our home, I always understood that I could run to my mother for protection, knowing she would still love me unconditionally. Her unquestioned motherly love instilled happiness and confidence into my young life.

But then, just when I needed her the most, my mother died.

I was a young child in the early years of school when they took her away from our home to put her body in the ground. In my despairing grief, I withdrew to such a dark place in my mind that my oldest sister, Nura, who endeavoured to console her younger siblings at the loss of our mother, feared that her baby sister Sultana would never smile again. Nura was so anxious that she kept a small diary of my daily behaviour. She shared this diary with me a few years ago, only a year before she, too, died, and upon reading her entries I came to know that my eldest sister did indeed carry the burden of parenting her siblings and assumed all the worries of a mother. In her diary she recorded her anxieties, writing words such as, 'Sultana has not smiled. Sultana did not smile today. Will Sultana ever smile again?' Indeed, my morose and unhappy demeanour lingered a frighteningly long time during that traumatic phase of our lives.

But eventually, it seems, things slowly began to improve, and I recall how Nura hugged me tightly as she placed her finger on the date in the diary when her little sister Sultana began to smile again. It had been precisely 201 days after Mother passed. Looking back, I recall the reason for my smile: my father had given me a half-eaten candy bar that my brother had carelessly discarded. To me, even this small token was better than being ignored.

My father's mind was wrapped solely around his son, Ali. His every whim was catered for, his every need anticipated. He did not notice his daughters.

But I noticed that he did not notice.

Even now, more than forty years after Mother was buried in an unmarked grave, the conflicting emotions of grief and joy exist together in my heart and mind. While I know no greater joy than when I reminisce about the days I spent safely enveloped in my mother's love, the intensity of the grief I experienced after her death has never left me and it always overshadows my happiest moments.

Truthfully, each year since my mother's death I have felt her absence acutely and have deeply regretted that she has not been at my side to experience important moments in my life. My mother did not live to see her Sultana marry a man she loved and respected; she did not live to see her beloved daughter grow into a mature woman or become a mother herself, giving birth to three babies. My mother never knew that her Sultana, who was a poor student, devoted her life to elevating the lives of other females by ensuring they had access to education. And she did not live to see Saudi Arabia on the cusp of the greatest social change in our history. As much happiness as the promise of social change is now bringing to my heart, it would soar to the moon if I was able to celebrate with my mother, a woman who lived in a time when females had so few rights that their infant children could be taken from their arms should their husbands demand something even forbidden by our religion.

My darling mother would be astonished by the litany of rights now promised to Saudi women by one of her many nephews and my cousin, Crown Prince Muhammad bin Salman.

I try to conceive of her happiness at such wonderful news, but I cannot get past my longing for her mother's touch. My lips are quivering, and my eyes are threatening to shed tears as I gaze at her stunning photograph, which is displayed on the wall in front of me. Although none outside her immediate family ever viewed her lovely face, for such a thing is considered taboo in our society, Mother was a legendary beauty to all the royal women who saw her unveiled. She had a flawless complexion, large expressive eyes, full lips and thick wavy hair.

Feeling the nearness of death upon me, I become emotional. 'Oh Mother,' I say in a voice that breaks, 'if I might lie in the same grave with you, then I would not fear death.'

That's the moment my daughters, Maha and Amani, enter the room where I am sitting. Thankfully both are in light-hearted moods and appear to be taking pleasure from the other's company, which is not their typical behaviour. When they notice the tears gathering in my eyes, both rush to sit by my side and try to console me.

'Mummy,' Amani cries, 'whatever is wrong?'

'Mother,' Maha says, as she lightly massages the back of my neck, 'don't be sad.'

I nod, whispering, 'You are right. This will be a day that brings my mother's love closer to my heart. How I wish she was here with us, rather than a beautiful photograph on the wall. Oh, daughters!' I cry. 'How I miss her!'

Both my girls hug and kiss me before staring reverently at their grandmother's striking image. But then, quite suddenly, Amani gasps and points at the portico above my mother's photograph, crying out, 'What is *that*, Mummy?'

My eyes follow Amani's gaze. 'Those precious stones are in honour of your grandmother, my darlings.'

This is the first time my daughters have seen the newly installed, impressive archway studded with expensive rubies above her picture. This arch is topped by a larger arch, in the centre of which is an emerald stone that is worth nearly as much as our palace. I recently removed this stone out of an extravagant necklace that my husband gave me for our twenty-fifth wedding anniversary. My husband has been reminded many times that jewels hold little significance for me, but he has failed in his efforts to cease his lifetime custom of seeking out and buying the most precious for the women in his life.

Often without telling Kareem, I sell some pieces to use in support of good causes, such as the building of schools or to provide funds for a girl's education. But never will I sell the emerald stone.

I recall the moment I first saw this magnificent jewel. I instantly thought of my mother. Emeralds were her favourite, due to their vivid green. The particular shade of this stone represents Islam to Muslims, so my heart told me that it was only fitting that I display it in a splendid manner near Mother's photograph. It is a meaningful way of honouring her and her love of Islam.

The beautiful photograph, given to me by my father before his death, has now been moved to my personal sitting room from the small room near the main entranceway of our palace. This happened for a good reason. At the first ceremony that took place with my siblings and nieces to honour the portrait of my mother and its display in my home, my brother Ali's daughter Medina disrupted our lives in a most horrifying manner. Prior to our hanging the photograph in the entranceway, Medina grabbed the large picture, shouting to all that her father was the only son and, as such, that he was entitled to have the only photograph known of our mother. She objected most furiously to the portrait residing with me! This, despite the fact that prior to his death, and during a family gathering when all his children were witnesses to his words, our father called me to his side to tell me that our mother had asked that her youngest daughter, Sultana, be the recipient of the photograph.

Medina succeeded in dashing out of our palace doors with the photograph and fled our property. Maha followed, giving chase and dangerously speeding a car through Riyadh's busy streets. My heart nearly stopped as I watched her driving alone and breaking the laws of our country. Had she been stopped by the police, the publicity would have been humiliating for our family. For certain, Kareem would have been forced to call in favours from royal cousins to keep Maha out of jail. Abdullah, Kareem and other family members chased after her and together they managed to retrieve the photograph safely, without damage. However, there were many close calls that nearly lost us the only known photograph of our beloved mother, including a near drenching with red paint. Ali's new wife was having her dancing room repainted and when Medina realized that she was cornered she grabbed those buckets of red paint to splash on my family. My husband, son and Maha returned to our palace covered in it, but the photograph remained untouched.

The close call, thanks to Medina's thievery, was so traumatizing that even after Kareem hired the most experienced security specialists to protect Mother's photograph I felt uneasy that the treasured image was only a few steps from the main entrance of our palace.

In fact, due to this specific concern, I had difficulty sleeping and would awaken several times during the night to hurry to Mother's photograph to make certain that it was still in its proper place.

After discovering his distraught wife lying beneath her mother's photograph three nights in a row, Kareem made the decision to move the picture to somewhere more private and secure. That is when he very carefully planned and hired engineers to construct a huge addition to our palace, a structure separately made as secure as the underground vault beneath the Bank of England in London, according to the experts hired by my husband. As added security, the structure is far from any of the entrances. One would have to run down many long corridors with a large framed picture in hand to escape from our palace.

In addition to finding a suitably safe space to display Mother's photograph, Kareem was also eager to find a location to house his ever-growing collection of commemorative artefacts and other precious items of remembrance relating to our families and our young country. Kareem said this collection was part of our heritage and it was vital, therefore, that we made every effort to protect it for future generations.

My husband is now on a dedicated mission to recover as many items from our past as is possible. For example, he has discovered and purchased seventeen copies of the Koran, some dating as far back as the early 1800s, as well as fifty ancient, valuable but very frayed carpets. He even claims to have the timeworn camel bags that originally belonged to our grandfather, King Abdul Aziz. These bags would be tossed on the back of his war camel when he fought enemy tribes in the early 1900s after he had recaptured old Riyadh from the al-Rashid tribe.

He has centuries-old wooden doors and windows that he treasures for their great beauty. He would often talk in great detail about the enormous amount of work carried out by skilful artisans who carved intricate designs into the wood. They would then use coloured dyes, made from berries that had been ground into a fine powder in wooden bowls, to further decorate the wood. Despite my doubts about their authenticity, Kareem insists that these were the doors and windows used on our ancestors' modest mud homes in the old city of Riyadh. Such an idea makes my romantic husband very happy and I have often watched as he opens and closes the door latches, taking great care not to damage them. He seems to derive the most pleasure from running his fingers over the carved flowers and plants. It is evident to me that my husband is escaping the present and returning to the days of our warrior grandfather when he does these things. When he is busily involved with our family's past like this, I slip away to leave him to his innocent pleasures.

Once when I shared stories of my grandfather's feats, a smiling friend told me that a sure sign of ageing is when our thoughts linger more in the past than in the present. If this is so, then I must acknowledge that my husband and I are now of the age where most would say we are no longer young.

Of our children and grandchildren, only Abdullah and his daughter, Little Sultana, have shown an interest in Kareem's obsession, but my husband frequently urges all our children to view the items and artefacts he has displayed and tells them the same stories repeatedly in the hope that their interest will one day emerge.

The most dazzling decorations are reserved for the room that houses my mother's photograph. Kareem set out on a global search for the most brilliantly coloured mosaics for the walls and the tiles on the floors. There are two windows in the room, with exquisite shapes and beautiful hues of glass. The most unique and expensive carpet in our palace has been placed upon the centre portion of the floor of this room. The ceiling is made of wood, with lovely friezes of Arab script encircling it. A specially made desk created by a European master furniture designer holds a copy of our rarest Koran.

Mother's Room, as we call it, is the most exclusive in a palace richly decorated with divine furnishings. Additionally, Kareem recalled that my mother was an avid gardener; she had a great love for the beautiful flowers she grew and arranged in massive vases throughout our home. My husband even added an expansive botanical garden to the structure, telling me, 'What better ornament could there be for your mother than desert roses and lilies?'

With all these elements, there is a depth of feeling in the room, a gentleness and grace that reveals the soul of my mother.

Recently, and for the first time, I can see that my daughters are captivated by the result of their father's intensive efforts. Their exclamations of joy and admiration for the work he has undertaken make me very happy.

In our married youth, many were the times I was frustrated by my husband's actions, finding him to be too self-interested to please me, but over the years he has shown me his sincere character, which I believe to be the best that a man can be. Perhaps his faultless brother Assad, who is married to my sister Sara and who, after many years of marriage, still loves her deeply, set a fine example and over the years he has influenced my husband. All I know is that with age Kareem's attentions turned inward to his home, his wife, his children and grandchildren. No longer was he as distracted by business and the world outside as he once was; he receives the greatest pleasure in planning brilliant surprises for those he loves.

Truly, I am a fortunate woman to have married Kareem al-Sa'ud. How pleased I am that I did not divorce my husband during our unpleasant years of discord.

Just as I am thinking to praise my husband to my daughters, who remain sitting closely by me, loud noises interrupt my attention. A variety of feminine voices and jovial laughter resonate through the hallway and into the room where we are sitting. My sisters and their daughters have arrived for the special function I have planned to display the new room housing Mother's photograph, as well as show the newly built structure filled with historical items. Ten daughters and one son were born to my mother, but of my nine sisters only seven, besides myself, remain with the living, for we have lost our greatly loved siblings Nura and Reema.

Today I am anticipating the attendance of four sisters, including Dunia, Tahani, Haifa and Sara, along with seventeen daughters of my sisters. Three sisters are abroad at the moment, as we are a family who travels the world. I do not yet know if any of the daughters of my three travelling sisters might appear. Ali's four wives and twelve daughters were invited, but none are expected. My brother is uneasy knowing that his wives and daughters might hear tales of his unruly youth or, indeed, criticism of how he continues to behave in an unseemly fashion today; therefore, he generally discourages their attendance at our female functions.

I admit that I do not desire to see Medina, Ali's daughter, who, as I mentioned, has already stolen my mother's photo once. She was later diagnosed as having a condition known as bipolar, which I hear from my sister Sara creates epic dramas in my brother's home.

Regrettably, my son Abdullah, his wife and two children are also travelling. This means his daughter, Little Sultana, who is soon to be twelve years old, will not be a part of this gathering. She knows more about her grandfather's collection than any family member and would be the ideal guide to give a presentation of the most interesting pieces. Alas, that is not to be.

Over the years Mother's eleven children have expanded into an enormous family, for when we count the children, grandchildren and great-grandchildren of our parents, we reach the large number of seventy-three immediate family members. My mother did not live to see or embrace any of her grandchildren, and for that I am particularly sad, for no one loved children with the intensity of our mother. How happy she would have been to be surrounded by all, reigning as the matriarch of our family gatherings. My mother is never far from my thoughts on such occasions.

My daughters and I hurry to wait at the doorway in the spacious room where Kareem has housed his artefacts. Here we will greet my sisters and nieces. Of my sisters, only Sara has seen my husband's antique collection, which Kareem is justly proud of.

As we patiently await the arrival of our guests, suddenly we are encircled by a flurry of activity and joyful laughter.

Dunia is the first to brush against me. 'Sultana, love! I have missed you!' Her large brown eyes are sparkling and her voice indicates a great affection that I know she is incapable of feeling; she dips her head without smiling. I have not seen my sister in nearly a year due to our conflicting schedules and I am not surprised to see that her face is even more youthful than her daughters', who are in their prime and beautiful. Sara had forewarned me that Dunia had spent the past four months in Switzerland undergoing various plastic surgery procedures. With this knowledge, I experience no shock in seeing the ageing Dunia without a single wrinkle, despite the fact she is ten years older than me. But I am taken aback by the appearance of my sister's lips. Dunia has had them pumped as big as possible and the result is painfully comic! When she leans down to kiss me on my forehead and cheeks, it feels as though a damp sponge ball is brushing against my face.

I am panicked, wondering how I might compliment her appearance, most particularly her lips, but I say nothing because Maha speaks for me. My daughter cannot restrain herself and yelps like a surprised puppy: 'Auntie! You look different! What happened?'

Dunia's eyes flash in anger, but she holds her irritation. 'Darling, I am the same as the day I was born. You have neglected me for so long that you do not remember your auntie. For shame, Maha.'

My daughter bites into her own lips as she stifles a snicker. I pinch her on her back, reminding her to heed proper manners.

In the past there would have been a danger of Maha pulling on those lips and making a joke of them, but thankfully over the years my daughter has learned to guard her tongue more carefully. Feeling my warning, her reply is restrained.

'Of course, Auntie. I have been absent far too long. I am sorry.'

The scene evokes a forgotten memory. The year before, Sara had told me that Dunia was attracted to the look presented by Angelina Jolie. My sister was desperate to be as beautiful as the famous Hollywood actress, however it is a goal difficult for most women of the world. Ms Jolie was born with her juicy lips, which means they look natural despite their size. My sister's abundance of injections now cries out for a surgical reduction. Dunia's small frame does not support oversized features.

I question how my sister succeeds in talking or eating normally with those huge lips. To satisfy my curiosity, I make a decision to observe Dunia when we take afternoon tea later in the day.

Of all my sisters, Dunia is the one most obsessed with maintaining a youthful appearance and trim body. Her latest attempt took my mind back many years, to a day when I was still a child and Nura was much like our surrogate mother. Nura and Sara, my mother always said, were the most kindhearted of her daughters, and now as an adult I can say she knew her daughters well.

My vision brought Nura back to life, for it was from her that I learned poor Dunia was cursed with unhealthy obsessions. While nine of Mother's daughters had strong appetites, Dunia ate with extreme caution, counting her bites and never allowing more than five to enter her mouth at each mealtime. Once I teased Dunia about her eating habits, laughing and saying, 'My sister, you are going to disappear you are so skinny. Can you not count over five? Or are you missing teeth and cannot chew?' I cringe now when I recall my cruel taunts at Dunia's discomfort. That's when elder sister Nura pulled me aside.

'Sultana, be kind to your sister,' she said. 'She was born with a curse – a curse to be the most beautiful woman in the world.' Nura made a sad face. 'But we know that no one can be more beautiful than our Sara. Dunia's unattainable preoccupation brings her depression and unhappiness that none of us can understand.'

Although I have become sympathetic to Dunia's obsessions, over the years she has still created a lot of shock in my mind. Dunia's unreachable desires are not limited to appearance alone. As I mentioned in an earlier book about my life, she has long been gripped by a passionate desire to create a jewellery collection to rival the famous assortment amassed by the movie star Elizabeth Taylor; her jewels recently auctioned for the enormous sum of $100 million. In fact, on the day of the auction my sister was the recipient of three of those jewellery sets, purchased by an agent so that my sister's name would not be known to the world. In our royal family, excessive publicity when spending large sums of money is not admired, particularly for the females.

The previous year, in fact, Dunia had pleaded with me to come to her palace to view her collection, but I could not gather the interest necessary to spend an entire day feigning excitement and complimenting my sister on her jewels.

The final analysis is that my sister Dunia is one of the most miserable women I have ever known. Her manic obsession for remaining youthful leaves her unsatisfied because there will always be a woman younger and more beautiful. Her second obsession of collecting jewels is nothing more than a desperate attempt to fill the void in her life with useless items that do nothing for the good of our world. A self-obsessed manner, greed and a constant striving for impossible goals has led to great unhappiness.

There have been occasions when Sara or I attempted to interest Dunia in financing schools in poor nations, adopting some poor families to support or sponsoring young women in their educational quests, but Dunia's eyes go blank and her face freezes rigid when one reminds her of the joy of charity. Other than her children and grandchildren, never have I known Dunia to help anyone. I am certain that the combined worth of my sister and her husband must total at least a billion dollars. What a pity they share nothing of their wealth to help those in need.

I am of the belief that an auspicious birth and a fortune to rival most in the world bring an obligation to be generous and open-hearted to others.

In the midst of this gathering, with Maha still attempting to stifle laughter and Amani gasping in disbelief, I look around to find Sara. My closest sister since I was a child is able to read my mind. After our eyes meet, she rushes to release me from Dunia, pulling her away to view the beautiful and priceless collection of Bedouin jewellery displayed on one full wall. I hear Dunia make bizarre squeaking sounds and suddenly realize that her new lips will not allow normal cries of joy. But I am most concerned that she might believe it possible to take some of the rare pieces of Bedouin jewellery for herself.

Hoping that Sara will keep her honest eyes on Dunia, I turn to my sisters Haifa and Tahani, who are holding hands and laughing gaily. The two have always been close and as children would weep if Mother suggested they sleep in separate beds. I recall those nights well when their cries would keep me awake.

I have a strong memory of slipping into Haifa's bed and whispering, 'Mother has gone to bed. She will never know if you return to Tahani.' My sisters were all obedient when it came to Mother's instructions. Haifa would gasp and turn her back to me at the audacity that I would suggest she disobey our mother, despite the emotional agony the two girls endured at having to sleep alone – separated from one another.

Haifa's reaction puzzled me, for although I dearly loved my mother I suffered no remorse at disobeying orders from any adult, even from my mother. I would only experience sorrow if my disobedience was discovered.

But Haifa was always a dutiful child, and since Nura's death Haifa is now the eldest sister in our family. She relishes the position, as she believes it gives her the justification to know all about our activities, and to suggest changes in our business and personal lives. But Haifa is such a precious woman, gentle and kind, and no one takes offence when she digs into our personal affairs or business matters in order to assist with various recommendations, none of which her sisters accept – although we each smile and nod in agreement with whatever suggestions she makes at any given moment, leaving Haifa to believe that she has helped us with her 'words of wisdom' and has saved each of us from what she believes are destructive habits.

Haifa's life appears to be happy, and she and her husband enjoy their seven children and nine grandchildren. Generally, her family spends most of the year in the south of France at their beautiful villa overlooking the sea, so it is pleasant to see Haifa in my home, despite her inquisitive ways.

'Sultana,' she now says with a frown, 'please, while I am in the kingdom, let us make time for me to come over and help you balance your charity books. I believe that you have taken on more than you can manage.' I chuckle and affectionately hug my sister, content to let her believe that I cannot successfully administer my accounts without her assistance. I smile in amusement but would never want Haifa to be aware of how she entertains me with her attempts to interfere.

'Of course, Haifa. You are too kind, sister. For sure, we will speak about this later.' I know that Haifa will forget the details and convince herself that she had indeed helped me with my accounts, and later in the year she will go into detail, telling Sara how she saved me from financial ruin.

Tahani glances at me and winks, knowing exactly my thoughts. Tahani is the sister who is so charming that all believe her to be the dearest friend in the family. Tahani does not have even the smallest particle of meanness in her body. Her only shortcoming is her inability to be on time for any appointment – be it a family business or leisure engagement. She is flighty in conduct and is always rushing to one missed appointment after another. That is why Haifa generally asks her driver to take her to Tahani's palace prior to any social engagement. With Haifa as her chaperone, Tahani makes our family gatherings on time.

Tahani is the mother of two sons and three daughters, and she enjoys an unusually close relationship with all her children, who insist upon seeing their mother at least once weekly for an extended visit. They love to gather together to entertain Tahani and share all their family news.

Tahani has a lovely face, with big expressive eyes and a bright smile. She does battle weight issues, but her husband constantly praises her beauty and threatens to leave her if she loses a single kilo. Their relationship is playful and delightful. They suffer none of the tense battles I knew in the early days of marriage with Kareem.

Sara often says, 'Lucky Tahani is on a life-long honeymoon with her husband.' It gives my family great satisfaction to see such contentment.

At that moment, Dunia pulls away from Sara to rush at Tahani, telling her, 'Darling sister, you must come with me to Switzerland. I have the most fabulous physician who performs miracles with liposuction.' Dunia pats Tahani's tummy with her hand. 'In three sessions, this tummy would disappear.'

Confident Tahani strokes her own tummy, laughing. 'And what then, Dunia? Lose my husband? He adores me just as I am. No thank you, sister.'

Haifa and Tahani share the funny moment and walk away once again hand in hand. Dunia stares after Tahani with a disapproving look. 'I cannot believe that I have an obese sister. It is a scandal, Sultana.'

Dunia then looks at me, glancing down at my body. Instinctively, I find myself pulling in a deep breath and holding my stomach as flat as possible, then realize what I am doing and exhale. Although I am not overweight, I am not the slim girl I was when I was a bride. Happily, I have no regrets at not making my appearance the foremost goal in my life. As a middle-aged woman, I have accepted that I will never again look as though I am only twenty years old. Being healthy is my first concern, for I would like to live an extended life and enjoy my children and grandchildren for as long as possible.

Sara takes Dunia by the hand, leading her away. 'Dunia, dear sister, you must not say such hurtful things. Not everyone can be as perfect as you.'

Dunia purrs with happiness that Sara has recognized her perfection.

My sister Sara once again has the ideal response to another's cruelty. Although it is a reprimand and Dunia recognizes it as such, there are no awkward reactions. Sara has gained the respect of all who know her as a great diplomat. As such, if she admonishes, everyone listens.

That's when Maha and Amani leave my side to join their cousins. I smile with pride as I watch my beautiful girls walk away. I am a realistic woman and can admit that while both have personality defects that have created havoc in our home more than once, I have lately seen signs of maturity, with a welcome lapse of their constant bickering. It makes me happy to think that perhaps each of my girls can finally enjoy the other's company.

The joyous sounds of young women at a party escalate noticeably when my daughters begin to greet all their cousins. I admit that I take special joy in hearing the loud talk and laughter of the next generation fill my palace.

Hors d'oeuvres are soon served. Although I have chefs who are artists in the kitchen gallery, on this occasion I have catered the affair from one of Riyadh's finest French shops. I am so pleased when I see that everything is impeccably prepared and beautifully displayed that I feel a tinge of regret that all is to be eaten.

I have no opportunity to study Dunia's munching capabilities with those large lips, for my sister refuses all the tempting morsels, accepting only a glass of cold apple juice, from which she never sips. I should have known that my sister would refuse all food, for, as I have explained, Dunia is terrified of gaining an extra kilo.

After refreshments, Maha makes a loud announcement, which is easily heard above the boisterous chatter and noise. 'Everyone! Follow your favourite cousin, please! My mother has something very special to show you!'

All those in the room laugh, for Maha is certainly unique and can be entertaining and witty if she is in a good mood. Her bold and forthright temperament has delighted her cousins more than once. In fact, all present would select her company over that of Amani, who even as an adult takes great pleasure in giving pointed advice to everyone around her. To my sorrow, Amani is an obstinate girl who truly believes she knows better than all and views every female cousin as a project. She likes to dispense advice with such haughtiness that it makes my daughter an unwelcome companion to most. I am sorry that my nieces think of Amani as someone to avoid, although I am pleased that on this evening Amani has softened her fanatical observations and annoying advice.

All assembled guests dutifully follow Maha and gather in Mother's Room. Amani walks quickly to accompany me, holding my hand. Once inside, I savour the moment, for I can easily see that all are entranced. I comprehend from the gasps, followed by excited chatter and smiles, that my sisters and nieces are ecstatic about the beauty of the chamber and the breathtaking manner in which Mother's photograph is exhibited. The display is the greatest triumph of the evening. There is not a single critical remark, not even from Dunia.

However, despite my happiness, I should have known better than to assume the best, for the evening had not yet ended.

*　　*　　*

Our gathering was so pleasurable that the hours passed quickly from afternoon to evening. I was agreeably surprised when none of the younger women made excuses to leave, as that is their customary behaviour when at a party with the older generation. Just as we were unwinding and beginning to relax into comfortable sofas in our largest sitting room, there was a loud noise that sounded like falling furniture.

Dunia struggled to scream – I heard only the slight whistling squeal escape from between those hopelessly unusable lips. Sara and I exchanged quick glances before bolting from the room, followed by our daughters, Maha and Nashwa.

Unsure of where the clamour arose, we first rushed into Mother's Room, where I saw a scene that caused my heart to race dangerously fast. There was Ali's wayward daughter Medina sprawled on the floor beneath Mother's photograph. At her side was a young woman in a black ninja suit with a head covering, also in black. Hers was the sort of costume that appears in movies featuring thieves who are attempting to rob wealthy hotel clients in southern France. This was a woman I had never before seen.

Then I saw a three-step ladder turned upside down on the floor near to Medina. Confusion reigned while I tried to determine exactly what was happening, but Maha instantly knew that Medina, once again, was there to steal Mother's photograph.

'You! Thief!' Maha shouted at her cousin, before pushing aside the black-attired stranger to lean down and yank Medina by both arms, straining to pull her to her feet.

Medina cried out in pain. 'Stop! Stop! My arms are broken.'

'Good news, Medina,' Maha growled, as she yanked more enthusiastically.

Medina shrieked loudly.

'Maha, no, I believe she *is* truly hurt,' Sara said, as she placed her hands on Maha's back.

'She is a known liar, Auntie. Do not let her act fool you. Besides, if she is not yet hurt, I will happily hurt her.'

By this time Haifa and Tahani, along with several nieces, were pushing into the room to discover the source of the commotion. All watched as Nashwa and Sara together tugged on Maha until she released her cousin.

I cringed and cried out when Maha gave Medina a swift parting kick to her bottom. 'Maha, no,' I pleaded. 'Please, no further violence, darling.'

Maha practically spat her words. 'Mother, it seems that Medina believes that all roads in Riyadh lead to Grandmother's photograph! I will teach her to avoid those roads!'

My daughter is one of the strongest women I know, both mentally and physically. She is aggressive for the right and aggressive against the wrong. When Maha is presented with a problem that needs solving, she will spring into action, regardless of any danger to herself. Neither Kareem nor I have ever been able to discourage Maha from doing what she believes is right – even if it means physical violence. At that moment I feared that Maha was dangerously close to seriously harming her cousin.

Medina has similar qualities, although she uses her emotional and physical strength to *do* wrong, rather than to *correct* wrong. Whether her misdeeds are wholly related to her bipolar disorder or she is simply a wicked girl, I do not know. But I do realize that when these two royal cousins clash there is valid reason to fear the outcome. Thankfully I was not alone with Maha and Medina or it would have been difficult for me to calm the situation.

Medina whimpered. 'My arms. My arms!'

'Medina,' Maha said in a strong, determined voice, 'do not fret about broken arms. But I suggest that you do worry about those grasping, long-fingered hands of yours that will be cut off in Deera Square if you do not cease stealing items that do not belong to you.'

'Maha! No! Do not say such things,' I told my daughter. I did glance at Medina's large hands. They are so large that they resemble the hands of a man. There is nothing feminine about my niece, in fact. Yet I shivered at the thought of blood spurting from her wrist if her hand was severed by the executioner's sword and knew that I did not wish her that harm.

I know more than I would like about the grisly punishments meted out at Deera Square, also known as Justice Square. Located in what could be described as a downtown area of Riyadh, it is known to all Saudi Arabians, and to many others arriving in our land from around the world, as the place where our criminals are punished by a hefty Saudi man brandishing a sword. Although there are other countries that inflict capital punishment for serious crimes committed, with the United States among them, for some reason our Saudi method of justice dispensed from the point of a sword seems more offensive to most than the image of those who are shot with a gun or have needles injected into their restrained bodies with powerful drugs that stop the heart.

I have always been extremely curious by nature and some years ago, after reading a Western newspaper article condemning my country for our methods of punishment, I conducted research on beheadings and the cutting off of limbs. While I am sad and sorry that such punishments are inflicted, I have no better plan of how to permanently stop murderers and rapists, for such hard-hearted criminals appear addicted to their crime of choice, leaving countless innocent victims in their wake.

As for beheadings, I have read that there are benefits over other methods of capital punishment. For sure, beheading causes an instant cringe-reaction in most, but whether the choice of weapon for beheading is a guillotine or a sword, both are swift methods of ending a life.

From what I have read, the French guillotine is the more efficient. Where a man swings a sword, mistakes are known to occur – there have been times when it has taken the Saudi Arabian executioner three or four strikes to separate the head from the neck, meaning that the death was gruesome, long and painful. The guillotine does not make such mistakes. It is a precise device built to hold a weighted and angled blade.

After the criminal condemned to death is placed in stocks with the neck positioned carefully below the blade, death comes in a matter of moments. When the blade is released, it falls fast to decapitate the criminal in one clean cut. The French were so thoughtful that they even placed a basket in a perfectly aligned position so as to catch the head. Thankfully, the French stopped displaying severed heads long before they ceased to use the guillotine in 1981, when they abolished capital punishment.

We Saudis are not quite so organized as the French.

Our criminals are taken on Fridays after the morning prayers to Deera Square, where large crowds are encouraged to gather to be reminded of what will happen to them should they commit a grave crime. The most serious crimes in Saudi are murder, rape, adultery, armed robbery and drug trafficking, all of which result in a sentence of death by beheading. Other lesser crimes include theft, which will cost a repeat offender one hand. Then if the criminal continues to steal, he or she will lose a second hand, then a foot, then a second foot – although I have never heard of a thief so persistent that all four limbs were lost to the sword.

I have heard from family members who attend these events out of curiosity that the crowd displays a festive attitude. Onlookers eagerly anticipate the arrival of the police. The criminals are pulled from the cars, one by one, at which moment those about to die will see the man and the sword, made of steel and four feet long.

The executioner, who has been known to give interviews about how he trains for his job, and how he feels fortunate and honoured to have such a career, appears eager to begin his day's work, or so I have been told. I recall reading an article about one Saudi family who held what they believed to be a coveted position as official executioners. As the father aged, he trained his son to follow him in his chosen vocation.

In Deera Square, the condemned are placed on a fixed spot, with a drain nearby, so that the head may roll into it.

Once the criminal is in position, the executioner lowers his blade and jabs at the neck of the condemned. This is done purposely, as the one about to be executed is super tense by this time, waiting for the strike. The poke by the sword causes the prisoner to lurch. When he jerks, the executioner is poised to strike. He very quickly lifts the sword high in the air and then swings it back down with such power that onlookers hear a thud about the same time as they see spurting blood.

When the head is so violently removed, the body of the prisoner snaps up before slumping to the plaza ground. That's when several men rush in to lift the body on to a stretcher. One of the men will grab the head and wrap it in a cloth, placing the head beside the body. Only then does an announcer on a loudspeaker tell the crowd what the criminal did to deserve the ultimate punishment of decapitation.

The executioner will then wipe the blood off his sword, sheath it and walk away, a happy man who gets satisfaction from his job.

When it comes to thieves, the prisoner lives, but if he survives the cutting off of a limb the worst of the punishment is yet to come. They say that the prisoner screams the loudest when the stump is dipped into boiling oil to stop the gushing of blood.

The bloody scene in my mind's eye repulses me and makes my body stiffen. I am brought back to the moment, knowing that I would never allow Medina to lose a hand, even if she was so vile as to steal my treasured photograph.

When I have recovered my composure, I see Sara kneeling beside Medina. She speaks in a calm, quiet and kindly voice.

'Medina, love, what were you trying to do?'

Medina is still weeping in pain, but nothing can diminish her defiance.

'I came to take what is my father's property.' Medina glares at me with loathing. 'She is the thief,' she snarls. 'Not me!'

'I will not allow you to speak such an untruth, Medina. Sultana is not deserving of these stones you are throwing. I was there when our father told Sultana that our mother had specifically asked that her youngest daughter receive the picture. Mother knew that no one would suffer more than Sultana when she died – for she was very young and vulnerable. Mother also understood that Sultana's love would ensure the proper handling of the only photograph that captured her likeness. All these things have come to pass, just as our mother envisioned. Your father has no right to the photograph, although he should be pleased that he can come and see it whenever he pleases.'

All those gathered around began to shout at Medina, their voices intermingling so it was impossible to understand who was saying what in the clamour. But it was clear that all were disappointed with Medina for her disrespect of my mother's wishes.

Medina contemplated her aunties and cousins, who were furious with her actions, and suddenly she broke into loud sobs, calling for her own mother and father. In an instant, she went from being loud and obnoxious to a tearful young woman filled with regrets.

This is how one with bipolar problems behaves, I thought to myself. But I said nothing aloud, for I was not certain if Sara had confided this information to any other sister.

It was at this moment that the ninja girl who had accompanied Medina stumbled and pushed her way out of the room. For the first time, I noticed that her hand was holding tightly to a small black cloth bag. What was in that bag, I wondered.

I was mainly concerned with getting her out of our home. We did not know her identity and I was not pleased that she was running around freely in a palace filled with expensive items. She was an obvious burglar or she would not have accompanied Medina. Perhaps she was the mastermind, I suddenly thought.

'Maha,' I shouted, 'please call security and have them find that girl and hold her.'

I looked at Amani. 'Darling, go and find your father. Tell him he is needed.'

Medina's hysterical sobs were growing louder with each passing moment. Sara and I quickly forgave her, but we were the only ones to react in sympathy.

Haifa telephoned Ali on her cell phone, telling him in a loud voice, 'Ali! Brother! Come to Sultana's now. You need to collect your daughter. Alert your medical staff to open your clinic. Medina has been injured while committing a crime.' Ali, like many of the royals, has a personal team of doctors and nurses who operate a medical clinic in the grounds of his palace.

That's when three of our male servants rushed into the room. They had heard the uproar and come to assist. Understanding that the family were not in danger, they began to sort out the room, lifting the stepladder and straightening the various pieces of furniture that had been displaced when Medina crashed to the floor.

I was shaken by the incident, realizing for the first time that Medina could have been seriously injured or killed had her head hit a hard object. Had that happened, it would have been a true tragedy.

Although Ali's palace is located a full thirty-minute drive from our own, within a few minutes he arrived with two of his sons.

'I am sorry, Father,' Medina mumbled, while looking into his face. 'I thought they would all be gone.' Her voice was low, yet we all overheard her telling words.

Tahani asked the obvious question. 'Ali, exactly where were you when Haifa called?'

Ali blushed red but refused to reply.

At this moment Sara's eyes met my own and we both grasped an unwelcome truth. Ali had obviously been nearby, and he and his sons had been involved in the potential theft of Mother's picture! They had been waiting near our palace to protect Medina and help her escape once she had the photograph in her hand.

Ali busied himself, focusing his attention on Medina. He lifted one of her arms and she screamed. 'It is broken! Both my arms are broken!'

'Who did this to you, daughter?' my brother asked with an angry edge to his voice.

Medina looked at me with an evil gaze. Finally, she spoke her lies. 'It was my cousin, Maha. I came into this room to enjoy a moment of quiet with my grandmother and I was attacked without reason by Maha. I believe she has broken both my arms.' She paused before saying, 'Maha really should be arrested for assault, Father.'

Medina was making fresh enemies every minute.

I stood aghast, thinking how it is that in a huge family such as ours only one or two members of that family can create complete lunacy that affects us all. I can find no words to describe my sorrow for the harm Ali and his family constantly create for me and my daughters.

My sister Sara stood to her feet, looking hard at Medina and then at Ali.

'My brother, take your daughter and leave before I contact the police and have your daughter arrested.'

Sara turned upon Medina in exasperated scorn. 'Medina, you are no longer my niece. Your lies are gaining momentum. Your lies are harming the reputation of innocent people. I will not stand for it. You tell your father the truth, that you were climbing a ladder to steal my mother's photograph when you fell and broke your arms. Maha only became involved once you were discovered here.'

Haifa and Tahani gathered round Sara. Haifa told Ali, 'Your daughter is lying. Your sisters are telling the truth.'

Tahani gazed sadly at Medina, who glowered back at her auntie. 'Ali, brother, you need to spend some of your wealth on treatment for Medina. With the passing years, a troubled young girl has now become an intolerable delinquent.'

Ali's lowered eyes watched everything with a look of gloomy suspicion. But he remained silent as he contemplated the multitude of sisters and nieces, recognizing that he was vastly outnumbered.

Ali motioned for his sons to help him lift Medina. The three of them carried her from my home without expressing a word of apology.

That's when Kareem came rushing through the corridor and into the room.

'Sultana! Amani told me that a theft was interrupted. What has happened?' Kareem seized me by my shoulders as the pitch of his voice rose so high it was shrill. 'Tell me now. Were you hurt? Was anyone hurt?' Kareem paused, suddenly remembering his hobby. 'Has someone stolen a part of my collection?'

'Kareem,' I replied, 'put your mind at ease. Your family is safe, other than Medina, who has broken both arms.' An expression of relief passed over Kareem's face. 'And,' I added, 'your collection has not been touched.'

Kareem smiled broadly. My husband truly believed that everyone valued his antiques just as he did.

I explained further, 'Mother's photograph remains untouched.' Pointing to the stepladder, I said, 'Medina was attempting once again to steal Mother's picture. But she met with failure due to her own clumsiness. See . . .' I gestured towards Mother's picture, a smile coming to my face for the first time since Medina had alerted us to her presence. 'Mother is safe.'

'Yes, Mother is safe,' Haifa laughed.

That's the moment Amani screamed.

I shuddered in fear and turned to look at my daughter. What now?

'Mother, Father, look! Look! The stones. The stones!'

'The stones?' I repeated. Then I saw what Amani had detected. Both archways over Mother's picture had been relieved of their expensive stones. The rubies had disappeared, but most importantly the huge emerald had vanished. Looking as closely as I could at that distance, I could see where a sharp instrument had been used to extract the stones from the woodwork.

Kareem grabbed me by my waist. 'The stones. The stones are gone!'

'Medina has the stones,' Tahani muttered.

That's when the last image of the girl in black attire came to my mind – her clutching the drawstring bag.

'No! Not Medina! No! The ninja girl! She is the one who ran away with the stones.'

My husband looked at me as though I had finally gone mad.

'Ninja girl?' he repeated.

By this time Dunia had rushed in to find the reason for the deafening chaos. When she comprehended that the irreplaceable emerald stone had been stolen, my sister fainted. Sara and Maha's night grew even more challenging when they insisted upon accompanying the servants taking Dunia to our medical clinic on the palace property, for when my sister fainted and fell she burst open her upper lip.

Kareem, Amani and I instructed our servants and security staff to search every corner in the palace. Hours later the ninja girl remained on the loose, either hiding in our palace or having escaped our grounds.

All these calamities demoralized me. I felt a violent shiver pressing against my heart and mind. Seeds of indignation were growing in my mind, threatening all that was happy in my life. I was tormented by the futility of any attempts to reason with my brother and his daughter, both of whom were overcome by envy and covetousness, twin emotions that poison the natural harmony that exists between most in any family. Tonight, for the first time, I recognized that Ali and his daughter were not just difficult, I believed that they both needed psychiatric help.

My brother, Medina and the ninja girl would have to wait until the sun rose on another day, I told myself. In the knowledge that the security staff were monitoring our home and the grounds, I felt safe and collapsed into bed later that night. My last thoughts should have been of my mother and the flawless triumph of the night, but due to the lunacy that exists in my family, nothing was as it should be.

'But madness will not prevail,' I whispered as I closed my eyes.

Chapter Three

The Mystery of the Ninja Girl

IN A BURST OF HEROISM, Maha alone captured the ninja girl.

But I knew nothing of her gallantry as Kareem eased me from sleep by delivering gentle kisses on my forehead and hands. 'Darling, please. Wake up. It is early for you, I know, but we have much to do.'

Still drowsy, yet still enchanted by the man I married, I felt no irritation, but instead smiled, for I do not resent adoration. Besides, I was calmed by a temporary memory loss of the upsetting events of the prior evening. All things bad had vanished during my deep sleep. 'My husband, I must sleep until noon,' I said, yawning.

'Sultana, we do not have the luxury of time. If that girl leaves the property and makes her way back to Ali's palace, we will never see those jewels again. We must act quickly!'

That's when a vivid memory of the previous night flooded my mind with such force that I was suddenly thrown into an unspeakable agitation. 'The jewels!' I cried out. 'Mother's jewels!' I stumbled out of bed and scrambled to find suitable clothes to wear. I knew we would have to search the property, and our grounds are extensive, so I would wear something comfortable. That devious girl could be hiding anywhere.

Kareem stood up. 'While you ready yourself, I will ask if any of our security people have seen the girl.'

Never have I dressed so rapidly. Soon I hurried out of my quarters, walking briskly to find my husband. Just when I was considering whether to turn left or right at the next juncture, I caught a glimpse of Maha and her father hurrying down the corridor in my direction.

I was momentarily startled to see Maha up so early. When I'd retired at midnight, my daughter had still been at the medical clinic with Sara and Dunia.

Recalling how painful my sister's injured lip appeared to be, I asked, 'Maha, how is Dunia?'

'Sore. She is very sore. Those lips are creating immense pain. She is flying to Switzerland this after-noon after the doctor told her last night that she must have a surgical reduction of her lips or she will con-tinue to have such painful incidents.' Maha made a face expressing puzzlement. 'The doctor questioned the professionalism of the physician who performed the procedure; in fact, he was angry that Dunia had pursued something so radical as this kind of cosmetic procedure.'

I shrugged, sorry to hear the news but overwhelmed at that moment by more pressing matters than Dunia's dangerous choices in her inane attempt to stay young for ever.

That's when I first noticed that Kareem was smiling widely.

'Tell your mother, Maha.'

'Tell me what?'

That's when I observed that Maha was holding both hands behind her back. My daughter's eyes sparkled with delight. Like a small child, she laughed with an open mouth as she lifted her right arm and dangled the drawstring bag before my eyes.

'*Maha! Really?*'

'Really, Mother. Here are the jewels. All are here!'

Speechless, I hugged my daughter before clasping my husband, then embracing my daughter a second time.

I cried out, '*What? How?*'

I heard amusement in the tone of his voice when Kareem said, 'It is a *long* story, Sultana. But let us not stand in the corridor.'

I agreed. 'Yes, let's sit somewhere comfortable and have a hot tea and some nourishment. With all this excitement, I have had no time to eat or drink this morning.'

Kareem smiled. 'I wish to hear the whole story. I do not yet know every detail. I only know that our daughter performed a miracle while we were sleeping.'

I stood with my hand over my mouth, so happy I could barely restrain myself from dancing. I am sure such a thing would thoroughly shock my husband, as I have never considered taking up wiggling about on a dance floor, as our country is quite conservative on that matter. While women do dance at weddings where there are female guests only, we do not dance easily or routinely, as our Egyptian sisters are prone to do, so I kept my feet still.

As we sat at the small breakfast table, Maha carefully placed the drawstring bag in the middle of the table, where all our eyes could keep it in view.

I very contentedly sipped my tea, listening to Maha tell how she had found success.

Maha told us, 'First of all, Mother, I will give you a bit more detail about Dunia and how it was I came home from the clinic earlier than I expected. Your doctor and his nurses were startled by Auntie Dunia's injured lip.' Maha let out a sad chuckle, expressing no sympathy for her aunt. 'We waited by her side until she regained awareness after having anaesthesia. Much to Auntie Dunia's despair, the doctor demanded that his patient remain overnight since the anaesthesia would not wear off for a few hours, but she might awaken in great discomfort. Auntie Sara was her usual calm self and requested a second cot for the room, where she said she would rest, while waiting for the morning sun, beside her sister.

'Auntie Sara also insisted that I return home in case you were waiting for news of Dunia, and also so that I could sleep in my own bed. Therefore, I reluctantly left them.

'When I entered the palace, the security team were all relaxing with coffee while sitting back with their feet on footrests. Their conduct led me to assume that the criminal had been apprehended. I was astonished when told otherwise – that twelve well-trained guards could not find one woman.

'I questioned the team and although I was told that each unoccupied room in the palace had been searched and then locked off, and that every corner of the grounds had been investigated, I felt uneasy.' Maha smiled at me. 'That ninja girl, as you call her, was small and dressed all in black, including most of her face, so I presumed that she would find it easy to slip from place to place in the dark of night without being easily detected.'

Maha paused, having a sip of tea, then clearing her throat. 'I knew then that I could not retire, for I would not rest.' She shook her head. 'How could I, Mother? The evening had been so perfect. And you were so pleased and happy with all that you had done to honour your precious mother. I could not bear the thought of seeing what I knew would be disappointment flash in your eyes if the jewels were not recovered.'

Kareem reached out to stroke his daughter's hands.

I felt tears forming in my eyes, thanking God that I had such a daughter. Maha, for all her tough exterior, has a soft interior. The theme song of her life is to protect those she loves. I knew that my child had suffered a great rage that a stranger whom we did not know had entered my home and had attempted to abscond with precious jewels that belonged to our family. It was doubly offensive because the jewels were displayed in honour of her long-dead grandmother.

Having questioned the security men, Maha took matters into her own hands while all in the palace were sleeping. With enormous courage, she set out to find the thief. Our home *is* doubtless a fine palace, yet it is not nearly so large as most owned by my royal cousins. After excluding the rooms occupied for the night, there were only thirty-five rooms for my daughter to search.

'Mother, first I set out to do exactly what had already been done. I searched every room, other than those inhabited by sleeping family or staff, for I knew that if the thief was in an occupied room, someone would spot her. So I was disappointed when my palace search was unsuccessful, for I knew that looking through the grounds would be much more complicated.'

I exhaled, eager to hear the rest of this adventure.

'But I was determined, Mother. The thief would not go uncaught or unpunished. I knew that Uncle Ali and Medina had most likely forgotten their partner in crime, never once considering the girl's plight, for both are so selfish. The thief had been abandoned! But I was concerned that once hysterical Medina calmed down and received treatment for her broken arms she would remember the jewels, and who had them. I feared they would return for the jewels, if not for Medina's accomplice.

'I then moved on to consider the grounds, and where someone might conceal themselves in darkness. Father,' she smiled and said, looking at Kareem, 'you have created gardens that are a green paradise, with so many bushes and trees that there are hundreds of corners in which one can take cover. A thief will feel at home in all that green camouflaging. Thinking about the height of the metal barriers surrounding the grounds, and the number of guards on the two gates, I assumed the thief would remain hidden, waiting until the morning hours when there would be much activity with the comings and goings of visitors and staff and other palace workers. I felt confident that was when she was intending to slip away with the valuables.'

I groaned, reflecting on how close we came to losing Mother's jewels, which is how I thought of the rubies and the emerald. I wanted those jewels to surround Mother's picture so long as the earth turns on its axis and civilization exists.

'So,' Maha said, 'I knew that I must carefully devise a plan. But first I hurried to my room and put on jeans and climbing boots. Then I went outside and assessed the surroundings. I almost instantly decided on the spot where I would wait for the thief to appear.' Maha chuckled. 'I am glad I took that rock-climbing course in Italy last year. I was fit and prepared for catching a thief. I climbed that beautiful tree with white flowers – you know, the one that is not so tall but has lots of limbs, leaves and blooming flowers to hide someone who does not want to be seen.'

'Maha!' I said, covering my mouth with my hand, trying to imagine my daughter climbing trees in the dark.

'Let her continue, darling,' Kareem said, as he gently rubbed my shoulder with his hand.

'Well, Mother, all I had to do was wait. I had a great view in that tree. No one could reach either gate without my seeing them.'

'And?'

'Well, I remained very still until daylight, and what I lived to see was nothing that I had expected.' Maha smiled at the memory. 'Suddenly I heard a sound that startled me. This ninja girl was *very* smart. She had obviously walked the grounds to find the transportation she felt would not be questioned. Thinking like the thief she is, I am sure she was hoping that the guards would assume she was of our family.'

'What did you see, sweetie?' I asked, eager to know the end of this exciting story.

'Mother, you will find this hard to accept as the truth, but I was alerted by the clatter of horses' hooves striking the stone drive. I could not believe what I was seeing when I saw that the thief had released our horses from the stables. She was making a low but shrill noise like I have never heard before. That bizarre sound caused the horses to stampede.

'Staring in shock, I saw her swinging around on that large cream-coloured mare that is slower than the other horses and tame. Even so, ninja girl was brave to attempt the ride because it was clear she had no experience and was barely clinging to the horse. She had not saddled it, but had put on a harness. She was straight on target to pass through the back gates.

'I remained calm. I thought about making a bold leap to land on the back of the mare as they passed beneath, but quickly realized that if I missed my target I would have no time to recover and would fail in catching her. Therefore, I took a few deep breaths and calmly jumped from the tree's lower limb a few strides before the mare passed me. Luckily, I stayed on my feet and with the help of God was able to leap on the mare's back and catch it by the bridle. How I managed to convince her to slow I will never know. I was in a struggle to stay on the mare because the girl tried to fight, but, truthfully, she was so stunned by my attack that she was useless in battle.'

Maha glanced at her father. 'Thank you for insisting that all your children become skilled riders. All those lessons cured my dread of the big animals, and when I needed to know what to do, it was automatic. All those long hours of training to jump on and off the backs of horses was of great benefit in this case.'

Kareem could not suppress his laughter. 'You are most welcome, Maha.'

My husband and I had parented our young children differently. While I protected them from any potential harm, he prepared them for the challenges of life. Together we accomplished much, providing our children with a sense of protection and unconditional love from their mother, while their father imbued in them an intellectual determination and independence that would serve them well for unexpected life events.

Maha carried on. 'About then I heard excited shouts from the guard gate. The horses were running so fast, but were trapped with nowhere to go because the gates were closed.'

'Maha,' I said more than once. 'Maha! Thanks be to God that you were not injured.'

'Not a chance, Mother.'

Kareem pressed for more detail. 'What happened then?'

'Ninja screamed, as she struggled to get away, but she was so slight in size that I grabbed her almost the same time I stopped the mare. I was not gentle, I admit. As I leapt from the mare, I pulled her off and on to the drive. The fall knocked the breath out of her lungs and I had to beat her on the back to start her breathing normally.

'She attempted to run away the moment she steadied her balance, but I yanked off her head covering and seized her by the hair. She was not going anywhere unless she was willing to forfeit every hair on her head.

'She was begging to be released. She pulled the drawstring bag out of her pocket and babbled that she had plans to stop at the guard gate and return the jewels, which was a huge lie. She and I both knew that she was hoping to startle the guards and gallop through an open gate. How she would have manipulated riding a horse from our palace to Uncle Ali's without being questioned, I do not know. The police would have captured her immediately.'

'True, daughter,' I said. For women in Saudi Arabia at this time are not allowed to trot through the city streets atop any animal, whether horse, camel or cow. She would have been arrested – that is a great certainty.

'She pleaded that I take the jewels and let her go, which I would not consider,' Maha continued. 'I could barely look at her because the urge was so strong to beat her up, but I knew that I should not. I am large. She is small. It would have been an unfair competition.

'By this time, two of the guards came running to discover what fool had released all the horses. When they saw me clinging to the thief, they were thrilled and offered to take her into custody, but I refused. The thief was going to answer for her crimes.'

'Where is she now, daughter?' Kareem wanted to know.

'She is locked in the storage room next to the kitchen gallery – and I have the only key, which I took from Cook,' Maha said smugly, shaking her head and I am sure marvelling at the idiocy the woman had shown by agreeing to steal from a royal palace in a country where the punishments are very severe. We had no knowledge about the girl. Was she Saudi? Was she a relative of one of Ali's wives?

Kareem was reading my mind. 'The girl must be interrogated.'

I nodded in agreement but did not verbally respond, as I turned my attention to my daughter. I was most concerned for her welfare after such an ordeal.

'You are a hero, darling,' I announced to Maha, thinking to myself that her burst of heroism alone captured the thief. 'No one but our Maha could overpower and capture this criminal,' I said, as I looked to Kareem for confirmation. 'Thank you, darling. Thank you.'

Kareem agreed, looking at Maha. 'Your mother is right, Maha. You, and you alone, saved the jewels.'

Maha is not a person who is comfortable receiving a lot of compliments, even when she deserves them. She gestured with her hand, as if to say that it was all nothing and what she had done was a routine matter. You would have thought my daughter leapt from trees and apprehended criminals every day.

'What I did was for my mother and my grandmother,' she said with a shrug. 'There is nothing I will not do for either.'

I kissed my daughter three times until she finally laughed and pushed me away.

Maha had a new thought just at that moment. 'Oh, I forgot to tell you both, in the drawstring bag holding the jewels there were several small instruments made of steel that are meant to dislodge items from wood or stone. Father,' she said, 'somehow Uncle Ali or Medina had heard about the precious stones and came prepared to steal the jewels, along with Grand-mother's picture.'

Kareem looked startled because it is unusual for Ali or members of his family to visit our home, although we do see them at family functions on occasion.

That's when I reminded him, 'Kareem, two of Ali's sons recently came by, looking for Abdullah, who they did not know was in Europe.' I shrugged. 'Our servants would have no reason to monitor Ali's sons, although I would have been notified had the visitors been Ali or Medina.

'I am thinking that the boys wandered around in the palace during their visit. Most likely they saw the on-going renovations regarding Mother's picture. That is the only explanation for my brother's family to know about the expensive stones. None of us would have suspected that they would report back to their father and that he, Ali, would get the idea to steal the rubies and the emerald!'

'Sultana,' Kareem said, 'from this point, we must tell our employees that neither Ali nor members of his fam-ily are to be allowed in the palace unless we are notified and meet them at the front entrance.'

'Yes, husband, I agree.'

Kareem drummed his fingers on the table. 'All right. Now, what should we do with this girl, Sultana?'

I pondered the problem. It would be easiest to return her to Ali and Medina and forget her, but I feel crimi-nals should not be treated lightly or they will remain criminals. Yet, if we turned her in to the police, she would be charged as a thief. Since the crime of theft by taking was layered with other complications, such as valuable jewellery and an attempt to escape, and finally a struggle with the royal princess who caught her, the girl was sure to receive a stiff punishment. Most troubling, the case would end up involving my brother and his daughter, and while I am very familiar with his character, I do not want the entire Saudi world to know of his eccentricities. I also felt certain that he and his daughter would focus solely on trying to blacken the name of my daughter, who was the hero in this story.

As angry as I was, I had no idea what Medina had told this young woman. Perhaps she believed that all the items she was asked to take really belonged to my brother.

'Kareem,' I said, 'I believe that before any decisions are made, you and the head of our security question her to discover her story. Then you and I can make the final decision together.'

I desired to know Ali's role in the malice of the crime. The last time his daughter Medina had stolen Mother's picture, I was told by Sara, Ali had been so furious at its return to me that he had spent many months praying daily for me to go blind so that I might not be able to enjoy Mother's image ever again. Although Ali and I had been more cordial over the past year, I knew that the slightest cause for anger could take my brother to a dangerous place. I have preserved a lively remembrance of my childhood and, from the time we were young, my brother and I were natural enemies. From those early days, he chose the excessive role of tyrant – a role he would play throughout our lives.

For the first time, I considered that perhaps Medina was a greater danger to our safety than Ali. While he could be hot and hostile in a matter of moments, he would often be quick to leave his complaints behind. On the other hand, Medina seemed to be an unusually cold and calculating woman – swift to act without thought or consideration of any consequences. I know her bipolar mental health problems do not help in this regard, but I have noticed that when I look into her eyes I feel as though I am looking at nothing.

'And that is what I will do, Sultana,' Kareem said, interrupting my unpleasant thoughts, as he took a last sip of tea before walking away.

I brushed aside all the grievances of my childhood to share a happy smile with my daughter, feeling as jubilant as perhaps people do when they suddenly win a large cash lottery prize. We walked arm in arm into my bedroom to admire Mother's jewels before putting them away in the huge safe in my closet.

*   *   *

The following afternoon my sisters Sara, Haifa and Tahani, along with my two daughters, organized a visit to my palace for no reason other than to offer support after the turmoil of the attempted theft of Mother's treasured picture. While Sara had been kept informed of every twist in the outlandish tale of the two clumsy thieves, Haifa, Tahani and Amani had missed the most exciting details of the night's events after the family party ended.

Maha updated all while I listened in silence, quietly assessing the various expressions on the faces of those I love.

At the end of the tale, I filled in the final blank when Haifa said, 'For sure, you are going to press charges, Sultana.'

I exhaled. 'My darlings, Kareem and I have made a decision not to report Medina or the ninja girl, named Nawal, to the police.'

All were initially quiet, even Haifa, whose eyes had grown huge in surprise. I knew that all but Sara expected to hear how the two thieves would suffer, spending time in a dank prison cell or perhaps living the rest of their lives minus a hand. But that was not going to happen.

I explained why we would not press for punishment, wishing to persuade them that our decision was appropriate and had been based on a feeling of humanity for Nawal.

'I will say that I find the meaning of her name ironic. For sure, she was no gift or favour to our family! But once Nawal was questioned, compassion replaced the anger both Kareem and I felt in our hearts. Kareem had the head of his security question the girl, and she could barely respond due to her fear. She was little more than a child – a child who easily volunteered all the information without much prompting. Indeed, Medina had convinced her that Maha had first stolen the photograph from Ali's home and that it rightfully belonged to him, as the only son of our mother. Nawal honestly trusted Medina's false words and believed she was taking something from thieves who were in possession of stolen property.

'Once we understood that she was operating under false information, and truly believed that she was doing nothing more than returning stolen property, our hearts were touched. Then, after we further investigated her home life, there was no doubt that we would *not* press charges.'

Maha made a clucking sound with her tongue. I knew that it would take a lot to convince her that we were making the correct decision. My daughter had been on the front line with the thieves and had little sympathy for Medina or Nawal.

I continued my story. 'Nawal's story is one that will create sympathy in your hearts. So now I will share those details with you. Medina met this young girl when she went into a lingerie shop at the Riyadh Gallery Mall.'

'Is that the mall located on King Fahd Road?' Amani asked.

'Yes, that is the one.' I knew that Amani was unfamiliar with most of the big malls, as she rarely shopped at what she considered to be vulgar, flashy places, as are all the modern malls in Saudi Arabia. Over the past twenty years enormous glitzy malls have erupted in our major cities of Riyadh and Jeddah, but Amani makes a point of continuing to shop in the ancient souks, as she believes that all Saudis should remain modest. The huge malls with the glittering lights and ultra-modern shops should not represent the country where our Prophet was born and where Islam was founded, according to my daughter. We should remain simple people, she is known to say to all who will listen. For sure, Amani lives as she moralizes. No one can accuse my daughter of being hypocritical. Amani lives in a nice home, but one that could never be called a palace.

She refuses to purchase frivolous items, including expensive jewellery, although she does not withstand her father's passion for draping lovely jewels around her delicate neck and wrists.

I continued my explanation of our reason behind our compassion for this girl.

'I have discovered that there are seven children in Nawal's family. Nawal is the oldest. To help with family expenses, Nawal's mother is employed as an assistant in a lingerie shop at the Riyadh Gallery Mall, as I mentioned. Medina had walked into the shop to browse the merchandise and met Nawal, who was there doing her schoolwork while her mother tended the counters. The two girls struck up a conversation and Medina took a liking to the girl, who was very quiet – and malleable. Nawal's family is a modest one, and I believe Medina was most likely curious because it is so different to her own.'

'Ali cannot claim to be modest in any manner and that is a certainty,' Haifa muttered, leading us all to take a moment to consider our brother's ostentatious lifestyle.

'Opposites do attract,' Maha said with authority.

'Most likely the family felt that a friendship with a royal could do no harm,' Amani remarked, 'because such friendships are rare and generally those who are not royal bestow a mantle of instant approval on those of the royal family.'

Not wishing to encourage my daughter to start a sermon on all the wrongs committed by the royals, I jumped in. 'Well, to shorten this story, Kareem sent one of our assistants to meet with the family. Once the parents heard the story of their daughter and how she was involved in a theft against a member of the royal family, the parents were instantly distraught. The mother pleaded for us to have mercy and not report Nawal to the police. The father turned against his wife, blaming her, as so many do in our country. Everything is the fault of the woman. We were told that the husband verbally attacked her and accused her of causing the problem by working in a shop where women's unmentionables are sold. The wife was a bad example for the children, he claimed.

'The husband did have a valid concern that if charges were filed he would be fired from his job at one of the automobile showrooms, where he worked as an accountant.'

In Saudi Arabia, as we all know, there is no leniency shown to those who get tangled in a scandal. Generally, the entire family suffers for the misdeeds of one.

'Before the meeting ended, the poor wife was forbidden to leave the house until she had direct permission from her husband. Then the most grievous command was given when the husband said that their three daughters were to end their education once they had learned the basics – to be able to read and write.

'At the snap of his fingers, all their lives were changed for ever. When we learned the distressing report, Kareem had our assistant return to that home to try and appease the man by reassuring him that no charges would be filed. Our family only asked that Nawal no longer see Medina. Kareem and I agree that the two girls are in an unequal friendship where one holds the power and the other wants to please. We feel that

Nawal might continue being compliant in the face of such a strong personality as Medina.

'The father was grateful that we would not file charges, but nothing could appease his anger at his wife, or his daughter Nawal – anger that had been spiralling out of control since he had first learned of the situation. He was still sputtering in rage, according to Kareem's assistant, shouting that all should learn that freedom for women brings only shame to a family, for the women of Saudi Arabia do not yet know how to supervise themselves if given freedom. He asked Kareem's assistant to pass on his advice to all the royals he knew.

'In view of all that we discovered, we could see no benefit to further harm the women of that family.'

Maha's eyes were flashing in a combination of sympathy for Nawal and fury at Nawal's father. 'Oh Mother, I am so glad I did not beat her up. And you and Father were right in this decision,' she exclaimed. 'Those poor women. A tyrant is their guardian.'

Sara, Haifa and Tahani also approved of our decision to be merciful.

'Yes, Sultana,' Sara said, 'you were kind to those who need a little kindness.'

Haifa clasped her hands tightly together, still thinking of the husband's ferocious reaction. 'How fortunate we are to have husbands who respect their wives.'

'Yes, *respect*, and this respect circles back from their wives,' Tahani said, thinking of her own flourishing marriage.

Only Amani was uncertain as to the wisdom of our decision. 'Mother, when a person commits a crime, despite the reason behind that decision, or the circumstances that arise from the crime, retribution *must* be made.'

'I believe that this girl, Nawal, is suffering quite enough, daughter,' I said, with a deep and wounded sigh. 'The unfortunate girl's act has created enormous problems for her mother and her two younger sisters. I am sure she is suffering a great torment even as we are having this conversation. I was told that she is a very good student, and now her studies will cease. This will alter the course of her entire life. I do not celebrate this outcome, for I consider it to be a great pity.'

How I wished for my daughter to loosen her rigid outlook on every aspect of life.

'She has paid, Amani, and paid dearly,' I said with raised eyebrows, yearning for my youngest to show some small gesture of empathy, even for humans who make wrong turns in life. Amani, an animal lover, forgives animals any naughty misdeeds they might commit, but her benevolence does not extend to human beings.

Amani puckered her lips, thinking, but at least did not put forth a heated argument against all that I had said. It has been my experience that when my daughter feels she is right, there is no deterring her from creating a scene, no matter who might be a witness to our dispute. For the moment, she seemed to be less intent on continuing the argument.

'So,' Maha said, 'this conversation brings up the most pressing problem facing our new Crown Prince, does it not?'

'*And what is that?*' Amani said in a high-pitched voice, the one she uses when she is set to launch into a heated squabble with her sister.

'Well, Amani, we *finally* have a bold man in line to be our king, a man who will not falter when making what I predict will be an unpopular decision with the vast majority of men in my country.'

Amani choked on her fruit, all the while glaring at Maha, as though her sister was a woman with two heads. When she finally caught her breath, Amani was off and running, her temper flaring at what she considered her sister's grave hypocrisy. '*Your country?*' Amani said with scorn. '*Your country?* Saudi Arabia is no longer your country. Your country is now Europe and I believe that means you can call multi-countries your home!'

How someone so beautiful could look so ugly was the question that came to my mind. Amani had such an unattractive expression that she no longer held the slightest resemblance to the beauty she is.

I knew that I must end this dialogue before it gained traction or the entire afternoon would be wound around another of my daughters' famous fights.

'Amani! No! I will not have you intentionally choose to fight today. Your mother is exhausted from the fright she experienced last evening. Now, please, allow others to have a pleasant conversation, daughter, even if it is a serious exchange about the challenges that face so many Saudi women. It is our responsibility as women to care about other women and the obstacles they face.'

'Shall I leave, Mother?' Amani asked, with a stern tone.

'No, darling. Your mother wants you here. But, Amani, I do not have the strength to endure an emotional day after an emotional evening.'

Amani tightened her lips and nodded. She sat silent with an expressionless face as the conversation entered a popular topic, for most women in Saudi Arabia are thrilled over the promised changes coming from the palace of the Crown Prince.

Haifa and Tahani have little experience of the riotous fights that can occur between my daughters, so it took them a few moments to re-enter the conversation.

I became animated with good will for the man who was making everything I have fought for finally happen. Eager to express my support of all that he was doing, I said, 'Many good things are coming our way, dear ones. I feel it in my heart that all that is being promised will be delivered. It might not be tomorrow, it might not be next week, it might not be next month, but it is coming. And what is *it*? *It* is a wonderful social tsunami that will sweep over this land and alter the entire social landscape. Nothing will ever be the same again – for women, or for men.'

Maha raised a vital point. 'But the guardianship law, Mother. To me, it seems that he is ignoring the elephant in the room.'

'Elephant? What elephant?' a confused Tahani questioned. 'Does our Crown Prince now have an elephant?'

Mild laughter spread from one to the other.

'That is a saying the clever English first created, Auntie,' Maha told her with a smile. 'This is when there is something very obvious that is causing a big problem but no one dares bring it out into the open. Basically, it means that something as huge as an elephant is being overlooked in conversations.'

'I am not sure I understand, still,' Tahani said.

'I will explain further when we are alone, dear,' Haifa assured her.

'So right, Maha,' Sara agreed. 'Yet I believe that in good time we shall see this issue addressed.'

It was evident that Maha had given the subject a lot of thought. She vocalized what many of us knew lurked in the hearts of most Saudi men.

'Let us be honest. Most Saudi men do not want their women to drive. Most Saudi men do not want their women to travel without permission. Most Saudi men do not want their women to decide upon their own education, or select the jobs and professions they want to follow. Truthfully, most Saudi men love being in charge of *everything*. They have had this power so long that it will not be easy to let go. And men are the same the world over. Just think how long it took women in the West to push their men in order to win their freedom. Believe me, so long as the guardianship law exists, it does not matter how many other laws are changed. In this country, the man of the family will still hold all the power and he *will not* give it up easily.'

I winced, knowing that Maha had hit upon a very sad truth. Even as I sat in my own palace, speaking with my sisters and daughters, every Saudi woman, including the six of us, all princesses, was still required to have a male guardian. This guardian must be a family member, such as a father, brother, husband or son. The man serving as our legal guardian has the legal authority to make all the vital decisions of our lives, whether driving, voting, studying, marrying, seeking legal advice or going to court – even a decision to seek medical treatment is in the hands of men. So many limitations!

Maha's face was blushing red, for she is a woman who makes all her decisions and lives a life of accomplishment. She has no need for any man to tell her yes or no. She is a free woman.

Thankfully, Kareem informed both daughters the day they reached adulthood at age twenty-one that he was there for consultation and advice, but he trusted them to make their own personal decisions. He proclaimed that he was removing himself from the position of their guardian. Maha embraced her freedom and from that day was responsible for all matters in her life, while Amani came to Kareem for advice until the day she married, then she turned to her husband. To my satisfaction, her husband is not a tyrant and encourages Amani to use her own mind, although she has a tendency to seek her husband's approval on all decisions she makes.

Too few Saudi women have a father who feels as Kareem does. Most men cling to control out of fear their women will make a decision that will cast a veil of shame over the entire family.

Maha continued to stir the conversation. 'The government cannot go house to house and force all these stubborn men to allow their women to drive or vote or travel. The laws will probably be passed to do all the things women should be allowed to do, but those laws will only benefit those whose men are modern-thinking and who trust the women to make good decisions so as not to embarrass the entire family.'

'Well, there is no elephant being ignored in this room,' Haifa said with a burst of laughter.

Sara did not disagree with Maha, yet she had hopes that matched my own. 'Regardless of these true things you are saying, Maha, and these things we all know deep in our hearts, I am filled with optimism that Crown Prince Muhammad will know how to man-oeuvre a successful path through the minefields of this desert kingdom.'

'Minefields?' Tahani said with alarm. 'What mine-fields?'

Once more our Tahani had amused us in the midst of a very serious discussion.

All knew that we would re-enter this same conversa-tion later, but for now we were happy women, waiting for good things to come into our lives.

'We all have great expectations,' Sara said in her sweet voice.

'At least we can safely discuss our expectations,' I reminded them all. Not so many years past, even when I was a child, such a conversation would have landed an adult woman in prison, with hands shackled around a concrete pillar. This had happened to women in my country. But I did not describe those tragic events now, as there was optimism in all our hearts and I did not wish to deflate the emotions of my sisters and daugh-ters with sad stories.

After saying goodnight to those whom I love with my whole heart, I retired in a very happy frame of mind.

After settling in bed but before sleeping, my mind began spinning backwards through time. Images of my ancestors and ancient Arabia came once more into clear focus, like snapshots in a photo album. The pages flipped rapidly, yet all were illuminated. I saw infant girls being buried in the sand, adult women being stoned, girls and women beaten by their husbands and fathers. Then positive images began to overtake the negative, with smiling Saudi women working in important posts, travelling throughout the world, marrying men they love.

Then the pages stopped flipping in my mind and settled on a single image of two men bound together by blood and by history. I saw my grandfather Abdul Aziz embracing his grandson Muhammad. In that image, I gained an understanding. With that picture imprinted in my mind, I knew that the circle of life, from the time of ancient Arabia to the modern day, was nearly complete.

Would I, Princess Sultana al-Sa'ud, live to say that Saudi women had gone from being the most abused women on earth to the happiest?

This is my wish and my prayer.

For a better tomorrow.

Chapter Four

The Heart of Evil

AN ODE TO BASHIR ASSAD, current president of Syria:

> An unjust ruler asked a holy man, 'What is more excellent than prayer?'
> The holy man replied, 'For you to remain asleep until midday, that for this one interval you may not afflict mankind.'
> – *The Gulistan of Saadi* (*The Rose Garden*),
> Saadi Shirazi, 1258

The countries of Iraq, Syria and Iran are so powerful, and so near.

Of all the neighbours of Saudi Arabia, these three nations rank as the most threatening, intimidating their own citizens while menacing the general stability of the area. Most agree that political rivalry, combined with military competition, emanates from the leaders of these three nations rather than from the people, who are, for the most part, simply ordinary citizens pursuing peace and prosperity.

Most of those who have ruled these lands are more alike than they are different. The majority of them have begun their reign with buoyant promises of greater freedoms before quickly emerging as the natural enemies of their own people. This pattern of promises made and never kept has become familiar, with Saddam Hussein in Iraq, the Assads in Syria (father Hafez and now son Bashir), and Ayatollah Khomeini – followed by other equally ruthless ayatollahs – in Iran.

I am reflecting on each of these countries in turn and sense the desperate vulnerability of those who have been born in Iraq, Syria and Iran.

In Iraq, for example, the lack of ethnic unity has brought recurring strife, and that country's history, from ancient days to the present, has been a chronicle of anarchy. How many inhabitants of Iraq can hope to live a normal, productive life under the dangerous dagger of continuous war? None. No one has reliable figures relating to the number of Iraqis who were murdered after Saddam Hussein assumed power in that country in July 1979, ruling for approximately twenty-four years until 9 April 2003. This period of tyranny was followed by deaths brought about by the American invasion in April 2003 and throughout the occupation. The figures quoted from various organizations are staggering and range from a total of 500,000 to 750,000 Iraqis who died as a result of Saddam's Ba'athist regime, combined with the American invasion and occupation, which ended on 18 December 2011.

In Syria, the despot Bashir Assad, and those who opposed his dictatorship, have fought each other to a common ruin. Rare is the Syrian who has dodged the precipice of personal tragedy during one of the most violent and costly civil wars in modern history. The approximate death toll resulting from that country's ongoing revolution is now estimated to be between 350,000 and 500,000, with new fatalities added each day that the revolution continues. So many cities, towns and villages have been obliterated by the almost continuous and horrendous bombardment. It is hard to imagine the terror felt by the inhabitants – men, women and children – who have little or no hope of escape.

In Iran, the ayatollahs are like bullies, with deadly plans lurking beneath the surface – never so happy as when stirring controversy and seeking out someone with whom to quarrel. There have been ceaseless attacks upon their own citizens for the most mundane of crimes since the beginning of the current regime in 1979, when the Shah was deposed and the ayatollahs assumed control. Although extremely top-secret information so carefully guarded by the Iranian government makes it a formidable task to uncover exact figures of 'death by Ayatollah', the acts of violence have been unprecedented in Iranian history, according to historians and organizations who closely follow the massive number of human-rights violations there.

As far as other nations in the neighbourhood are concerned, since the coup d'état of the Shah, the Iranian leaders have selected Saudi Arabia as their favoured target, despite fighting eight years of war against Iraq to an undetermined outcome, as neither country could claim victory, although both, in my opinion, were defeated in reality by sheer exhaustion.

Although a lightly populated country such as Saudi Arabia does not seek confrontation with such populous neighbours, we must be prepared for war. Yet many in the West are of the opinion that we have no right to organize. This is incomprehensible when criticism arises only because our Saudi Arabian leaders seek to structure our military so that we may protect our cities and our people. Should we wait like baby lambs for a slaughter? Would that mollify those so hasty to criticize the efforts made to keep my country safe and secure from tyrannical forces?

There are other issues veiling these three nations that cleave closest to my own heart and mind. This crucial problem affects all aspects of family life, for I am speaking about the deterioration of women's rights. Although I have been the first to identify the debilitating issues affecting Saudi women by the clerics and other extremists in our land, I always felt optimistic for Muslim women in neighbouring countries. At one time, all three countries made impressive gains against discrimination directed at women, but now they are rapidly moving backwards when it comes to this most important issue.

There was intimidation against Iranian citizens in general under the reign of the Shah, but women were not routinely targeted. Those olden days – oftentimes referred to as golden days – under the Shah seem like the purest freedom compared to the present, when the radical and seemingly hate-filled ayatollahs pursue women for special punishments without any justification at all, apart from the fact that they are women!

Prior to the revolution in Syria, women's lives were as near to normal as is possible in the Middle East. But now everything in conventional life has changed. The revolution has scoured the land of all that is good, erasing the slightest respect for females. It is said that Assad's all-seeing security forces now routinely arrest, harass and even rape young girls, boys and women.

In Iraq, during the secular days of Saddam, women were sampling a refreshing sense of freedom in the workplace and in public life, despite the ever-increasing threats of war emanating from the president's palace. Eventually the world turned against the regime and opened up the ancient country for today's most menacing terrorists, ISIS. Women in today's Iraq yearn for the personal freedoms they once tasted.

As time passed, the world continued to watch as these three nations plunged ever nearer the precipice of war. As radicalism triumphed, toleration waned and governments have turned against women, once again seeking to control and contain them ever tighter.

The violence and political upheaval in these countries are occupying more of my thoughts, for fears in Saudi Arabia that extremists from Iraq and Syria will intentionally focus on peace-loving nations in the region are valid. Indeed, no one who follows the movements of Iran in particular can deny that it, more than any nation in this area, intentionally deposits fertile seeds of hatred throughout our entire region.

Iran is the acknowledged neighbourhood oppressor, seemingly eager to attack Saudi Arabia through those who are leading Yemen, one of our closest neighbours, with whom we share a border. It is imperative for Saudi Arabia to trust those who rule Yemen, as well as those who live there, which we cannot do at this time.

There is a second motive for my focus on these three nations. My daughter Maha has become personally involved with a small group of women who are reaching out from behind the scenes to assist their refugee sisters in Syria and Iraq. While they are not currently occupied with any Iranian cases, they are aware of the tribulations many women face under the harsh rule of the clerics.

During a recent visit to the kingdom, Maha set up a meeting with two trusted cousins, with a plan to interest them in joining the group since both cousins spend most of the year in Europe, where the group had been formed and carries out its responsibilities to save female refugees whenever possible. With profound pleasure, I had donated a substantial sum of money to the cause, as much financial assistance is required when courageous men are called upon to go to Syria to help in the rescue of women trapped within the war zone – and who require rapid removal from the country or from one area to another, out of reach of Assad's military forces.

As of the date of the Riyadh meeting, Maha's group had rescued only three women, but none would have survived without assistance upon leaving Syria. All were young women in their late teens or early twenties, with many years of life stretching before them, and now they would have the opportunity to live in safety and make their lives worthy of the sacrifice others made. Regrettably, I was told by Maha that two young men lost their lives while saving the women.

Reflecting on so much sadness, as I sat sipping tea in the larger of my two offices, I admired my daughter at my desk as she meticulously reviewed her notes. She noticed nothing other than the material she was examining. I watched affectionately while detecting the worry line deepening between her brows. Maha was devoted to the cause of saving lives and her new-found wrinkle was telling.

Maha was undoubtedly lovely to my eyes but, even more, she is a confident woman who cares little for beauty and favours intellect over the trappings of wealth and a life well lived. Never have I felt more contented than at that moment knowing that by raising such a daughter I have ensured good deeds will continue to stream from our palace long after Kareem and I are no longer with the living.

When my secretary escorted Maha's two cousins in, Maha rose to her feet to welcome them. Both girls were smiling and appeared pleased to be in our home. Although each had covered her hair with a black scarf, and both were wearing abaayas with attractive and colourful embroidered designs, a popular mode of dressing these days, neither was veiled, a new habit being embraced joyfully by many of our young women. I could never recall meeting these two, although they are of the royal family, albeit not from our family's tribe, the Aniza.

Arabia is, and always will be, a nation of tribes, although the men of my family are slowly moving away from distinguishing themselves from any tribe in the country. They say the al-Sa'ud are in reality 'every tribe', as the rulers of our land. As such, they formally represent each man and woman in the kingdom. However, despite the royal family's intentional avoidance of tribal divisions, the knowledge of such historical ties hangs over the head of every Saudi, whether royal or non-royal, and most likely will never diminish, for it is challenging to erase a proud heritage.

'Mother, please meet my friends. This is Lala. This is Shabane.'

'I welcome you to my home,' I said, as I strained on my toes to make physical contact with each girl so that I might place light kisses on their forehead and cheeks. Like many of the younger generation, these girls were very tall, reaching at least a full head above my own.

'Please, do make yourselves comfortable. Is there anything you need?'

Both demurred with charming smiles.

'Well, tea and refreshments will be served momentarily.'

My assistant helped in removing their scarves and abaayas, while Maha moved two chairs closer to the desk where she was sitting.

I sat once more in my easy chair, thinking that we would enjoy a relaxed exchange of conversation before business and I would learn more about these two young women, but on this day there was no unproductive time spent on affable chatter, for when my daughter is immersed in any solemn issue, she goes without delay to the heart of the topic.

'Yes, ladies. Welcome. I was so pleased when we were speaking earlier to learn that you both share my concern regarding the current toxic environment in Syria, relating to the safety of innocent girls and women who are being targeted by the government that should be protecting them. I hope that after hearing about the three rescues we have made you might become a part of our group in Europe. Our club consists of four women at this time, but hopefully you will unite with us to increase our numbers and our ability to help more women to a new life without continual jeopardy to their safety. Although we have the funds, be warned, it is hard work, and attention to detail and good organizational skills are required for successful rescues.'

I sat quietly, ready to absorb the stories of the three women who would not be alive today but for my daughter and her friends. And for that I feel the greatest joy. That I have raised such a daughter, a bright and sophisticated young woman whose principal aspiration in life is to ensure the well-being of other women, lifts my spirits and makes me hopeful for the future.

Maha looked at each of us in turn. Her manner was melancholy, as though she was reflecting on the tragic stories that she must share.

We all looked on in anticipation without speaking.

Maha cleared her throat. 'Here we are, ladies ...' she stated in a soft but firm voice, jangling her gold bracelets for emphasis. 'Safe in our little world in this kingdom for a part of the year and then enjoying months of luxury living in Europe. We are some of the most fortunate women in the world.' She blew out a noisy breath. 'Others are not so fortunate.'

My daughter, I knew, was struggling to share the distressing stories. She slowly rubbed her forehead. 'I must apologize before I begin, for none of us have been accustomed to such horrifyingly graphic truths. What I am about to tell you is so dreadful that none of us can even try to imagine what it would feel like to live through such gruesome trauma. These stories, though, tell of the life of so many of our Muslim sisters.' Maha's voice indicated a deep emotion. 'Mother. Lala. Shabane. Here is the unveiled truth: at this very moment, *this very moment*, girls and women are being arrested for no cause, taken from their families, driven away from their homes, dragged into dark prisons, taken alone into darker rooms, handcuffed to bed railings and raped by multiple men. *Yes, at this moment, girls as young as ten, and women as old as sixty, are being raped by one man after another!*'

My daughter lowered her head and closed her eyes, attempting to shake off her emotion. She took a moment before clearing her throat once again. 'And if they survive, they will need help. These are the girls and women we must try to save.'

Lala squirmed, her hand over her mouth.

Shabane appeared frozen.

Both, I was certain, were shaken by the mention of rape against any female, no matter the age, for in our society nothing is more damaging to the life of a woman than to be a victim of rape. Most women living in our region, in fact, consider death preferable to rape. There are many explanations for this psychological agony. Should a female be raped, the woman's family suffers tremendous shame. In many cases, the family blames the victim for her own rape. If a woman is married, her husband will most likely leave her. If she is engaged, most likely her husband-to-be will jilt her. If she is not yet engaged to be married, she will never be engaged. Perhaps she will be a victim of murder, for it is not uncommon for brothers of rape victims to kill their sisters in the belief that their death will eliminate the shame upon the family.

The intense humiliation attached to rape is the same all over the region, whether a girl is born in Saudi Arabia, Syria, Iraq, Afghanistan, or a whole host of neighbouring countries. There is nowhere a female can escape the disgrace of being raped.

Maha selected a document from the desk. 'Most people who follow the news are aware of the indiscriminate bombings on Syrian cities and villages for the sole purpose of terrifying the population. Citizens there have also been the victims of chemical weapons. But for Syrian families nothing is considered more destructive to life than the sexual violence being used by the Syrian regime against girls and women. That, I have been told, is one of the main reasons so many families take dangerous chances to flee the country. Information about such rapes travels faster than wild fires and when ordinary families hear about the kidnapping, imprisonment and rape of innocent girls and women, they start packing, making every effort to escape the areas targeted by the Syrian government.'

With a faraway look in her eyes, Maha stared into the distance. My heart told me that my daughter was reliving the tragedies she had heard from the women she had helped to rescue. She shook her head lightly before meeting our eyes once more.

I clicked my tongue in sympathy. Never could I recall seeing my Maha more emotionally torn.

My daughter's eyes met my gaze for a moment and I willed strength into her body, so she was able to continue the heart-rending tales that, once known to a person, can never be erased from their memory. Although I am a mature woman who knows more than most when it comes to the abuse inflicted on females worldwide, both young and old, I knew that I would remain awake for long hours on this night, remembering the graphic incidents I would soon hear.

Maha gave me a slight smile prior to recounting the personal stories that she had to share for all to know the extent of the crisis facing so many girls and women in Syria. I sensed correctly that my daughter had regained the power necessary to carry on.

'Now I will share with you the stories of the three whom we have rescued. First, I will tell you about the most darling woman, sweet and smart. Her name is Souzan.

'Souzan was only a fifteen-year-old schoolgirl at home doing her homework when Assad's security forces surrounded the neighbourhood, going house to house to supposedly arrest members of the revolution. They were after the men, but the men were in another area of the country arranging for an attack upon a government building.

'Souzan's mother had left their home for only a few minutes to visit a neighbour. She was often a visitor at this house since the husbands of both women were deeply involved in the Free Syrian Army, an important fighting group who are well established in their attempts to dislodge Assad's regime. Souzan's mother was desperate to discover the latest news of her husband, as she had heard nothing for a month when generally he sent word weekly as to his safety. Souzan recalled that her mother's entire life rested on hope – hope that her husband would not be killed, hope that her children would remain safe, and hope that the civil war that was destroying untold lives would soon end.'

'Her hopes are our hopes, daughter,' I said in a low voice.

'Yes, Mother, you are right. All who know anything about this vicious war pray for an end to the misery and suffering. I have read reports stating that the Syrian civil war is the most destructive in modern history, and I now believe that to be so.'

I shook my head in regret for the Syrian people, for indeed I know too much about the Syrian civil war and the tremendous tragedy the war has wrought on so many innocent people.

'Unknowingly,' Maha said, 'Souzan's mother picked the worst possible time to leave her home and children.

'The first sound that alerted Souzan to danger was the reverberation of tanks. The dictator Assad and his military routinely use tanks to block off streets. The frighteningly loud clamour of these machines accelerating with metal against the rock road was so fearsome that women's voices shrieking for their children became louder than the noise of the tanks! The neighbourhood was quickly locked down, with shouts heard that no one was allowed on the streets, or even in or out of their homes.

'A young and terrified Souzan was the adult in a house with five younger children. Her equally alarmed mother found herself confined in her neighbour's house, only feet away from her children but unable to reach them.

'Souzan felt numb from her head to her toes, but vividly remembers the loud knocks on the door. She did not respond to the incessant pounding because her mother had warned her against opening the door unless she heard her mother's special knock. This was a way of letting the children know it was safe to answer the door. That knock was three quick hits, followed by silence, and then five additional hits, made as fast as possible.

' "Those who are dangerous to us do not strike the door lightly, my children," she told them, "but instead will knock it down with tremendous blows made by angry hands and kicking feet. Never answer. Make them kick the door to the floor, children. They are known to shoot whoever answers the doors to intimidate all remaining within. Do not let yourself be a target. Hide under the mattresses in the storage room. They will be in a hurry and perhaps will do nothing more than give a cursory look."

'Souzan knew that the extreme noise of the banging was definitely not her mother. Distinctly recalling her mother's exact words, she acted quickly, jumping to take her younger siblings to the room where their mattresses were stored. She succeeded in hiding three brothers and one sister underneath, warning them to remain quiet. Since they were very young, aged just three to nine, Souzan did not feel confident in their ability to remain hidden and her fear became a reality before the tragedy ended. The youngest was an infant sleeping in a crib. Just as Souzan gently lifted the infant to make a run to join her hidden siblings, the door gave way and the house was instantly swarming with six big men, all armed, and all red-faced with anger.'

Shabane slumped in her chair, trembling. 'Please, do hurry and tell us what happened. My imagination is causing my heart to flutter in fear.'

Lala's face was ashen when she blurted out, 'Did those men rape her in the house in front of the children?'

'Ladies, I am not here to provide you with sweetness. These stories are heart-rending. So, please, gather your courage. As far as Souzan's abuse, I will tell you in good time. The end of the story should help your nerves, for Souzan survived and she is now safe.'

Lala nodded. 'You are right, Maha. The successful conclusion is where my mind will dwell, but I am now dreading hearing the rest of this frightening story.'

Maha tightened her lips. 'You must be strong to know such stories, for if you join our group, you will have knowledge of many such tragedies. Listen,' Maha leaned forward and narrowed her eyes, 'we all know that the heart of evil is what we are dealing with. Assad is that evil heart, but evil is like a vapour and spreads to all who are around it or who simply follow its orders. These men who do Assad's malevolent deeds have inhaled his evil and are equally guilty!'

I was moved by my daughter's words and could not help but interject. 'You are speaking a sad truth, my daughter. Indeed, the government of Syria is the heart of evil. As we all know, Saddam Hussein's regime was guilty too of many crimes against his own people, and during the most horrific days of his regime innocent adult women were raped, but there were never reports of government-sanctioned rape of children coming out of Iraq. But in this regime the Syrian government is actively targeting young children, who are seized from the safety of their homes and taken away from their parents to be brutally raped, and in some cases tortured and murdered.' Although I, too, was unable to imagine such unbelievable cruelty perpetrated against the most helpless victims possible.

'We are becoming distracted,' Maha said, with a hint of impatience. 'I will return now to a woman who deserves to be heard, and that is Souzan.

'One of the men who was obviously the leader of the security unit shouted to Souzan, "Where is your father? We want your father. Tell us where your father is hiding and we will leave you." The man then gave a hand signal to his crew, who fanned out to search the small home, room by room.

'Souzan, who had been sheltered for her entire life by her conservative parents, and who in fact had rarely had a conversation with a man not of her family, was so frightened that she found she could not speak a word. Although she was conscious of moving her mouth, trying with all her might to speak, to tell the angry man that her father was working, she could make no sound.

'Souzan truly believed that was the truth, as all the children had been sheltered from their father's military activities by their parents. Souzan had even pressed her mother with her worried questions but had been reassured that her father was safe on a job in a neighbouring city. With the war, there was unlimited need for electricians, which was her father's profession. His high-quality work restoring electricity to damaged buildings was the only reason he was away for long periods of time, according to her mother.

'Souzan's silence further angered the man, who pushed her to the wall, screaming his threats so loudly that the female infant in her arms began to wail.

'Finally, Souzan was capable of uttering a few words in rapid succession: "My father is working. He is working. He is an electrician."

'"And your mother? Is she working, too?"

'"No. No, next door. To borrow six eggs."

'Then the moment Souzan dreaded occurred. She shivered when she heard the cries of her younger siblings. The situation grew more tense with the actions of Omar, the nine-year-old boy, who considered himself the man of the family because his father had lovingly told him that he, Omar, was the protector of his mother and younger siblings when his father was away. Thus, he began to kick and scratch the men who were roughly shoving and pushing his young sister and two younger brothers into the kitchen where Souzan was desperately trying to convince the man who was questioning her that, indeed, her father was working.

'Out of fear that the men would harm her younger brother, Souzan shouted to Omar to stop resisting and thankfully he obeyed her. But when the head man observed the children, he became even more invigorated, and Souzan assumed it was because he had more children to intimidate.

' "Hiding? Why were these children hiding? Have you committed a crime? Is that why these children were hiding? Only criminals hide," the ugly man said with a smirk.

'Souzan stuttered, "No, no, no. They were playing a game, a hiding game. I was about to play looking for them. They were frightened of the noise."

' "Playing games? Well, sister, I am not playing games. Tell me where your father is *at this moment*, so we can go and collect him. Your father is an enemy of our great country. You should tell us his whereabouts willingly." Then his voice grew more gruff. "Tell us what we want to know, or you will regret it."

'Souzan was helpless, clinging tightly to her infant sister while keeping an eye on the other siblings. The second daughter of the house, a three-year-old girl, began sobbing and crying out for her mummy. Her pitiful tears appeared to enrage the man even more.

' "So, you will not tell us where to find your father?"

'Souzan repeated what she believed to be true, that her father was at work.

'The man shook his head back and forth, calling her a silly girl, then Souzan saw him make a motion to one of his men before telling that man, "You are free to do what you like." Souzan glanced in panic at the second man, whose face, she said, displayed the most sadistic expression. For certain she believed that the man was mentally unbalanced because he began laughing while striking the younger children, whose screams appeared to energize him, causing him to beat them with his baton with intense enthusiasm.

'That's when the head man took the infant from Souzan's arms and roughly placed the crying baby on the floor. The man started smiling and sneering at her and then, grabbing Souzan by the arms and pulling her out of the room, told her that she was going with him to have some fun.

'The last image Souzan remembers of her younger siblings is that of the mentally deranged man kicking them with his boots. Souzan believes that all the children being beaten were unconscious, other than Omar, who was so brave that he was crying out while butting his small head into the big man's stomach.'

I shuddered, struggling to hold back tears at the bravery shown by that young boy. Hearing quiet sniffles, I glanced to see that Lala and Shabane were both weeping.

Maha looked around the room with a hint of disappointment on her face. While she expected her audience to share her anger, she was faced with weeping women unable to arouse a single threatening shout.

'I will tell you only a few more details because the images I have in my mind I do not wish for you to have in yours,' Maha exclaimed. 'But I shall give you a brief outline of what happened to Souzan from the time she was kidnapped until now.

'A very terrified fifteen-year-old Souzan was forcibly dragged out of her home, thrown into the back seat of a security vehicle and driven out of the neighbourhood. She was transported to a large grey building, which she quickly discovered was a prison, and was swiftly isolated in a room with a large bed. Motionless from fear, she sat on the cold floor, waiting, knowing that something unspeakable was about to happen to her.

'Soon after being locked into the room, the man who kidnapped her burst in with two other uniformed men, loudly ordering them to prepare her. Those men grinned and then leapt on her, stripping her of all her clothes until she was standing naked.

'The kidnapper snapped at the subordinates, telling them to hold her.

'And so, our fifteen-year-old innocent Souzan was tossed on to the bed, held down by two brutes, raped repeatedly, first by the kidnapper, then his subordinates, and then by six other men who were called into the room to participate.

'This violation of her young body never ceased during the six months she was held prisoner. She became pregnant three times, and each time medical personnel at the prison performed an abortion.

'Souzan had no information helpful to Assad's regime. She was basically a child, with nothing to offer of importance. The truth is that the bodies of young girls are given as prizes to the men upholding this evil regime. Souzan was being held as a sex slave for those venomous men, nothing more.

'During the time Souzan was held captive, the government security repeatedly visited Souzan's anxious mother with orders that if her husband turned himself in they would release Souzan. But, they threatened, if her husband refused to exchange himself for his daughter, they would next take away the three-year-old toddler. The fate of her children was in her hands.

'Meanwhile, Souzan's mother had discovered that her husband had been killed during a mission against government troops, so she could do nothing but tell the truth, that her husband had been killed. She pleaded with the authorities that her husband would never stay away if he knew what was happening to his family. If he was able to, he would willingly turn himself in and save his daughter.

'Government security claimed not to believe her, but obviously they had information of their own that Souzan's father had indeed been killed during a battle, for they revisited the family one day hinting that for a certain sum paid to the kidnapper, who was their supervisor, Souzan would be returned to them. This was a poor family and they were being blackmailed by those in power. Of course, the sum was more than the family could raise, but by coincidence our contact heard about this family's story and notified us that we had the opportunity to help a young girl be released from torture in prison.

'We said yes, of course. After some complicated organizing, we arranged to have the funds sent from Lebanon into Syria. Once the kidnapper received the ransom, Souzan was freed and taken to her mother. To me, the speed with which she was dispatched meant that they had moved on to other victims.

'Although alive, Souzan was emaciated and, not surprisingly, was mentally distraught. Although disbelieving and miserable upon learning about the truth of her father's life, and his death, she experienced great happiness when she discovered that her younger siblings had survived the beating, although Omar suffered a concussion that endangered his life for a time. With her mother's patient encouragement and support, Souzan was determined to heal from her ghastly ordeal, if for no other reason than to be able to declare victory over the evil men who had nearly killed her.

'Tragically, the family remained in danger because the kidnapper was greedy. Once the family had paid the large ransom, that vile man believed that he could continue to milk them for money. He reappeared with a warning that without an additional payment he would return to take Souzan and the three-year-old daughter together to prison for special treatment.

'That's when we knew we must move the entire family out of the country and as quickly as possible. This happened only recently, and I am pleased that no one was harmed in the process. The family is now living in Jordan. Souzan is receiving medical treatment. The children are all in school, and we provide a stipend to Souzan's mother for family living expenses.

'I cannot say that Souzan will fully recover, for she is now withdrawn and only cares about her studies and being with her family. But she is now seeing a psychiatrist and he believes that she will regain much of the confidence she has lost, although her recovery will take much time.'

Lala and Shabane were clearly moved by Souzan's story. When they gathered themselves, they spoke as one, saying, 'Yes, yes. We will join your group, Maha. And we will do all we can to help.'

'I knew your answer would be positive,' Maha said quietly. 'I know you both as compassionate women.'

Lala stood, and Shabane did the same.

Lala said, 'Maha, I am very sad and sorry, but I can hear no more today. I am deeply upset by all I have heard. If your two other rescues suffered such abuse,

I must postpone hearing these miserable tales until tomorrow, or another day of your choice.'

'But these stories are not so miserable, Lala,' Maha protested. 'They would be much more miserable if we had not met with success.'

'I do not deny that a rescue adds relief to these stories, but still, it is very painful to imagine any young girl undergoing such violent sexual attacks.'

'I, too, have had too much pain today,' Shabane added. 'I must postpone added pain, my cousin.'

Maha reluctantly relented because she had been successful in convincing both to join the cause. 'Yes, OK then. I will call each of you tomorrow.'

After the usual drawn-out goodbyes, Maha escorted her cousins to the door. She quickly returned to me, eager to get the pain out of her system. 'I will tell you about the other two rescues, Mother,' she announced.

I quickly stood. 'Darling daughter, I love you with all of my heart, but I too prefer to postpone further pain. Your mother will find it impossible to get these stories out of her mind to make room for peaceful sleep! Truly, Maha, sleep will not come if I am subjected to additional stories involving violence against young women.'

Maha grudgingly agreed. 'It is fine, Mother. Thank you for helping me with this important mission. And I do hope that you find it possible to remove these tragic scenes from your mind and sleep well tonight. I must go out now, but I will see you in the morning.'

While hugging my daughter, I gave sincere thanks to God that we were living in Saudi Arabia, a country that has not been visited by war and violence since the days my grandfather fought battles to bring Arabia's tribes together as one. I did not wish to even think about the possibility of my daughters or granddaughters experiencing the nightmarish circumstances currently endured by equally precious Syrian girls. It is just too terrible to contemplate.

Despite my efforts, sleep failed to come. As I had known, my mind would remain centred around Syria and the despot Bashir al-Assad. I recalled Kareem once saying to me that the son would follow the father and possibly equal him in violence and that true peace would not come to Syrians so long as the Assad family ruled.

My mind then drifted to Souzan, and other Syrian girls and women. I became angry and disturbed by the events that were happening so near to my beloved country. All in this region know that the women of Syria can be dazzling, with their lovely skin, bright eyes, full lips and slim figures. But whether they are great beauties or not, no woman should be subjected to the kind of trauma Souzan suffered – men in power, who in this instance behaved no better than the most brutal beasts, should pay the price for such barbarism.

And so I spent the remainder of the day contemplating the incredible effect of war and violence upon the lives of innocent women.

Indeed, nothing a writer could share would appear exaggerated when it comes to the violence that some men enthusiastically commit upon women.

Although all humans must allow hope in their hearts, my experience with humanity and the systematic exploitation of women had narrowed my hopefulness into a sliver so small I could not feel the slightest hope.

Chapter Five

Kareem: A Kitten's Kiss

ALTHOUGH I FELT THE GREATEST yearning to drape a cloak over what I had heard of Souzan's meandering path from loving childhood to her torturous time in Syria's prisons, the dear girl's ghastly experiences were impossible to erase from my memory. The morning after our meeting I awakened weary from a restless night. Yawning, I stretched my aching limbs and kept my eyes shut. I naively wished that when I opened them the world around me would be shining with startling splendour and the sorrows of the Syrian people would have settled in the recesses of my mind.

This was not to be.

During my lifetime of humanitarian work, I have heard countless tragic tales. I have spent many sleepless nights dwelling on the misery of those who have suffered intentional cruelty at the hands of other humans. Over time I have come to understand that I must not dwell too deeply on the agony of what I have discovered, otherwise I would sink into despair, limiting any ability to resume my work. And no matter what might be occurring in my life, I have always been determined that my work must continue.

When I finally opened my eyes, there was no splendour to see. The tales of the previous evening had displaced the glory of an early morning in sunny Riyadh. Instead, the sorrowful faces of Syrians, with their blood-stilling shrieks and moans of pain, remained *in* me, affecting every breath I took and each step I made, as I roamed through my home. I compelled myself to scrutinize the various projects Kareem was organizing to enhance our lives, but the beauty surrounding me failed to relieve the gloomy images in my mind.

I took a moment to peer in the main sitting room, where we generally entertain guests not of our family. It was a hive of activity. Kareem had searched for and found some of the most talented Saudi artists, and these men and women were sketching various beautiful desert scenes which we had enjoyed during our years of travelling throughout our country. Later those artists would paint those sketches on vast framed canvases, which we would then hang throughout the palace. Although I had a huge interest in the undertaking, on that day I failed to appreciate the many hours of hard work and skill involved in such an important project. Truthfully, my mind had shifted, becoming fully engaged in thoughts of how I might convey to Maha the need to avoid more grisly narratives, at least for a few days. I felt anxious and was shrinking from a second meeting to hear the stories of the remaining two victims saved by my daughter and her friends. Despite my pride and pleasure in the fact that she had personally aided others to rescue three women whose lives would have most likely ended had they not been liberated from Syria, I knew that I must convince Maha that I had no further need of evidence to persuade me that the regime was so wicked that the entire world should come together and relieve Assad of his self-anointed power. I asked myself then why this had not already happened. I pondered the fact that Saddam Hussein was ultimately overthrown and executed for his deadly crimes against his own people, but for those in possession of the complete statistics it is clear that Assad is even more venomous, even more ruthless than the Iraqi dictator.

I felt some guilty relief when Maha's cousins texted my daughter to report that they were departing Riyadh earlier than expected to return to their apartments in London. Later, they promised, they would connect with Maha's group in Europe. That would be when they would hear further stories of successful rescues, they pledged.

I smiled to myself, knowing that the girls had been clever, taking flight, escaping Saudi Arabia for Europe. They, too, had no need for further stories in order to induce them to throw in their lot with Maha. They clearly recognized how useful their help would be to my daughter.

Maha was satisfied, as her goal to increase her group's numbers from four to six had been accomplished. There would now be additional minds to manage requests from those desperate women who needed to flee the catastrophic remains of Syrian cities and villages.

It is not only the people of Syria who have suffered during the reign of the Assad family. While visiting

London in 2012, I recall how I wept as I read an article in the *Guardian* newspaper, written by a reporter named Kevin Rushby. He wrote sorrowfully of the 'cultural casualties' in Syria, Iraq and Afghanistan.

The situation is even more grim in 2018.

History itself has been obliterated, as many of Syria's historic relics have been lost to the missile and bombing attacks of a government that should be obliged to protect all its citizens.

Damascus and Aleppo, two of humankind's earliest continuously settled cities, are in Syria. Famous worldwide for their ancient history, irreplaceable artefacts and haunting beauty, parts of Damascus are now annihilated, while much of Aleppo has been razed to the ground.

One of the first of the cultural fatalities was Aleppo's Souk al-Madina. The souk was built during the Ottoman occupation of Syria, in the fifteenth and sixteenth centuries, and was a UNESCO world heritage site, but the souk's cultural and historical importance failed to discourage Assad's attacks. His military was ordered to use their artillery to shell the souk, which it did. It was completely destroyed, centuries of history becoming little more than rubble in a matter of hours.

There have been other cultural losses in these cities and many others, which now resemble the ruins of Afghanistan, a country also rich in history but now sadly devastated, the result of long years of violence, from the nine-year war with Russia and the violent civil war that followed that country's withdrawal in 1989 right through to America's bombing and occupation.

War? I loathe war with all the passion I have in my heart, as do most sensible people, but somehow discussions and discord between nations all too often lead to nothing more than destructive violence.

* * *

When I learned that Maha had departed our palace for the day to visit with another group of cousins, I chose to enjoy a proper English tea prepared by our chef from London. Unsettled by my thoughts of war, I relaxed in a comfortable spot by the indoor pool, where I could sip tea and try to think positive thoughts. The rumblings of my stomach reminded me that I was ravenous. Yet I ate little after selecting from the tiers of goodies set out before me – my favourite little crustless sandwiches, which were chicken salad, and goat's cheese on cinnamon raisin bread. I eyed the warm scones, clotted cream and strawberry jam, but despite my hunger could not enjoy the feast. I resolved to eat more later, when I felt calmer and less agitated by all I had heard from Maha.

In the quiet of my palace, I found myself reflecting further on the former glory of Syria, knowing that time relieves all agonies and that the season will come when the people of Syria will not be ruled by a despot without care or concern for the welfare of his citizens or the protection of the country's ancient historical sites. Such encouraging thoughts about what the future must hold eased my burdened mind.

My recent method of visiting ancient times through the power of my thoughts was the most rewarding and soothing, for it took me back through the history I had learned over the years from my family, as well as from my love of reading.

No written records remain of the earliest days of civilization that impacted the land once referred to as Assyria, but evidence has been found that indeed it was occupied by early humans around 100,000 years ago. I have read that ceramics, crude tools and human skeletons have been discovered that support this theory. Climate change, or meteorological conditions not limited to our modern age, is believed to have influenced the humans living in Syria to adapt their lifestyle. Moving from merely hunting for food, they began to grow their crops in the rich soils of the fertile plains that spread from Mesopotamia, which comprised the Tigris–Euphrates river system, and through the eastern parts of Assyria, becoming settled in small villages and cities.

Once hunters become farmers, the men are at home more than they are gone, freeing up time to dwell on needed inventions and objects of beauty, and that is what happened in Syria.

At that moment, as I recalled so much of what I had been taught as a child, Kareem interrupted my thoughts, which were firmly focused on Syria. His voice was loud, as he searched for me throughout our palace. 'Sultana? Sultana? Where are you?'

I felt a flush of frustration, for I was just feeling the sensation and wonder of Syria, but then I heard the low laughter of my son, Abdullah, who was amused over one thing or another.

My irritation instantly vanished. 'I am here,' I happily called out, as my eyes hunted for their two tall figures, knowing that any moment they would walk through the wide and open archway leading into our indoor pool area.

Never am I annoyed when it is one of my children who is disrupting my contemplations. My son had been on a lengthy holiday to Europe and I had not seen him for nearly a month, which felt an eternity to his mother, despite his being an adult man with children of his own.

'Ah, Sultana, there you are,' Kareem said, before kissing me on my forehead and pulling up a chair to sit beside me. My husband reached for a plate and began to fill it with the roast beef sandwiches, his favourite, as well as a few specially made custard cream biscuits.

'Mother!' Abdullah smiled, as he popped a candy into his mouth. 'I have missed you.'

I laughed with pleasure. Nothing can match the joy I feel at seeing one of my children after a long absence. 'Son, come,' I exclaimed, as I patted the chair on the other side of me.

Abdullah pulled the chair slightly closer to me, as he settled himself and leaned in to kiss me on my cheeks and forehead.

Kareem gave me a probing look. 'Darling, tell me, how did your meeting go with Maha and her cousins?'

My smile faded into a grimace. 'Please, please do not ask.'

Abdullah frowned, feeling displeased that I was upset, although he was the family member who had pushed against his father for Maha to remain working in Turkey with the Syrian refugees who had fled the war to seek aid in that country. That excitement had occurred in 2015, three years previously. 'What, now?' he asked.

Kareem shifted uncomfortably, hoping that the current problem would not remind Abdullah of the huge row between them over the topic of Maha's presence in what Kareem considered a dangerous situation.

I paused before giving a minimal account of my concerns. 'Just so you know, it is not *my* troubles that are disturbing me, Abdullah, so do not worry about your mother.' I inhaled before continuing with my concerns. 'Truthfully, I am distraught over the grave danger so many women and their young families are facing in Syria. It is bad enough for the men who are at war, but I am talking here about the innocent and vulnerable women and children.'

'So, Maha gave you the details?' Kareem asked in between bites of his sandwich.

My jaw dropped as I looked in surprise at my husband. 'Our daughter already described the rescues to you?'

After their serious argument regarding Maha's work at the refugee centre in Turkey, I was startled that Maha had confided in her father. Quite obviously the two had moved past their major dispute.

'Yes, last week,' Kareem said, nodding his head. 'I asked her not to tell you the specifics, Sultana, as I knew you would be just as you are now – disheartened, upset and lethargic.'

Despite my best efforts to hide my sadness, my husband could sense my mood and I felt defensive. 'I may be disheartened and a little upset, but I am not lethargic.'

'If you say so,' Kareem said.

Abdullah asked, 'Mother, can you share the particulars with me?'

I shook my head. 'No, son, I think not. These are stories I do not want etched in your brain. Maha is doing all things possible to assist and relieve the women whose stories come to her, so you could do nothing but fret. Thankfully, she is doing this work from Europe, so she is in no immediate personal danger. But unless there is a need to know, or there is some way a person might help the situation, I would say that it is not fitting or healthy for anyone to be aware of these shocking stories.'

Kind and loving, Abdullah has never been one to seek out distressing tales, nor does he push when his parents say no, so he accepted my decision without further comment. I smiled and patted his hand. My son spent his youth in a palace with three excitable females, his mother and his two sisters, Maha and Amani. Perhaps that explains why he appears so happy to be married to Zain, a good woman with a quiet and calm temperament.

'But, son, please do tell me about your holiday. I insist.'

For the next hour, I had joyful moments hearing about Little Sultana and Abdullah's youngest child, his son, darling Feisal, and the fun events they enjoyed in England and France.

Little Sultana is small in stature, like her namesake, but has a huge personality and, despite her young age – she is almost twelve years old – is very busy working on projects to help the world. She is a natural activist and amazes us all with her mature attitude. Little Feisal will soon be five, a most precious child, full of sweetness and a joy for life, not unlike his father in so many ways. He is a big boy who promises to one day overtake his sister in size.

When my many questions about my grandchildren finally ceased, Abdullah stood, saying, 'But now I must leave. Little Sultana is waiting for me to deliver her a pet kitten.' He chuckled. 'She entrapped her mother at a weak moment in France, and Zain finally agreed that our daughter could have another pet.'

'A kitten? Will her little bunnies be in danger?' I questioned, with genuine alarm.

The year before, our animal-loving youngest daughter Amani had given her niece two utterly adorable, sweet baby bunnies; they are of the Netherland Dwarf breed. They are very small and named Tess and Lucas. Little Sultana had insisted on researching the most popular names in the Netherlands to make the babies feel at home in their new surroundings. She also maintained that one was a boy and the other a girl, and that they were in a romantic relationship, although Amani assured Abdullah that both were female and the lack of babies had reassured us all.

Tess and Lucas had so delighted my granddaughter that I was sorry I had not presented her with the little animals myself. Those rabbits enjoyed complete freedom to romp around in Little Sultana's private apartment. My granddaughter guarded their safety as carefully as a mother protects her babies.

Believing that rabbits and felines were natural enemies, I feared a cat attack that would harm the little creatures so loved by Little Sultana. Should that happen, I knew that we would have a very sad little girl on our hands.

Abdullah calmed me. 'We called two well-known small animal veterinarians and were told that the best cat to befriend rabbits are the Persians, and that if a Persian kitten is brought into the rabbit family while very young, all should be well. While on holiday, we ordered a white Persian kitten from a respectable breeder in Europe and it arrived on our plane just today. Little Sultana overheard us discussing the cat delivery and now my daughter is too impatient. The last I spoke with Zain, I was told that our daughter was discussing the kitten with Tess and Lucas, and was stressing the importance of welcoming a kitty friend into our home. Little Sultana is confident the three will be perfect companions.'

Kareem shifted in his seat but said nothing, although I knew my husband's thoughts as well as if they were my own. My husband is not a lover of animals, although he claims to be open to tolerating our grandchildren's pets. He probably also felt that it was an extravagance to fly a kitten from Europe on a private jet, but he said nothing.

Prior to Abdullah's departure, I reminded my son, 'Abdullah, please bring your family and come to dinner tomorrow evening. I cannot wait any longer to see the children.'

'Of course, Mother. We shall see you tomorrow evening, then?'

'Yes, please.'

'Little Sultana may not want to leave her new kitten.'

'By all means, the kitten is invited to dinner as well.'

Kareem stiffened and his eyes flashed. But still, he said nothing.

Although when my children were young, many were the times I had grumbled about my daughter Amani's obsession with animals, which often turned our palace into a den of total chaos, over the years I have adjusted to the new reality that many young people have an unusual affection for animals. Our grandchildren would be surprised to know that in our youth animals were rarely pets; they were kept for a specific purpose – such as camels for transport, or dogs for security. Now I feel no aversion to my grandchildren having and loving pets, and bringing those pets into my home – Saudi Arabian people and our habits have drastically changed over the course of one generation – but Kareem is less keen and still cringes in protest.

Yet I know he would never criticize anything about our grandchildren, all of whom he loved from the moment of their birth with his whole heart. Should Little Sultana bring in a herd of baby goats, or ten kittens, Kareem would surely suffer, but would not openly criticize or prevent them from entering our palace.

After Abdullah departed, Kareem approached the topic of Maha's Syrian activities once more.

'Sultana, let us discuss Maha's latest project.'

'Let's not, husband. I am just now beginning to feel less upset and more normal.'

'But, Sultana, I can tell you some specifics without the emotion. Then I will casually tell our daughter that you are aware of her successful rescues and that there is no need for further discussion with you, at least not any time soon.'

'Well, I am not a child, Kareem. I can cope with anything Maha needs to share. And I want her to know that I support her work. That is important to me!'

Kareem made a clicking noise with his tongue. 'When I first saw you today, you were pale and had a tremor in your hands. Now you are much improved, more settled. You know how I worry about you.'

I smiled. 'Our son is like a tonic. He brings me happiness and makes any bad memories or thoughts fade away.'

Kareem would not cease in his sudden determination to protect me. He frowned. 'I must spare you the full stories that Maha appears so determined to share with anyone who will listen. She is becoming obsessed with the problems these women are facing. But she is young and healthy, and I know that she will withstand whatever is placed in front of her.' Kareem paused. 'But you, Sultana, you take such things very intensely. I am worried. Your health might be adversely affected.'

By now I was feeling a flush of worry. Why was my husband suddenly so concerned about my health? Did he know something I did not know? Had he spoken with a doctor about my hand tremors without telling me? In Saudi Arabia, our men are still very traditional about many things. As a result of the guardian law, husbands have been given the right to share confidential information about their wives with physicians. Then, should a wife be diagnosed with an illness, the husband will be the first to hear from the physician, even before the patient.

I stared at Kareem without speaking.

'Sultana?'

'Have you spoken with a doctor about my tremors? Am I suffering from a terminal illness, husband? If so, I demand to know.'

Kareem always squirms when a conversation makes him uncomfortable. He was visibly doing so now.

Finally, my husband became truthful. 'Sultana, no, I truly know nothing about any terminal illness. And I have not spoken with any doctors about your health. But I have noticed that you have a tremor in your hands. I believe you should take it easy. And,' he hurriedly added, 'we should make an appointment to see a doctor in London to have some tests.'

My husband had shocked me.

I stared at him and he stared at me.

Then I lowered my eyes to gaze at my hands, hands I no longer felt pleased to show. In my youth my hands had been soft and smooth and appeared to be the hands of the girl or young woman I was. The years have done little to bring wrinkles and spots to my face, for Saudi women have beautiful olive-coloured skin and we take no pleasure in baking in the sun in order to have a dark tan. As a result of this, our faces generally remain youthful, with few wrinkles. But now I must admit that my hands appear to be older than my years. While ageing is natural and gives me little worry, I do not welcome the way my hands have started to tremble unnaturally.

Unexpectedly, both hands began to noticeably shake, appearing much worse than previously. I had sighted this movement on more than one occasion but had forgotten the abnormality the moment something new drew my attention. There is always so much going on in my life, I do not waste time thinking about myself and

135

every little twinge or ache that I might experience. After all, I am no longer a young princess! But now my husband had put a big worry in my mind and had given me cause for concern. As I concentrated on my tremor, somehow it made matters worse, more pronounced.

'Why, Kareem? Why did you choose to say this to me on this day?'

Kareem squirmed again.

'Stop that squirming!' I ordered in a sharp tone.

'I am not squirming.'

'Yes, you *are* squirming, and you squirm like a child each time you are in an unpleasant conversation.'

My husband laughed. 'Sultana, you are shaking, and I am squirming. We are a perfect older couple, darling.'

I snarled, preparing to snap.

'OK, darling, perhaps we both need some medical tests,' Kareem said, with a tight smile.

Rather than do battle, I smiled too. Over the years mine has become a less volatile personality, which is a good thing for my husband.

Then, after a very lengthy pause, he confessed his apprehension. 'All right. I will tell you. Last evening I was worried, as I assumed Maha was revealing many gruesome details about those poor girls she has helped to save. I, too, was disturbed by those stories. I knew that you would suffer more than most. After you retired, I came to your room to see for myself how you were reacting. You were in a sort of fog, not fully asleep, not fully awake. You did not acknowledge me, so I sat beside you for a time.

'My darling, your hands were trembling, shaking badly, even when you were at rest. That is when I knew that we must go for medical tests. That is when I began to connect emotional traumas with your shaking.'

'What do you think it might be?' I asked, a tinge of fear recognizable in my tone of voice. As a human being, nothing is more unsettling than believing one might be facing a serious illness and possibly premature death. I know only too well that even those with great wealth are helpless when faced with incurable disease. Although I could not fathom the idea of Kareem confronting old age without me, for we are a couple who have unspoken emotions, yet we each depend upon and need the other. Truthfully, I was most distressed at the possibility of leaving my children and grandchildren without their mother and grandmother.

He shrugged. 'It is probably nothing to worry over, Sultana. You seem well otherwise. You are not in pain. You are not losing weight. I believe we will find a good explanation for this trembling problem.'

I gazed at my husband with true affection. After years of marriage and three children, we had mastered many problems and our bond had grown stronger. My love for him has never diminished and yet, at that moment, I felt vulnerable and alone. Generally, I face all of life with a feeling of power and strength – willing to take on difficult matters with resolve and commitment – but something felt different on this occasion. We were both weary and agreed to retire to rest so we could face our problems with renewed energy.

We are a couple who generally enjoys the other's company very much – until we sleep. After a few years of married life we acknowledged that we slept more restfully when we slept alone, and so we retire to our own individual suites for naps or for sleeping. On this particular afternoon I was pleased when my husband insisted on staying with me until I slept, for I needed him with me – I needed him to be nearby.

And so I fell into a deep slumber with my husband cuddling me.

*   *   *

Kareem and I were so exhausted that we both slept through the afternoon and evening. The following morning I felt revitalized and Kareem and I temporarily parted so that both might shower and prepare ourselves for the new day, but agreed to meet for breakfast by the pool.

An hour later when we met as planned I noticed that at first he looked intently at my hands.

'No, they are not trembling,' I said with a smile.

'It was the cuddle cure,' he replied, with a smile of his own.

After eating pitta bread, boiled eggs and yogurt, and drinking sweet tea, I felt my strength return.

'All right. Tell me a few facts about those rescues, Kareem. Maha will go into every detail and my strength will ebb if I hear the specifics of yet another girl or woman who was violated.'

'Yes, you are right, Sultana.'

'All right, then. I am ready.'

Kareem exhaled. 'These stories are the most tragic because all are young girls or women who were taken from their homes, from their parents or husband, and kept isolated and tortured.' Kareem asked, 'Which of the three did you hear about?'

'Souzan. The teenager kidnapped, imprisoned and raped repeatedly.'

'Right. She, at least, is with her mother and siblings in Jordan. While she will never be the same girl she once was, she does have a chance to live something close to a normal life.'

'Normal? I do not think so. You know from our societies that no man will marry her. She will never have a husband or children, something most women want. So I would never say she will live a normal life.'

'I take your point, darling. But she is with her mother. She is with her siblings. She is receiving medical attention. She is safe. At least she is alive!'

'Only that – she is alive – nothing more, at least for now.'

Kareem had a sad look on his face but said nothing more.

'What of the other two girls, Kareem?'

'One was a young mother. I cannot remember her name. I believe she was in her early twenties. She was the mother of a toddler and had also given birth a few months before she was taken. Her husband was not fighting against the government, but her uncle was caught transporting weapons. He managed to run away from the government security forces after he had been identified but had no way of alerting his family to vacate their home; he knew security would come and they would take others if he was not there.

'The young mother had no knowledge of the event and very innocently walked over a couple of streets from her home to visit her aunt. Thinking she would be away only an hour, she left her infant with her mother but took her toddler along, as her aunt had a similarly aged child and the toddler enjoyed play time with his cousin.

'The young mother's fate was linked to bad luck. While she was visiting her aunt, the security forces crashed into the house. Unable to find the husband, they took hostages, the young mother and her toddler son. This reaction is routine for them, from all that I know from security reports I have read.

'The other toddler had successfully hidden when the noise of the crashing door frightened him. The wife of the hunted man was left behind, as the security misunderstood and believed they were taking the wife and child of the one they were tracking. Therefore, they mistakenly took the wrong woman and the wrong child. As much as the uncle felt remorse that his niece and great-nephew had been kidnapped, he refused to turn himself in to release them.'

Kareem lifted his shoulders. 'And, from what we know, the Syrian government never lives up to its promises, so it would have been a wasted life anyhow.'

'And the young mother and her child?' I asked, dreading to know what I was about to discover.

'The young mother had a similar experience to Souzan. She was held as a hostage and was beaten and raped. She was finally released approximately six months later, but here is the real tragedy. She never saw her toddler son again. The security forces actually denied taking the child. They claimed that the mother was hallucinating. Although she was reunited with her infant, over time this baby had come to believe her grandmother was her mother. Sadly she failed to recognize her mother. The entire family was in danger because once someone is taken into custody the Syrian government never forgets them. They return time and again to ask for bribes or to threaten the family with brutal consequences.

'This entire family was set to go to a camp in Lebanon, but once Maha's team was involved they were taken to Amman, in Jordan, the same as Souzan's family. That is where they are now living.

'Unfortunately, the young mother has broken down many times, unable to forget her toddler son and what he must have endured. She wants to see his body and that alone will help her to move to a position of being able to heal. The unknown is unbearable. She is most afraid that her son is still a prisoner and is being tortured and is crying endlessly for his mother. The last sight and sound of her son was when she saw his little face, terrified, and heard his pitiful cries. Then he was very roughly taken away. I assume they killed the child, but there is no way of knowing.'

'Oh, Kareem,' I cried. 'How can these men inflict this horrendous pain on innocent women and children? Do they not have families? Can they not put themselves in the places of these mothers and their babies?'

'Such a man I cannot imagine, Sultana. I really cannot.'

We both sat and stared for long moments, my thoughts focusing on our little Feisal. I would go mad should he be taken away to be tortured by such brutes, dying while screeching for his mother. It was almost too much to contemplate.

'And the other girl our daughter saved?'

'The third victim was a child, Sultana. A thirteen-year-old girl. She foolishly joined in a demonstration against the government being held in her city. Assad's security swooped in and captured and arrested fifteen or twenty of the teenagers, those too young to understand that they should run for their lives. The young girl was a victim of savage attacks. In fact, she has undergone four operations to repair her assaulted body and the surgeons say she will need at least two more. Due to the tension of the situation, her parents divorced. The father blamed his daughter for her arrest and rape, saying that if she had been home where she belonged none of it would have ever happened. So, the father is no longer involved in their family life and this is increasing pressure on the mother, who is trying to raise six children with little or no help. But at least Maha is taking the financial pressure from the mother's mind. I cannot remember if this family is in Jordan or Lebanon, but I do know that Maha prefers to keep all the families she supports in the same country. Whether she will be able to manage that feat remains to be seen. All the countries taking in refugees are baulking at taking more, other than Turkey, as you know.'

I could barely abide the pain of thinking about these young women. And I was so far removed from their much greater anguish and pain. I was nothing more than a woman in a country far away who could easily spare the funds to help them live. I could not fathom the enormous strength required by these Syrian women and their families just to persist with life, minute by minute, hour by hour, day by day, enduring pain that must feel unendurable.

I decided to escape to my apartments. 'Kareem, your wife is retiring for a nap. I shall see you tonight when our son and his family come for dinner.'

Kareem's face looked old for the first time in our lives. He, too, was suffering greatly just from knowing these stories. But even as my husband suffered, he saved his worries for me, his wife.

Later that evening I felt some small joy when I entered our sitting room to see my son and his family. My eyes searched for my husband and I could not restrain my laughter when I saw him cooing at a small white kitten that was perched on his shoulder and sniffing his face.

Little Sultana was looking on with tremendous pride. I overheard her exclaim, 'I knew you would love Chanel, Grandfather. You cannot have her, but you can kitty-sit when I travel.'

I watched with immeasurable amusement as my most loving husband managed to hide a grimace.

But he was squirming . . .

Chapter Six

Doctor, Doctor

As Abdullah and Zain were leaving our home after their most pleasant visit, Zain nudged her husband, coyly asking him, 'Abdullah, have you told your parents?'

'Zain! No, of course not. I was going to share our news for the first time tomorrow, as you and I planned.'

Zain smiled her sweetest smile. 'But I wish to be with you when you tell them, husband.'

That's when Little Sultana began to jump about from her mother to her father. 'What? What news, Mama? What news, Baba?'

'I do not believe this is the best time, Zain.' Abdullah squirmed, as he struggled to block his daughter from stamping on his shiny designer shoes. My son has always been very particular about his clothes and how he looks, maintaining a smart appearance at all times. His squirming prompted a smile from me, as I looked from Kareem to our son. Abdullah was definitely his father's child.

'Zain, we will want to talk about this news for longer than a bulletin, given as we are departing.'

'No, I want you to tell them now. Your mother will sleep very nicely tonight if she knows.'

On hearing this I allowed my excitement to grow, realizing that their news was apparently positive. I had several ideas regarding various pieces of information that would make me happy. I wondered if Little Sultana had won the school prize for reading the most books, or if sweet Feisal might be attending the special school for royal toddlers, which I had highly recommended to Zain after learning from my sister Sara that her grand-children were registered there, and they had enjoyed it and had progressed well.

But I stood quietly without interrupting, as that is my new habit.

Kareem was not quite so patient. 'What news? Now you must tell us, as we will feel we are hanging in limbo until we know.'

'Zain, see what you have started.' Abdullah sighed as he shook his head. 'All right, but I am not going to tell you as we stand in the door saying our goodbyes. Let us return to the sitting room.'

Little Sultana skipped, then remembered her kitty, Chanel. She looked for Edna, who was a wonderful nanny employed from the Philippines to help Zain with our grandchildren. Little Sultana spotted her standing quietly behind Kareem. 'Edna, please can we go and bring Chanel from the car. She will want to know this news, too.'

Kareem, who had been kitty kissed numerous times over the course of the evening, interrupted. 'Sweet girl, your little kitten is asleep in her carrier. She is surely exhausted from her international flight. Let her sleep, sweetheart.' Kareem looked at me for support. 'Sultana, don't you think it best that Chanel learn this news after she has rested?'

I struggled not to tease my husband, and for a moment considered insisting that Chanel be returned to visit longer with Kareem, but I resisted my inclination to be naughty and instead was a good wife. 'Of course, Little Sultana, any baby will be tired after a long day of travel.'

Little Sultana puckered her lips, frowned, but then agreed. 'All right. Chanel did seem tired. I will tell her Mama's news tomorrow.'

Soon we were seated around a table in the sitting area. Abdullah did not waste a moment. He leaned in to his wife and touched her shoulder before caressing her hand.

'Zain and I are so very happy. I will not keep you in suspense. We are going to increase the size of our family – not by one, but by two. We are expecting twins!'

I sat without moving or speaking. I felt a flush of complete joy. But then, unexpectedly, my heart began to beat very fast, too fast. It was beating so fast I realized something was very wrong. My hands began to shake, then I fainted.

* * *

The following morning I stirred under thin bedcovers after a fitful night's sleep filled with what I believed to be nightmares of losing control of my mind and my body being touched by strangers. I soon realized that the nightmares were my reality.

I looked down at the sterile, beige-coloured coverlet over my body. I was sleeping in a bed that was not my own. I peered around at the room to discover I was not alone. There was a woman I did not know sitting at a table in the unfamiliar room organizing some documents. She was in a nursing uniform and it was becoming clear to me that I was a patient in a hospital. Although the room was very chic and decorated with expensive furniture, it was a hospital nevertheless. Disorientated, I blinked several times to try to make sense of what was happening to me and then glanced at my arms to see that I was receiving fluids.

The nurse glanced in my direction and smiled. Too late I tried to feign sleep.

'Awake, are we?' she said with an accent I did not readily identify. She didn't speak in a typically British way, as we have a number of citizens from that country assisting us in managing our properties in England and in helping us at our various homes, and her pronunciation was different to theirs. She was a woman with European features, dark blonde hair and light skin.

My croaky, rough-sounding voice surprised me when I asked, 'Where am I?'

'You are at the royal hospital, Princess, the King Faisal Specialist Hospital and Research Centre.'

I looked around again and realized this was true. I am quite familiar with the hospital. Seeing my confusion, the woman added with a wide smile, 'My name is Pamela, but everyone calls me Pam. I am from Canada and I have worked in this hospital for the past five years.'

'Where is my husband?'

'The prince stepped out to meet with your doctor. He said that if you were to awaken I should tell you that everything is going to be all right and not to worry. And he will return shortly.'

'Go and get my husband, now.'

'He said he would return shortly.'

'My husband, please.'

'Yes, of course. I will tell him that you are awake, Princess.'

After the woman left I studied my surroundings. My room was spacious and would be considered luxurious by most. I had been in this hospital several times since becoming an adult, so the ambience felt familiar.

As I lay back on my pillows, waiting for Kareem to arrive, my mind drifted back to how this hospital came to be built and the stories that had been passed down through the family about it. Even kings have dreams, and the royal hospital where I was now a patient was one of my uncle Faisal's dreams come true.

After he became king in 1964, Uncle Faisal made the financial health of the kingdom his first priority after his brother, King Saud, who was the first of Grandfather's sons to assume the throne, virtually bankrupted the kingdom with his unrestrained spending. King Saud's excessive splurging was so out of control that there was full agreement within the family that he should abdicate the throne in favour of his brother. After several years of King Faisal's careful budgeting and austere spending, the kingdom, aided by the oil wealth, finally rested on a solid financial footing.

Saudi Arabia had a promising future due to the oil under its soil, but the lives of its citizens were poorly lived when Uncle Faisal came to power: there were few schools and hospitals – little of the modern world had penetrated our desert kingdom. While the royals were educated, few of the less fortunate Saudis benefited from education, and adequate healthcare was nearly non-existent. Therefore, King Faisal's second priority was to improve the daily life of ordinary citizens, whether through high-quality education, improved medical care or the introduction of technology.

Television, for example, came very slowly to the kingdom – not until in 1965, as I have been told, for I was a very young child at the time. Tragically, a fanatical prince who believed television to be evil attacked the headquarters of Saudi television and was killed in a shoot-out with security guards. It was an incident that would affect the lives of all Saudis for some years because the brother of the dead prince was determined to take revenge.

Meanwhile King Faisal had moved ahead with his progressive plans to transform his outdated country into an advanced, modern kingdom. Everything Saudi Arabia can boast of today began with King Faisal, including the hospital where I was receiving care.

In 1970, my uncle Faisal donated the land where the hospital now stands. I recall how my father once told me that Faisal, his half-brother, impatiently studied all the plans and enthusiastically awaited the opening of the ultra-modern hospital, which was set for 1975. But Uncle Faisal failed to realize his dream, for he was shot dead by the brother of the zealous prince, who had long plotted his revenge. Poor Uncle Faisal never lived to see the reality of the medical centre he had envisioned for his people. And so it was in 1975 that King Khalid, who followed King Faisal, officially opened the hospital.

'Thank you, Uncle Faisal,' I whispered, thinking of what it had become over the past forty-four years, all the additions and renovations that had been carried out. These days there are beds for more than a thousand patients and the hospital currently has many ongoing major projects, such as the King Abdullah Centre for Oncology and Liver Diseases, as well as the Emergency Medical Services Building. No finer hospital exists in the entire kingdom.

As I lay in bed thinking of old times, my thoughts became more lucid and I recalled the previous night's events, which felt like faded memories slowly becoming clear and filling with vivid colour in my mind. At that moment I remembered the most divine ending to the enjoyable evening spent with my son and his family. Prior to what I now realized was evidently a medical emergency, I had learned the nicest news imaginable, that our son and his wife were going to be the parents of twins. Their family would grow from four to six in only seven months.

'Twins!' I said aloud.

Just then Kareem walked rapidly into my room and rushed to my side. 'Darling, you are awake.'

'What has happened?'

'Do you remember anything?'

'I do remember my hands shaking very badly and I felt very weak, and then nothing more.'

'You passed out, Sultana.'

'It was from excitement, for sure,' I said, wishing to downplay the event. 'We are going to have twins in the family.' I spoke in a gleeful tone. 'Twins!' I gazed at my husband with, I am sure, an expression of yearning. 'I cannot be ill, Kareem. Not now. I am sure it is nothing serious. The thought of these twins to come will create a cure for certain. I just want to go home and rest. I will get better.'

'I fear not, Sultana. Something is wrong, sweetheart. We must find out why you have these hand tremors and why you blacked out.' When he saw my look of complete despair, he reassured me. 'I have spoken with the doctor and there are many non-threatening health reasons to explain the tremors. So now, while we are here, we are going to run tests to find the cause and treat it and cure you. Then, when your mind is at rest, you will enjoy the twins so much more!'

'But I do feel well.'

'The doctor found your heart rate to be elevated, Sultana. Combine that with the tremors and there must be an underlying cause.'

I exhaled, feeling tears coming to my eyes. I was as frightened as I had been years ago when I was told I had breast cancer. Although a lot of time had passed since that occasion, and I was considered permanently cured of that particular cancer, like many others who have had similar problems the fear of a new malignancy rarely leaves you. Those days, while fighting cancer, I had experienced sheer terror at the realization that I might leave my small children without their mother. Now I felt similar alarm at the idea of leaving my grown children and their small babies.

I wanted to live. I wanted to see my son's twins, now due to arrive and to bring such joy to our family, and in only seven months. I could not abide the thought of missing holding two newborn babies in my arms at once, for I am a woman who loves all children, but most especially those of my blood.

I dreaded what the tests might show, although I knew that I must submit and face whatever was to come for me in my future. Many millions of women worldwide each year confront the catastrophic reality that they will not have the good fortune to remain with their children or grandchildren as long as they would like. I often tell myself that I am no different from any other woman in her hopes to live without disease. But I admit that I am self-interested when it comes to my health and do not wish to live with the health struggles that impact so many women on this earth.

But at that precise moment I was helpless and could do no more than any other woman in the world who yearns to live for her family. Wait, and pray for God's mercy.

*　　*　　*

'Cancer again!' I muttered in disbelief.

It had been a month since I had fainted and had been rushed to the hospital. During that time I had endured hospital tests, medical consultations and surgery for stage one papillary thyroid cancer. Surgery is the definitive treatment for my grade and type of cancer. In another few weeks I would undergo radioiodine therapy for the purpose of detecting and destroying any remaining cancer cells.

During those long weeks of endless medical worries, a growing consciousness of my own mortality lingered in my mind. I sat uneasily on the sofa in my hospital room, drinking warm tea in an attempt to dissipate the cold feeling within me. I could do nothing to conceal the anxiety that I am sure was clearly etched on my face. The initial feeling of excitement that had engulfed me over the joyous news of my daughter-in-law's pregnancy with twins had been replaced by an overwhelming sadness and a longing to leave the hospital, which I was set to do that very afternoon.

I really could not believe that I had been diagnosed as having a double medical problem. First the doctors discovered that I had hyperthyroidism, which had caused the tremors. The hyperthyroidism was a blessing, however, for the tests searching for the cause of the tremors had discovered a small growth in my thyroid, which was tested in the hospital laboratory and revealed to be malignant.

I had thyroid cancer.

While it is rare for a patient to have both hyperthyroidism and thyroid cancer, it does occur. This was my fate.

I was so grateful that my husband, who had been so alarmed by my fainting, had insisted upon me receiving serious medical attention without delay. Kareem, my doctors told me, had most likely saved my life; medical intervention had led to the discovery of early stage cancer, curable if detected and treated without delay.

Although my husband suffered every moment with me, leaving my side only when it was absolutely necessary for him to do so, I saw a spark of genuine joy cross his face when the doctors credited him with saving my life.

Never once did I doubt that my husband was as devoted to me as a man can be to the woman he loves. 'Thank you for coming back. I really cannot live without you, Sultana,' Kareem had whispered to me as I had slowly revived after the anaesthesia. Although most husbands would not be allowed in a recovery room, being a prince in Saudi Arabia has benefits. I was startled when my eyes met my husband's loving gaze so soon during recovery. Despite the fact he was wearing a surgical gown and a mask, I instantly recognized him. I could barely return his smile, as my drowsy brain was not yet fully functioning.

I smiled, reliving that moment, still drinking my tea when the door burst open and my happy husband bounded into my room.

'The prince is here to collect his princess,' Kareem said with laughter. 'Here, let us have proof that you are my true princess.' With those words, Kareem raised a beautiful jewelled shoe that was clasped in his right hand, a shoe that appeared to be glass.

Behind him my son laughed loudly and reached out with his hand. 'Really, Father, is that a glass shoe? I must see it.'

'No, my son. Only the true princess can touch this shoe.'

Then I watched in wonder as Kareem knelt at my feet and slipped the shoe upon my foot. It was a perfect fit, although it was made of acrylic material rather than glass.

'Ah! There is no doubt. This woman is my princess,' he said, looking up at Abdullah. Then my husband surprised me with a kiss upon my lips, in full view of our son, who blushed, for he had never seen his father kiss his mother on the lips. In Saudi Arabia, we keep our most intimate moments private. Never will anyone see Saudi Arabian couples displaying affection in public, or for that matter even in front of their own families.

Kareem then looked at his son and confirmed the words he had spoken to me earlier. 'Son, I cannot live without your mother. When I was young and first married, I was a fool and thought of little other than enjoying what it means to be a man in this country. But over time I came to see that I am the most fortunate man in the world to have married your mother. Yes, my wife is very beautiful, but that is not the most important aspect of her appeal. Your mother is intelligent, interesting, caring, and she is a woman who has changed the world we live in.'

'Kareem, stop!' I demanded. 'You are embarrassing me.'

'No, Sultana, I want my son, and the rest of our family, to know that you are more than a wonderful mother and wife, you are a woman who is truly unique. You, my wife, are one of the few royals not spoiled by idle wealth. You have used your wealth to save many people from poverty, from ignorance, even from death. You have raised children who think of others more than they think of themselves. I repeat: you are unique in this world, Sultana, and truly, a most inspiring person.' Kareem continued, 'How bored I would be with any other woman. Your mother, Abdullah, has been for me a prolonged feast.'

'Well, Mother is definitely not boring,' Abdullah said, his face still red with discomfort at seeing his father carry on.

Kareem totally lifted my spirits. 'I do love my glass shoes, husband. But I want to go home, and it is not possible for me to walk out of the hospital in these heels!'

'I will carry you in my arms!'

'You will not!' I was suddenly fearful that my husband would create an embarrassing scene in front of the entire hospital staff. Other Saudi Arabians in the hospital would be mortified on his behalf. 'You, Abdullah!' I nodded at my son. 'You go and ask the nurse to bring the wheelchair. This woman, unique or not, is going home!'

Kareem laughed and looked relieved at my sudden awakening! Perhaps he recognized once again the 'true Sultana' – the determined, strong woman he married.

When Abdullah rushed from the room, eager to remove himself from his newly emotionally energized father, Kareem laughed at his retreat, then looked at me with renewed affection. 'Honestly, Sultana, this was too much of a fright. Thanks be to God that we found the cancer in time. The doctor just told me once again that he does not believe you will have further problems. He says a stage one in this particular cancer is almost always curable.'

'I, too, am relieved, Kareem. I could not bear the thought of leaving you or our children and grandchildren. All are so precious to me.'

And then my husband gave me a gentle kiss on my lips, one that would have been improper for our son to witness.

And so home we went, where I was greeted by Maha and Amani. My girls gave me the welcome news that they had made a pact that never again would they argue in front of me, despite their enormous differences of opinion. From this moment on, I would never again find the need to separate them in a verbal or physical altercation.

'Now, this news means that my operation and cure was meaningful,' I replied. It was such a relief to me, for nothing in my family life has caused more distress than the constant squabbling between my girls.

I was so content to be home again and sat with a quiet happiness, looking at my husband and three children, giving thanks for life as the beautiful desert twilight turned to evening. How grateful I was to have a chance of more years to be with my family and to continue my work. How many children might I educate, or lives might I save, with the years that I hoped to live?

While sitting there, I made a silent vow to increase all efforts to help others. I was so ecstatic to still be with the living and now, with the promise of more years to come, I considered breaking into song. But since I am a woman without the talent to sing, I restrained myself and spared my family.

*　　*　　*

After returning home I rested frequently and during that time watched more television than usual. Yemen, due to the current conflict, dominated the news. During the days following my release from the hospital, I had many thoughts, memories and questions in my mind about one of our closest neighbours.

Yemen, once known as Arabia Felix, was at one time a wealthy little kingdom, rich in frankincense, myrrh, cinnamon, gum and precious stones. There was a successful caravan trade via land with parts of Asia and thriving commerce by sea with India and Egypt. The kingdom was so wealthy that the legions of Augustus of the Roman Empire desired to absorb it, but the heat and disease of the region decimated those soldiers and Arabia Felix remained independent, at least for a time.

The future was not so kind to Yemen.

A brief exploration of Yemen's history reveals that the little kingdom has been beset by upheaval and uncertainty for centuries. It was absorbed by other empires, such as the Ottomans and Great Britain in the 1500s and 1800s, with the determined Ottomans returning to the northern sections of the country, creating havoc in their quest for dominance. A century on, in the 1960s, Yemen split into two countries, then in 1990 it was reunited, only to be threatened with separation once again. Al-Qaeda interfered in Yemeni business in the early 2000s before the Houthi insurgency brought violence, war and death to many innocent people from 2004 until the present time. The multiple bomb attacks, clashes and renewed clashes that litter its modern history are far too many to list. Most recently Iran, a dedicated enemy of Saudi Arabia, has found it agreeable to their foreign policy plans to support the Houthi movement, which champions Yemen's Shia Muslim minority. Iran is encouraging them to commit war and violence against their rival, their Sunni neighbour Saudi Arabia.

Iran is the evil next door.

My own country is now involved in the business of Yemen, for we cannot abide a close neighbour who carries out malevolent orders originating in Tehran. Despite the marches and outcries against us – many originating in the Western world – we Saudis believe that our actions can be compared to that of the Americans during the Cuban Missile Crisis, a hard-fought, dangerous battle of wills between the American presidency of John F. Kennedy and Russia's Nikita Khrushchev leadership in October 1962. It was a crisis that deflated like a pricked balloon when the Americans threatened nuclear war. Although war was averted, the United States made it abundantly clear to the entire world that such a close neighbour could not, and would not, be allowed to have the nuclear ability to attack America.

In Saudi Arabia, we have a similarly volatile relationship with Iran. There is little doubt that if we do nothing now, all will pay a bigger price in the future. For certain, we Saudis would be overrun with Iranian attacks from Yemen, which would instigate a much bigger confrontation in the region. To date, Saudi Arabia has been assisted by the United States, the United Kingdom and France with logistical and intelligence reports.

From my own research, I know that nearly 10,000 people have been killed and nearly 60,000 have been injured since the beginning of this war in 2015. Most people believe that Saudi Arabian bombings are the cause of each death in Yemen, but this is not true. Many

Yemeni people have been killed or wounded by the Houthi – menacing rebels with authoritative attitudes and bullying behaviour. They besiege and overwhelm residents of villages and cities who do not join their cause. Chaos prevails, and it is difficult, if not impossible, to know the exact figures of who is killing whom.

But never doubt that the human cost in Yemen strikes sorrow and horror in the hearts of Saudi Arabians, for the Yemeni and Saudi people have been more friendly than unfriendly for most of our history. On a personal level, numerous Yemeni people have worked in our homes and, on some occasions, educated Yemenis have managed our businesses. We are friends with that country's people.

Such interest and activity in a small land with few resources is creating violence, war and death for its blameless people, those who have no interest in the greater politics of the area. Iran should tuck its political ambitions in its pockets and take them home, allowing Saudi Arabia to swoop in to bind the wounds of the Yemeni people, then all would return to normal in this area.

I mourn for these innocent victims of war. As readers of my books well know, my sister Sara and I have enjoyed special friendships with two extraordinary women from Yemen.

Italia is the great beauty who was once married to Kareem's father. Although the marriage was not a success, such was Italia's charm that he bestowed enormous wealth upon her at the time of their divorce. Italia was such a beauty in her youth that she was married off frequently and for large sums of money, paid to her family. Her divorce from Kareem's father finally produced enough wealth for her to do as she pleased with her life. What made her happiest was being able to help as many females in Yemen as possible, as Italia has a noble character. She improved the lives of many girls and women, whether with their education or helping them to divorce an abusive husband. She even assisted some women to access the kind of medical care that is beyond the reach of most.

Since the very beginning of the civil war in Yemen, I have maintained contact with Italia and had recently learned that she had received millions in aid money from rich Saudi royals to enable her to continue to ease the burdens of those caught up in this dreadful, continuous conflict. But during our latest communication Italia had sounded desperately sad.

'Princess, the war is too broad and the combination of the Houthi and Saudi bombings – along with the worsening famine in Yemen – is making it impossible for me to help all but a small number of injured and displaced people,' she said. 'I have the funds, Princess, but I am finding it impossible to get the proper documents to cross the blockades and negotiate the checkpoints manned by the rebels.'

There are other women with similar ambitions – women who are dedicated to the cause of helping the Yemeni people. But as with every civil war, where each part of the country is embroiled in conflict, the enormous challenges never end. And they are *enormous* challenges.

Fiery – whom I named 'Fiery the Fearless' due to her plucky personality – is the second Yemeni woman with whom I bonded. She is a brilliant woman and highly educated. She held a senior position as a college professor in Yemen, but she was opinionated and blunt, and the sharpness of her tongue made her many enemies. Eventually, she was fired from her post but remains a bright and vibrant woman who says exactly what she thinks, regardless of the consequences. Such women have difficulty surviving in any part of the world, but more so in Middle Eastern countries, where women can carry on with their work, including humanitarian projects, so long as they are not too loud with their voices and not too brilliant with their brains! They must also take care not to upstage the men they encounter, even if they are lazy and incompetent and do nothing more than sit around, drinking tea and ruling over others.

Italia claims that she and Fiery will be coming back to Jeddah to see Sara and me again very soon, and I eagerly await hearing their personal stories to find out what is really happening in the villages and cities of Yemen. My only fear when it comes to Italia and Fiery is that their ardour and passion will endanger them both.

For all who read this, I hope that you pray, as I do, that the multiple conflicts in Yemen will ease, that the people will recover from the ongoing anarchy, and that they will heal and grow strong so that they might take back their nation from the squabbling factions that wreak havoc on their homeland.

Chapter Seven

Destroy the Guardianship Law

'SULTANA,' KAREEM SAID, as he held out an expectant hand to pull me near to him, 'your feeling heart is the foundation of many of your troubles.'

I did not accept his hand, nor did I move closer. Despite our true love for one another, my husband and I often disagree, for he is a man with strong views but is married to a woman who has equally strong opinions of her own. Also, my husband is vastly different from his wife when it comes to charity, for he saves his greatest generosity for members of his family, while I derive the ultimate pleasure from helping the helpless, the majority of whom are strangers to me and who come to my attention through the efforts of others who are familiar with the work I do.

I was feeling exasperated, for Kareem and I were repeating the same words to each other for at least the fourth time since my illness three months before. But our conversations were becoming more heated, as my husband continued to push me to turn some of my charities over to our daughter Maha, so that we might enjoy more time together.

'Kareem, when I believed that I might pass from this earth sooner than expected for a woman of my age, I knew then that I would not only continue my charities but that I would increase my efforts in helping those in need.'

Kareem clicked his tongue in annoyance. I could feel his impatience. 'Sultana, living with you leads me to believe that our world is made up of nothing but abuse against the helpless. Yes, yes, yes, this earth we live on is populated with many abusers. And yes, I do know that there are many women in need of help. But Sultana, *one lone woman cannot reform the world*! After our frightful experience with your health, I had hoped you would work less and enjoy more leisure time with your husband, children and grandchildren.' Then he stared at me for a few moments before laughing loudly. 'Sultana, you should see your face. Those black eyes of yours are overflowing with fire!'

I chuckled. 'Would you prefer that your wife be deceitful and wear a mask, never telling you how she feels?'

'Well, no, Sultana, and I have never had a moment of concern that you do not tell me *exactly* what you are feeling at all times.' He exhaled. 'Ah, Sultana, of course I should have known you would never stop your charity work; however, I would be a happier husband if you might divide your week, working perhaps only four days and devoting three days to family. Why is this reasonable division not possible? Let us compromise, please.

'My darling, you have the most caring heart, filled with empathy for others. But do not forget that you have a strong and determined daughter who is displaying her own caring heart. Maha has begun to devote much time to several projects that make a difference in lives. Give your daughter an opportunity to expand her charity work. Maha will be a perfect assistant to relieve you of some of your more tedious duties.'

I pursed my lips and frowned a little while thinking through all that Kareem had said, but I did not immediately react, for I have discovered that when I make sudden decisions I often live with regret.

My husband's expression became very sad. 'Sultana, one day we will be gone from the earth. It is written. No one lives for ever. We, too, shall one day pass from our earthly life. We, too, will be buried in the sands of our country. This is written. Your daughter, or someone else you trust, will need to have full knowledge of your charities and how they operate so that your good works will continue without pause.'

I conceded this point, at least, for I had felt nervously close to my own mortality over the past few months. I thought to myself that Kareem was right.

'Yes, husband. I hear what you are saying. Only fools do not plan for the future, even if that future does not include them.'

I shrugged, knowing that Kareem only had my best interests in mind. Truthfully I would enjoy more free time to spend with my grandchildren, especially with the highly anticipated twins arriving in only four months.

'Yes, it is best for Maha to know all that I do and then, in a few years, Little Sultana will be a perfect assistant for her.' My heart suddenly felt full emotionally, imagining my daughter and my granddaughter carrying the torch of generosity after my passing, continuing my work helping those of a different generation, those not yet born perhaps, but those who would one day be abused and would need help.

I felt a twinge of excitement at the idea of working closer with Maha. She had become a dream daughter, devoting much of her life to charity work. In fact, I was so proud that Maha was following in my footsteps by organizing several charities of her own.

While my thoughts strayed to all that might be possible working more closely in collaboration with Maha, Kareem waited patiently for me to respond. When he extended his hand for the second time, I accepted it and we embraced each other.

'You make me very happy, Sultana,' Kareem told me with a smile. 'I look forward to spending more time with the woman I love.'

Just then both our phones began to buzz with great intensity. When each of us rushed to retrieve our devices, we collided and nearly lost our footing. We both laughed with pleasure. While we were planning more leisure time in our lives, it was rewarding to know that others still needed us. Kareem no longer worked in his chosen career; he had once been an attorney in his own legal office, but after retirement had begun various business projects with his brother, Assad, the husband of my sister, Sara. There were occasions when Kareem, Assad and Abdullah took trips abroad to oversee some of those projects.

'It is Assad,' Kareem said. 'He is asking me to meet him at his office.'

'Sara is texting me,' I replied. 'She is rushing over and says there is an urgent matter she must share with me.' I felt a sudden panic and quickly considered the possible problems she might be facing. I only hoped that no one in her family had met with an accident or was seriously ill.

'I will see you for dinner tonight?' Kareem said.

'Oh, yes,' I replied. 'I will be here.'

And we happily parted, for we had amiably compromised, for one of the few times in our married life.

*   *   *

I was not happy for very long.

Sara walked into my home within the hour and her tear-streaked face told me that indeed something terrible had happened.

'Sara!' I rushed to her. 'Are you unwell?'

'Sultana. No. No, I am well – I am well physically, at least. But my heart is broken.' Sara shook her head vigorously, as though trying to rid her mind of something very bad. 'Sultana, the past is coming back to us. The past is repeating itself.'

'What past? What do you mean, Sara?' During our years of being close sisters we had met many challenges. I could not imagine which event from our past was now coming to plague us once more.

'There is a big problem with daughter Sabrina's friend, Nona.'

'What? What?' Perplexed and anxious, I raised my hand to my forehead, as I tried to recall all I knew about Sabrina and Nona's friendship.

My niece Sabrina was Sara's youngest child, only fourteen years old, a baby who came unexpectedly when Sara believed she was no longer of a child-bearing age. I had a lively remembrance of the day Sabrina was born. In a sumptuous lounge area of the hospital, a waiting room which was reserved exclusively for members of the royal family, both Kareem and I thought Assad had lost his mind as he leapt for joy in the nearby delivery suite and then danced around the waiting area on hearing the news that Sara was recovering from childbirth nicely and they had an unusually small but healthy baby girl. Assad, unlike most Saudi men of that time, always claimed to be happier with his daughters than with his sons, and Sabrina, we believe, quickly became his favourite child.

Like a beautiful little doll, Sabrina was born delicately small and remained petite the rest of her childhood and teenage years. Her size prompted most to aspire to protect her. Considering that she was the baby of the family and ultimately spoiled by her parents and her siblings, Sabrina had never created the least problem. She was sweet, lovingly devoted to her family and, in fact, seemed contented with their company alone. She did not seek out friends and did not make friends easily. The little girl Nona, as far as I could remember, was Sabrina's only friend.

Sabrina had met Nona at school four or five years ago. I could not remember many details about her other than she was a very cute girl with a bubbly personality. She was not of the royal family, although her father was a wealthy merchant with various successful businesses in Riyadh and Jeddah.

'Come, Sara. Come and sit. I will call for sweet tea and when you feel calm you can tell me what is going on.'

'I do not believe I will ever be calm again. This entire situation has brought back to my mind and heart every cruel thing that occurred in our childhood, as well as those heartless events inflicted upon us when we became adults, Sultana.'

My interest was now intensely piqued, for since meeting and marrying Assad, Sara had very firmly closed and locked the window to the grimmest memories of our childhood. The tragic episodes of the past no longer existed for Sara. While she spoke of our childhood, she limited her conversations to the most pleasant memories of our younger years. I know that my sister used this avoidance mechanism to prevent further mental anguish because she had a most agonizing experience when she was only sixteen years old.

Sara, like all of Mother's daughters, was a very sheltered and conservative girl who knew nothing of adult life. Without a doubt, she was also the most physically stunning of Mother's ten daughters. She was so beautiful, in fact, that rumours of her acclaimed beauty travelled throughout the entire kingdom.

In our youth, all females wore a veil unless strictly cloistered in a family setting or at any party or social gathering where males were banned. At weddings, for example, all attendees removed their veils other than the most zealous conservatives. The truth is that weddings were and are where Saudi mothers look watchfully for potential future brides for their sons. Sara began attending weddings with Mother and our older siblings when she reached puberty. And so it was that many women saw Sara when she was only fourteen and set their minds on accomplishing an important mission: providing a beloved son with a wife who was clearly the most exquisite-looking girl in the kingdom.

I remember hearing my older sisters excitedly whisper that families from Riyadh, Jeddah, Mecca, Medina and Taif had approached our parents, pleading that Sara be given in marriage to one of their sons. Several families even said that they would sell their properties to raise the appropriate dowry.

Dowries for brides have always been paid in Saudi Arabia, and beauty, sadly enough, was and is one of the most important attributes Saudi families seek in their brides. Sara's beauty created such a raging tsunami of dowry offers that our fabulously wealthy but materialistic father took note, became immersed in gaining the most money possible from Sara's desirability and demanded complete control of Sara's marriage choices. Although most Saudi mothers generally have a say in the selection of their daughters' grooms, this was not to be the case when it came to Sara. I recall that my father informed my mother that he, and he alone, would determine who Sara would marry.

Against Mother's tearful objections, Father set up a marriage for Sara to the highest bidder. That happened to be an extremely wealthy merchant from Jeddah, a man who was already sixty-two years old. Sara was to be his third wife and she was told that she would be withdrawn from school, even though she was a brilliant student. The prospect of this marriage brought no benefit to Sara, but she had no choice in the matter and her opinion was never sought. Even though our Muslim teachings say that a girl should be asked if she accepts the one selected for her, and she has the right to say no, in those days not many girls were bold enough to contradict anything decided by their parents.

And so my sister, who was sixteen years old but emotionally and mentally still a child, found herself trapped in a marriage to a brutish man forty-six years her senior.

Sara was taken to Jeddah to live in a home as the third wife of a most undesirable husband. She was forbidden to contact her family, and after months of sexual abuse she tried to commit suicide. Only then was she allowed a divorce and was permitted to return to our home. Shattered by her appalling experience, Sara became reclusive and sad, a delicate and anxious young woman who withdrew from the world. It was not until she met Assad, Kareem's brother, that Sara eventually emerged from the fragile shell she had built around herself. The two fell in love and have been devoted to each other since their first meeting.

* * *

Mother and Sara had both been powerless in the face of such firm control because all females in Saudi Arabia must have a male guardian, generally their father, but the 'ownership of the woman' can be passed to a brother or uncle, or when she marries to her husband. Prior to our marriages, our insensitive, avaricious father was the guardian of all his daughters and there was no possibility of changing this fact of life.

To understand how limiting life is with a guardian, it is important to know the facts of guardianship in Saudi Arabia. The guardian has the right to make most decisions on behalf of the females in his custody. Females require their guardian's permission for all major aspects of life, such as whether they will be educated or seek a career. They are required to have written permission from the guardian to open a bank account or to travel. Even elective surgery is forbidden unless the woman can produce a letter from her guardian. Most particularly vexing, the guardian has the full right to say whether a woman can marry, and who she can marry. Then a guardian must give permission if a married woman seeks a divorce. If guardianship is passed from the father to the husband, this contradictory situation requires a wife to have written permission to seek a divorce from the man she wants to divorce. Absolute power and control define the guardianship laws in Saudi Arabia!

Tragically, while there are laws giving men guardianship rights, there are no laws written to protect women against abusive guardians.

Any intelligent person might ask, why do Saudi Arabian men cling to the tradition of maintaining such tight control over the women in their family? According to most Saudi men who are asked, they believe that there is a dire necessity for a male guardian since they believe women lack the capacity to make their own decisions.

Thus Sara, like many other Saudi girls, was married against her will to a man she had never met; this man, who was suddenly her legal guardian, was able to do what he wished with his young bride.

Maddeningly, the guardianship law remains in effect to this day, although it is applied differently in each family, according to the decision of the man who is the head of the household. If the man is sensible and sensitive, as is my husband, and feels no need or desire to control the women in his life, the guardianship laws are somewhat less frustrating for those being guarded!

* * *

Sara sat sipping her tea, but she was so distraught that her hands were trembling.

'Sara, darling, can you tell me what has happened to Nona?'

My sister grimaced but nodded. 'Yes, I can tell you, Sultana, although I am unhappy to pass this story to you.'

'Why? I am your sister. We have no secrets.'

'Of course, that is true, but this story is so very sad. You have been ill and now you will lose much-needed sleep over Nona's heart-rending situation.' Sara raised her eyebrows. 'Assad pleaded with me not to add this burden to your heart, but, Sultana, I could not bear it alone.' She sighed. 'If only our dear sister Nura was still with the living, she could ease this weight on our hearts.' Sara gazed at me with a sad smile. 'But Sultana, now we only have each other with whom to share our deepest secrets.'

I reached for my sister's hands, holding tight to the woman I loved as much as I loved my own children.

'Tell me. Perhaps I can do something to solve this problem.'

'If only, Sultana. But yes, I will tell you without giving you every detail. But this story is so painful that I must sit back and close my eyes. I am too weak to sit upright and look into your eyes while I speak.'

Startled by Sara's unusual request, I glanced around the room, scrutinizing the various chairs and sofas, recalling that Kareem had recently purchased two reclining chairs, although no one had ever reclined in them until now.

'Of course. Sit here, in this reclining chair. And there is a second one.' I smiled at my sweetest and most beloved sister. 'I will recline with you.'

Sara moved to one of the two chairs in the sitting area. I sat in the other. We were close enough to hold hands, and we did. And there we reclined with closed eyes, my sister speaking while I listened, absorbing every word and imagining the scenes she was describing.

'Poor Nona, Sultana. She was once a happy girl who enjoyed visiting with Sabrina and spending endless hours in my daughter's apartment, absorbed in sketching fashion designs. Those girls were too feisty, planning to one day leave Saudi Arabia and study fashion design in Paris. Surprisingly, Nona already had researched the various schools and had decided upon the Institut Français de la Mode. It has a good ranking in the fashion programmes. I believe the Institut ranked third, but I am not sure. I would have financially supported Nona had she applied and been accepted. The girls were getting quite excited, really, believing they might work with some famous designers until they could set up their own fashion house.

'I studied their designs, and while Sabrina appears to be involved in fashion plans only to please her friend, Nona is quite talented actually, and with appropriate financial backing and hard work most likely would have been a success. Over this past year, however, this talkative, cheerful girl slowly turned into a morose and unsociable introvert. While she still visited Sabrina at least once a week, I noticed how the two would retire to listen to sombre music, usually Chopin's *Funeral March*, a most haunting piece of music. The girls listened to it over and over until I asked Sabrina to tell me what was behind their sudden interest in such dark music. I felt concerned for their mental well-being, to tell you the truth. It seemed so unnatural for two girls of their age.

'Sabrina said she was simply trying to please Nona, that she in reality did not enjoy listening to that over and over. I pressed Sabrina further, but my daughter said she was uncertain why Nona had become so glum. She truly had no knowledge of what was behind her friend's gloomy disposition, or what she had been enduring, at least not until last evening when Nona sought refuge in our home.'

'Refuge? Why?'

'Sultana, Nona's father has been sexually molesting his daughter since she was twelve years old.'

My closed eyes flew open. 'What?' Sexual assault on a daughter by her father is not something one hears about often in Saudi Arabia. If such a thing happens, it is generally hidden by all family members.

'Nona believes that her mother knew, or at least had reason to suspect that the hours her husband was spending with his daughter were not entirely innocent. The beastly man had built Nona her own separate apartment several years before and when his wife questioned the time he spent alone with Nona, he claimed to be helping her with her schoolwork and term papers, as he also asserted to have been a top-ranked student at university. He was preparing his daughter for great things in mathematics, or so he said.'

'Oh, Sara. And the mother did nothing?'

'From what Nona told us last evening, her mother is routinely raped and beaten by her husband. The woman is living in terror for herself and can find no courage to fight for her daughter.'

I sat upright, so incensed that I gripped Sara's hand with a strength I never knew I had.

'Sultana,' my sister shouted, and pulled her hand away.

I looked at Sara, whose eyes had momentarily popped open from the pain. She was rubbing her hands together, but still reclining and soon closed her eyes once again. Her behaviour would be considered bizarre by those unfamiliar with her full story, regarding the sexual abuse and physical violence she endured at the hands of her first husband. But I knew that Sara had been so scarred by the trauma that she had found ways to soldier through the toughest moments. If keeping her eyes closed while she discussed the acts inflicted on Nona that once she had experienced herself made it possible to relay the details, then I felt confident she had correctly assessed what she could and could not withstand.

'Sorry, Sara, sorry.'

'That is not the worst of it, Sultana.'

'No?'

'No. Nona recently discovered that she is pregnant.'

'Pregnant?'

'Yes, pregnant by her own father. Nona finally confessed everything to her mother yesterday. Her mother confronted her husband when he arrived home for the noon-time meal, but all she gained from her new-found courage was to be beaten severely. Nona says that her father punched her mother in the face, knocked her to the floor, then kicked her. Her mother lost several teeth and has some broken ribs, along with numerous cuts and bruises. She was not allowed medical treatment and is now locked in her room, forbidden to come out. She is a virtual prisoner in her own home. Her husband has retrieved all her communication devices, so she cannot call her mother or her sisters. He has a guard by the door. He has told his wife that he would never allow her a divorce, so she is trapped in that marriage, most likely until one of them dies.'

'And Nona?'

'Her father told her that she will be getting an abortion. There are numerous back-alley abortionists to be found in Jeddah, or so he claims. He is bringing one of them to their home tomorrow.'

'Oh, Sara.'

Sara was silent for a long moment. 'Sadly, that is not the worst of it, Sultana.'

I leaned in to my sister. 'What, Sara, what could be worse than being raped and getting pregnant by your own father and forced to get an abortion?'

Sara's voice was flat and unemotional. 'Her father has arranged a marriage. Nona is going to be married within ten days of having an abortion. The creepy man her father has chosen works in one of his companies and is known for abusing his wives – he has three wives already – and Nona will be his fourth.'

'No, no, no,' I said, exhaling. 'We must do something.'

Sara was right. This horrifying incident nearly mirrored her own experience. This poor girl was just being passed from one disastrous situation to another.

'Nona is hiding out at our home, but her father called Assad and he is threatening to notify the authorities that we are harbouring a minor against the wishes of her guardian. He is pressuring my husband to turn Nona over to him, saying that he will tell everyone that Assad is the father of Nona's child.'

'Surely he will not do that!'

'Well, he can, but we are not worried about that point. Assad is meeting with Kareem now, and they will come up with a plan, I am sure. This man cannot harm Assad. My husband is well known throughout the entire family as a decent man who is faithful to his wife. And of course we do not believe that Nona's father will be so stupid as to start advertising that his daughter is pregnant. That would raise suspicions too close to home.'

I shook my head, inhaling and exhaling loudly. After a moment of thought, I was not worried about Assad either. His reputation is sterling, and in addition he is exceptionally close friends with one of the members of the ruling family. This association would protect my brother-in-law from such a false accusation.

It is worth noting that in Saudi Arabia anyone who gives false testimony can be subjected to eighty lashes.

In my country, a person's good reputation is taken seriously, and it is considered a crime to falsely accuse anyone of anything unlawful. Nona's father would risk a very painful punishment should he dare to threaten Assad's impeccable reputation in public.

'How are you going to help Nona, Sara?' I asked.

Both of us knew that the guardianship law gave Nona's father the right to seal his wife in a room for ever, if he so chose. No one would free her. The guardianship law also gave him the right to marry his daughter to anyone he might select. No person would or could intervene. Neither would the government intercede in a man's decision with regards to the women he 'protected' as their guardian.

Even if Nona wanted to go to court to reveal her father's sexual abuse, she would not get very far, for she would not be allowed to report him to the authorities 'without the guardian's approval'. Therefore, if her father refused Nona the right to report him, she could not do so. Even if she managed to convince a court to hear her complaint, no one would believe her word over that of her father. Although women may now testify in court, their testimony is still considered to be worth only half that of a man, so in the case of conflicting testimony, the male will always be believed over the woman.

In my country it is nearly impossible for a female to be treated fairly, so long as all women are treated as children and men have the right to control every aspect of their lives.

At that moment my eyes were clouded with a mist and my entire body began to tremble, although this feeling had nothing to do with my previous medical problem. I was shaking from an anger so great that I was losing control. How can any sane person believe it is a good idea to allow one person – a male guardian – to have control over the females he is supposed to protect? It is a system that must be changed for any real progress to be made in the rights of women in Saudi Arabia.

'Sara? I must ask again, how will you help Nona? You must be aware that your home is the first place the father will look for his daughter; he already suspects that she is hiding there with Sabrina.'

'Perhaps we will fly her out of the country,' Sara said, her eyes closed tighter than ever.

'If that is your plan, then bring her over here and we will fly her out on *our* plane. Her father will never assume that we are involved.'

'She does not have her passport. Her father has it locked in the family safe.'

'Oh, that is a problem,' I conceded. Even if we could remove Nona from Saudi Arabia, a passport would be essential for her to begin a new life elsewhere. While being a royal in Saudi Arabia provides many creative possibilities, once we have entered another nation we must adhere to the laws of that land just as all others do.

Clasping my sister's hand, I lay back once more and closed my eyes, trying to remain calm and to focus once again on what we might do to save Nona from an unforgiving life of pain, sorrow and abuse. This is what she would suffer under the domination of the brutish man her father had chosen to be her husband.

I spoke to myself, although I felt certain my words could be heard by Sara. 'The dread of hell should torment Nona's father every day that he lives.'

'Yes, you are right, Sultana. This is a man who would be an object of contempt even to a barbarian.'

That is when Kareem and Assad sauntered into the room, involved in an animated conversation. When they saw their wives reclining with closed eyes and clasping hands, they both looked surprised and more than a little concerned.

'Sultana, may I ask what you and Sara are doing?' Kareem enquired in a high-pitched voice that conveyed his astonishment.

I quickly pushed myself upright, while Sara remained prone with eyes closed. Despite the seriousness of the evening, I burst into laughter when I observed the look of disbelief etched on the faces of my husband and brother-in-law.

'You would never understand, husband,' I said with a smile.

Assad quickly regained his equilibrium and walked over to sit beside Sara. 'Darling, are you unwell?'

Sara sat up, looking sadly at her husband. 'I still have a pulse, at least,' she said with a tired smile, 'but truthfully I am drained of all energy, Assad. It has been a most traumatic day.'

'Let us go home.'

I sat on the edge of the recliner, then stood up. 'Where is Nona?' I asked.

Kareem shushed me, nodding at Sara, so I knew the news was not good.

'Has something happened to Nona?' Sara wanted to know.

Assad wrapped his arms around my sister and told her. 'Yes. I am afraid we have lost her. After I left to go to my offices, her father came to our home demanding the return of his daughter. He yelled until a frightened Nona came out of her hiding room and joined him outside. They left, driving off at high speed. I assume he has Nona back at her home.'

My poor sister was speechless with grief.

'We cannot save her?' I asked.

Assad shook his head. 'I do not see how. He has the law on his side, Sultana.'

'So she is going to be punished for a crime her father committed?'

At that moment Maha entered the room. She ran to her aunt Sara. 'I heard what happened. Sabrina called me when Nona's father appeared at your home, but I could not get there in time to take action. I am sorry, Auntie, I am sorry.'

Sara was inconsolable. With a faraway, haunted look in her eyes, I knew that she was reliving her child-marriage and the abuse she had endured. Painful memories flooded back to her and she trembled as she wept pitiful tears.

I was thinking of what Nona, the bright-faced and once happy girl, would soon suffer. She would have a less-than-medically-safe procedure in her own home to abort the child, without the care of a physician. She would most likely be raped repeatedly by her enraged father until she was given to a man she did not know as his wife. She would, essentially, be the property of a man already known to be brutish, a man who knew nothing, nor cared, of her dreams, her hopes, her ambitions. She would bear children with a man she did not love. In her misery, she would grow old before her time in a marriage filled with pain and suffering.

Maha was red-faced and angry, but she was loving and sympathetic with Sara. She spoke with emphasis. 'Auntie, you have my promise. My generation is going to destroy this irrational guardianship law. You will see this happen. Remember my words, you will see this happen.'

I thought that my daughter was trying to convince herself, for few men in our country will willingly give up the law that gives them the right to completely control the females in their home. But Maha was adamant.

'The time is soon coming when these so-called guardians will not be allowed to use the law to abuse the ones they are supposed to protect. No abuser will be supported by the law. *We are going to destroy this law!*'

Sara patted my daughter on her face. 'Yes, Maha. Yes, darling girl, you must destroy this law.' Sara paused, searching for the best words to unite her thoughts with her message. Finally, she spoke softly but firmly. 'But you must remember this very important point, Maha. You must put something better in place of what you destroy.'

Maha gazed at Sara with an all-embracing respect. 'You are brilliant, Auntie. *We must put something better in place of what we destroy.* And that we shall do! You have my promise.'

Chapter Eight

A Sprinkling of Stars

A MONTH HAD PASSED SINCE the disheartening personal calamity of Sabrina's friend, Nona. Despite all efforts, we had been unable to save the darling girl from her fate. From Sabrina, we had learned that during that month, Nona had suffered an abortion, and was quickly married to the man chosen for her by her criminally abusive father. The husband was proving to us that he was as heartless as her father, for he had refused Nona's pleas to contact her mother or her best friend.

The entire incident was a devastating blow to all who loved Nona, for due to the strict guardianship law that reigns over all females in our country we were helpless to save her.

Now, Dalal, one of our nieces and the daughter of our deceased eldest sister Nura, was having a crisis of her own. Sara had arrived at my home to provide the details.

While we waited for refreshments, I encouraged Sara, 'Go ahead. Tell me what has happened with Dalal.'

'Poor Dalal. You know that she is a very feisty girl and she will not accept behaviour that most Saudi women would ignore. Well, she is very unhappy in her marriage and wants a divorce.'

Even those women who are royal do not have the easiest time convincing the family authorities to allow a divorce, for our clerics, and our courts, generally side with the husband. I felt that Dalal had a challenge facing her, yet I knew she was bold and resourceful, and perhaps would succeed where others had failed.

Sara appeared nervous, but told me, 'Sultana, Dalal tells me that her husband has remained permanently adolescent mentally and morally.' Sara hesitated, pondering the message she was about to deliver. She then said, 'I remind you, Sultana, that I am only repeating what I was told . . .' A soft blush started on my sister's neck and moved up to her face. Then she whispered, 'Dalal says that he is neither a good provider *nor* a successful lover.'

Sara struggles with conversations involving sexual matters, so I was surprised that she did not expunge at least a portion of all that had been told to her by our niece.

Sara is the auntie with whom most of our nieces best connect, for no one is more patient, loving and understanding than my sister, and since Nura's death Sara has taken a special interest in Nura's children.

'So many of our men are not made for family life. You and I are some of the few so fortunate,' I said with a frustrated groan.

Sara nodded her head but said nothing; my sweet sister is reluctant to condemn our society for practically worshipping male children.

In my view, mothers must carry the blame for much of this idolization. Too often, when a Saudi male child is born, he is so treasured by his extended family that he quickly reaches the conclusion that he is superior to all other beings, both male and female. The mother – the one person intimately involved with a Saudi male from his moment of birth – should impede this improper mindset, but instead females are too often complicit with their husbands and other family members in instilling a feeling of self-importance.

There are, of course, valid reasons why Saudi mothers cannot control their elation after giving birth to a male child. When a female is born, many families mourn, failing to congratulate the mother, indeed often showing anger. This attitude springs from the fact that Saudi Arabia is what could be termed a 'shame society'. All things shameful affect the entire family and nothing diminishes their status more than the behaviour of their women. The most damaging is if a girl has a relationship of any kind with a boy prior to marriage – should she do nothing more than chat over the phone with a boy not of her family, she will gain a bad reputation. Other families will not allow their sons or daughters to marry if the family's women are considered impure. Guarding female behaviour is a tiring task, and if the girl's parents fail in their quest, then they will suffer. Due to the shame felt by improper behaviour, our entire society remains enamoured of celebrating the birth of sons only. Thus, when a male child is born, the mother is treated as a queen to have delivered such a human gem.

Such insulation from reality means that our young men too often become arrogant tyrants, cossetted by their families and caring little for anything other than seeking pleasure in their lives. How their egotistical conduct adversely affects others is not a concern to them and such arrogance results in ill-fated marriages. Although Saudi women are accustomed to accepting a secondary status in marriage, wives today are a little less passive than in the past and are often frustrated and unhappy with their husbands' arrogant, dominant behaviour – like women the world over, the Saudi wife wants a good, compassionate husband who will not only provide for the family but will lovingly care for her too. The discontent felt by many wives can lead to unending disputes that often precede divorce.

As I was pondering the state of marriage today, an unexpected voice confidently announced, 'That man should leave women alone and become a scholar!'

Sara and I exchanged puzzled glances before looking to see Little Sultana standing under the silk-covered archway which was the entrance into my bedroom suite. I was forced to bite my lower lip to keep from laughing, although the marriage problem tormenting Dalal was no laughing matter. After successfully stifling my urge to laugh, I asked, 'Little Sultana, when did you arrive?'

Zain had called me earlier in the day, alerting me that she was feeling unwell, and mentioned that her toddler Feisal would be staying the night with her mother. Zain wondered if I might enjoy having Little Sultana to spend the afternoon and night with me. There was never a time since my oldest grandchild was born that I did not relish every moment spent with her. Even had I been involved in the most urgent of business, I would have dropped everything to help my daughter-in-law Zain, who confirmed what I expected, that she was feeling miserable carrying twins. She was also feeling despondent because it had been necessary for Abdullah to leave the kingdom and travel to Japan for business. She did not like being without my son, even for only a few days at this particular time, and I fully understood her feelings. From what I knew of a pregnancy with twins, the mother was easily exhausted.

'Nanny Edna, Chanel and I were delivered by the driver,' Little Sultana told me in her very precious but serious voice. 'Edna is putting Chanel down for her nap.' Little Sultana explained to Sara, 'Chanel is still a baby and must have three naps a day.' She looked at her phone to check the time. 'I believe that I am twenty minutes earlier than scheduled, *Jaddati* (my grandmother).'

My gaze met that of Sara. I knew from the expression in her eyes she was thinking my exact thoughts. Little Sultana's maturity was remarkable.

Little Sultana puckered her brow in serious thought. 'If I am annoying anyone, I can have an ice cream while I wait. I will invite Edna and Chanel to have one too, because sometimes I interrupt Chanel's naps. Or I can read a book to Chanel while I am waiting.' She smiled. 'I have a number of options.'

Since she was a toddler, Little Sultana had been the biggest fan of the snazzy ice-cream parlour Kareem had built near to the indoor swimming pool. It was brightly coloured, with fun wall paintings of well-known children's characters from books, and there were various video games installed around the room, as well as a corner bookstore stocked with picture books for the youngest of the grandchildren, with more suitable books for adolescents. There were endless possibilities for entertainment in the ice-cream parlour and, now, with Little Sultana's visit, I knew Sara and I would have to continue our conversation later.

'Darling, you will do no such thing! Whatever would make you think you could annoy anyone in this house? Never! Never! I will not hear of you having an ice cream without us. Your auntie Sara and I will enjoy an ice cream with you.'

Sara obviously felt the same as I did. 'Indeed! An ice-cream treat sounds delicious!'

My granddaughter's bright smile was worth any interruption. With Little Sultana walking along between us, we three made our way through the palace.

Little Sultana suddenly paused, telling us, 'I am sorry that I listened to your conversation, *Jadda*, but I did not believe a child should interrupt what seemed to be a serious conversation. While I waited for you to finish, my ears could not avoid hearing what you said.'

I stooped to give my cherished granddaughter a quick kiss on her forehead. 'Do not worry, precious, but try to forget what you heard. You know that your father will be unhappy with me if he knew you had overheard conversations that were meant for adults only.'

'I will keep the secret, *Jadda*.' She pondered for a moment before continuing in a very stern tone, 'But if I were Queen Sultana, I would make it a law that all men who mistreat women would *never* be allowed to have contact with women again. Such mean men would live only with men and work only with men and play only with men. They would have to dream of women, for they could not see them.'

'That would be called a prison, little one,' Sara said with a smile. 'But, truthfully, you are right. There are a lot of men who are walking freely who should be confined.'

I nodded. 'A fine idea, indeed, Little Sultana. Perhaps that one law would solve a lot of problems. But do not forget your promise. You will keep this secret, that you accidentally listened in on our adult conversation, all right?'

I was stressing the point due to genuine concern for my son's reaction. When Little Sultana was only six years old, she had accidentally overheard an adult conversation when I was discussing an upsetting problem regarding a male abuser. A large part of the conversation centred around sexual abuse. My normally mild-mannered son had reacted with anger when his daughter began asking him inappropriate questions about a subject she should have known nothing about. Abdullah, astute as always, traced the conversation back to me and, despite the fact he knew that nothing had been told to his daughter intentionally, he was adamant that I should carefully guard my tongue, and the tongues of my assistants, if there was any chance that his young daughter was on the premises. I had been warned!

Now, once again, fate had placed my granddaughter where she was privy to a conversation that was inappropriate for her age.

'I already promised, *Jadda*. I will keep my promise.'

'We could use such a queen as this little one,' Sara said with a chuckle.

'Who is queen of Saudi Arabia, Auntie Sara?'

'Little Sultana, I am sorry to tell you that there is no queen in this country.'

My granddaughter abruptly stopped walking. 'No queen?'

'No queen, sweetheart. No. No. No. There is no queen in our kingdom.'

'But we have a king. Do not all kings have queens to help them?' She thought for a moment. 'Like in England?' Since Prince William had married Catherine Middleton, Little Sultana had followed the activities of the royal family of Great Britain with intense devotion.

'Sweetie, in Great Britain there is no king. The Queen rules the country.'

My granddaughter looked up at me for confirmation of what Sara was saying. '*Jadda*, there is a queen but not a king?' She paused once more. 'A woman rules the country?'

'Well, it is complicated. I will explain more to you later, sweetie. But as far as Saudi Arabia is concerned, your auntie Sara is correct. No, there has never been a queen of Saudi Arabia.'

I hesitated before saying the obvious, since I always felt embarrassment at the backwardness of our men's fondness to be married to more than one woman at the same time.

'Sweetheart, you know that in our country some men have more than one wife. Actually, our seven relatives who have ruled as king, including Grandfather Abdul Aziz and uncles Saud, Faisal, Khalid, Fahd, Abdullah and our current king, Salman, have all had more than one wife. Most of these uncles had four wives. A country cannot have more than one queen. Yet one wife cannot be queen if the others are not, as all the wives must be treated equally, according to Islam. So there is no queen.'

'My head feels confused about this, *Jadda*.'

'You will understand one day. And perhaps we shall soon have a king who only has one wife, and that wife will become our first queen!'

'Now that would be cause for a huge celebration,' Sara said with a big smile. 'I thoroughly approve of that!'

'Indeed, Sara, I agree. What joy it would be for Saudi Arabia to have one woman named as queen.'

Seeing my granddaughter's sweet little face and bright eyes taking in and absorbing talk that I knew her father would very likely feel was unseemly, I hastily changed the subject. 'But for now, ladies, let us have a nice ice cream and forget the tangled world of queens and kings.'

Any conversation about the state of marriage today in Saudi Arabia, whether within the royal family or among ordinary members of our society, would have to wait. There would be time enough to discuss this later with Sara and to hear more about the three women occupying our thoughts: Dalal, Sabrina, and her friend, Nona.

For now, the ice-cream parlour beckoned.

*   *   *

At the end of the day, when the setting sun was casting beautiful hues of gold and pink on Riyadh, by chance a party of female relatives gathered at my palace.

Sara remained, having mentioned that Assad was in Japan with Abdullah, and her youngest child, Sabrina, was visiting with Assad's nieces in Jeddah. While I relish complete solitude on occasion, Sara does not. I knew that she would be miserable being alone and saw she was visibly pleased when I encouraged her to spend the night at my palace.

Then Amani dropped by unexpectedly to tell me that her family was leaving for Norway in two days. Her husband was meeting with potential business partners from that nation and she wanted to select some jewels from her collection to wear on the trip. Both daughters have their own large safes in our home, filled with the treasures that Kareem has purchased for them since they were infants.

'Mummy,' she said, 'I am thinking of wearing that black pearl necklace and earring set.' She frowned as she pondered on the many jewels she might choose from and was now trying to remember. 'And perhaps that really nice ruby ring. The one circled by those shiny clear stones.'

'Diamonds. Those are diamonds, dear.' I smiled as I rolled my eyes. 'You know where the safe is, darling. The keys are in the top drawer of my desk.'

'Yes, I will get the jewels later,' Amani said, as she sat down to join us. 'I am tired, Mummy. I would like some tea and sweets, please.'

'Of course, sweetheart,' I said, as I pushed the small button that would alert the kitchen staff.

I was thrilled Amani was interested in wearing some of her jewellery. Rarely had either of my daughters expressed an interest in these items, so meticulously

collected for them by their father. I forced my tongue to
remain still, although I was excited and eager to know
what sort of function would encourage my daughter to
bring out her jewels. Kareem would be thrilled as well,
for I know he was disappointed that neither of our girls
was particularly keen to wear the beautiful necklaces,
bracelets and earrings he had selected. Because of that,
and their careless attitude towards these precious gifts,
he had insisted on keeping the jewels in our home and
safely locked away. Truthfully, Kareem also felt anxious that Maha would sell her jewels to finance her
charities assisting women refugees, and that Amani
would also sell her collections so as to give the proceeds
to an Islamic association.

I remembered the evening years before when Kareem
had insisted his daughters come to our home, where he
very carefully displayed each girl's collection of expensive jewels. He wanted our daughters to know the extent
of the time, thought and care he had given to their individual collections. He told them that night, 'Daughters,
even if you do not appreciate these precious gems, I
want you to appreciate the love your father has for you
and the time he spent gathering what he believed to be
the perfect pieces for each of you. I always considered
your colouring, your styles, and your likes and dislikes.
Should you ever feel the urge to sell your jewels for one
purpose or another, instead come to me and I will give
you the funds you need. And even if you do not wear
these jewels, I ask that you save them for your own children. I must have your promise on this point.'

Both girls had vowed to their father that they would
do as he requested, but Kareem had never felt secure

enough to allow them to take the precious jewels off our premises.

Now, with this business trip in prospect, I knew that my husband would be delighted to know that Amani was going to finally wear some of his gifts.

Just as Amani was sipping her tea and eating her sweet treats, Maha arrived unexpectedly from Europe, saying that her father had called and that she was prepared to meet with me to train as my assistant. Sara's eyes popped at this revelation, but she said nothing, knowing that I would fill her in soon enough. Amani, too, was surprised and clearly not amused, looking fiercely at her sister with irritation and what could only be described as a form of sibling rivalry.

Amani, for reasons unknown, has always been jealous of Maha, as my daughters are as different as two girls can be. Amani's dislike has earned Maha's dislike. Their spiteful relationship has been a challenge for the entire family, although after my latest health crisis I have seen their efforts to curb their outbursts, as I find their quarrels so disturbing and upsetting.

Just as I was about to explain to Amani that I could use her assistance as well, I was interrupted when my niece Dalal hurried into the room; she was clearly agitated and was speaking loudly and rapidly.

'I went to your home, Auntie Sara, and was told you were here. So here I am! I am sorry, Auntie, but I cannot live another night with my husband. I have left him. I am going to ask for a divorce.'

Little Sultana, still being a child, spoke without thinking, breaking her earlier promise to keep Dalal and her arrogant and petulant husband's problems a secret. 'I believe it is good that you have left him! I heard about your husband. Tell him to do this: go into a room, close the door, do a lot of thinking and become a scholar. He needs to forget about women.'

Dalal was so astonished to hear a child give such advice that her jaw was slack and hanging open.

'Little Sultana!' Amani said in bewilderment. 'Where did you hear such tales?'

'From *Jadda* and Auntie Sara.'

Amani looked at me. 'Mother!'

'My granddaughter accidentally overheard Sara and me talking,' I explained. 'It was an accidental oversight. I did not know that Little Sultana was in the area.'

Maha was laughing. 'Wait until Abdullah hears about this.'

'He is not going to hear about it. All of you, keep this to yourself.'

I considered my granddaughter, and with Dalal now present and talking of divorce I knew the evening would be for adults only. 'Little Sultana, can you please go to Edna and ask her to order your dinner? Tonight is special. You can have anything you want. Just tell Edna what you would like and she will order it from the kitchen. Have them prepare something special for Chanel, too. Then I would like for you to watch those documentaries I found for you, the ones you said you wanted on the history of England. Ask Edna to watch them with you. Then I will come in shortly to see how you are doing.'

'Yes, *Jadda*. I know that Chanel is missing me. We will eat our meal and then cuddle in bed.'

My smiling granddaughter then left the room as I endured Amani's look of disappointment that I had not been more cautious earlier. Just as I was going to try and soothe my most obstinate child, I was interrupted a second time when our doorman announced from the hallway, 'Madam Sultana, you have another visitor.'

Puzzled as to who might be visiting, I stood to make a greeting and was delighted to see that it was one of my most beloved nieces, Munira.

'Munira!' I cried out, as I embraced Ali's daughter.

When Munira was only a young girl, her father had forced her to marry a most horrible man who lacked any kind of moral compass. Hadi, her husband, was one of Ali's best friends and had spent his life abusing and terrorizing women. Tragically, his favourite target was the young and innocent Munira, who had been given to Hadi by her father. The horror of her marriage to a man the same age as Ali had tormented her, as well as all the women of our family, for many years, but finally when Hadi's lifeless body was lowered into the sands of Arabia after dying of a massive stroke Munira had been freed. Even then Ali had tried to claim ownership of his daughter once again, saying that Hadi had instructed him to regain guardianship. Munira, Ali said, needed a strong hand. But Munira's eldest son faced Ali with determination, insisting that he and he alone would be his mother's guardian.

My brother Ali, like all bullies, becomes a coward when faced by a powerful opponent, and Munira's eldest son was large and physically strong, with a forceful personality. We were amused to hear that Ali was so frightened after Munira's son paid him a visit that he fled Saudi Arabia. We were much relieved when he decided to take a tour of the Far East and was away for several months.

Mercifully, Munira's son loved his mother and was going to do all things possible to ensure that the rest of her life was peaceful and happy.

If only all guardians were so inclined.

Everyone present was delighted to see Munira. She had been away on an extended trip to Thailand with two of her children.

'Auntie, you invited me to come for a visit after my trip and, with the children busy with my grandchildren, I decided this might be the best time. I hope it is not an inconvenience.'

'Any time is the best time, Munira. My home is your home.'

Maha stood to hug her cousin. 'You are looking beautiful, Munira.'

That's when I noticed that Munira's physical appearance had changed dramatically. She had never been physically beautiful but was a pretty girl when her father gave her to Hadi. During her miserable marriage, she had become gaunt and frail, looking twenty years older than her actual age. Although she was not much older than my own children, she had been married so young and given birth to six children, one right after the other. Munira was still young when she became a grandmother. But now she looked lovely, with a delicate face, and she had gained weight and looked very elegant in her designer clothes.

'Yes, I am. I know. I am rested,' Munira said with a smile. 'At least that is what the surgeons told me to tell people who asked – that I had rested. But I will tell you the truth, while in Thailand my children arranged for some talented surgeons to do corrective surgery to my face and body. I have lived too long with the legacy of my terrible marriage.'

After years of constant beatings, Munira's face and body had been a testament to the viciousness of her husband's brutality. She had endured unending physical assaults, leaving her with rough and reddened facial scars. Her nose was broken more times than we could count. Her arms and ribs had been fractured or broken frequently.

'How wonderful for you, Munira,' Sara exclaimed.

'Are you thinking of marrying again?' Amani asked.

'Never! Never! I have been a slave once, Amani. Never again.'

'Of course, Munira.'

'I now get my pleasures from my children and grand-children. Travelling is a second pleasure. I cannot take more happiness than I now know!' Munira looked around the room. 'God is good,' she finally said with a big smile.

*   *   *

After the staff assisted Munira and Dalal in settling into their apartments in my palace, the six of us met for dinner in the courtyard centred behind my apartment. We ate in that small but lovely area, with lots of fragrant flowers, luxurious green plants and gentle fountains. It was a cool and relaxing setting. Most importantly, it is an enclosure for women only – a patio area not for the purpose of hiding women away but for keeping men out. In this beautiful setting women gather together and are free to say and do anything they please. There are no strict rules to guide our conversations.

The food was perfect, and the company pleasing. The evening was so joyful and enchanting, with stimulating conversation and genuine merriment, that no observer would have ever guessed that other than my two daughters all the women in attendance had been touched by enormous suffering and hidden anger. And all that grief and suffering was at the instigation of a man.

After eating, Dalal said, 'This conversation has been so interesting that I will be thinking about all that has been said here for weeks. I do feel that I have been to Thailand and to Norway and to Japan and back, but, now, ladies, I am ready to spill some beans.'

Maha, who, much to my displeasure, had brought her favourite wine to the party, and had drunk several glasses while pretending to her sister Amani that her glass was filled with grape juice, giggled and said, 'I believe you mean to say you are ready to spill *the* beans, Dalal.'

'Whatever, ladies, I am spilling some beans!'

Dalal was a cute girl with a big personality and now she showed us why she was the type who refused to live with an overindulged Saudi male tyrant for very long. She stood up and waved her hands around, looking like someone getting ready to fly, or perhaps someone hit by an electrical charge.

'If only my mother had lived, I would have nothing interesting to tell you on this evening because my mother would have cared who her daughter married and would have looked in every city and village to find someone suitable. But my darling mother did not live long enough and my fate was left in the hands of my father's most insensitive sister, who was only looking for more money for my father's pockets. So, let me tell you all about this man my father's sister found for me.'

Dalal was right about her mother. My older sister Nura would never have allowed her daughter to be married to such a monster. It saddened me to think of what poor Nura would make of this situation. We all knew that Dalal's husband was no Omar Sharif, a truly rare specimen of a man, exquisite and handsome and at one time the heart-throb of the East *and* the West. Even though Dalal's husband was not movie-star handsome, we had hoped that he at least had a pleasing personality, for many times a distinctive personality can lead one's opinion to change, as to a person's appearance, from plain to handsome, cloaking many unattractive physical features.

But obviously, from what we were about to hear, that had not been not the case with Dalal's husband.

'He is shorter than this!' She held a hand slightly above her stomach. 'His head is too large for his body – there are times I fear that big head of his will cause him to fall over. I believe his head swelled up like that from the lies his family told him about his handsome looks and wonderful personality. With such attributes, the world, clearly, was at his feet!

'Let's not forget his nose. His nose way too big for his face, reminding me of one of those proboscis monkeys. We saw those big-nosed creatures in Indonesia when we visited there, and I pointed out to him then that I had found some of his lost relatives! Later in the hotel room I paid for that remark when he hit me twice while I slept, although he got a shock when I woke up and hit him back three times – and hard!

'Ah, and those lips! He has lips so big that the lower drapes over his chin. I scream and push him away when he tries to get his lips close to mine. And, his brows. What brows he has! His brows are so bushy that on the night of my wedding I thought my auntie had arranged a marriage with Leonid Brezhnev's son!'

Maha could no longer hold her laughter. 'Those eyebrows! I have seen them!'

Even Amani was smiling. 'I have seen those monkeys, too.'

Dalal chimed in, 'Those Russian eyebrows could be given to some of those organizations that take donations for patients who have lost their hair to chemotherapy.'

Maha agreed. 'Yes, those brows are bushy enough to make a full bob.'

'Surely they could pluck them,' a kindly Munira suggested, causing Maha to double over with laughter before falling out of her chair.

'At times like this, I am soooooooo happy to be a lesbian,' Maha screamed.

'Maha, please,' I warned her.

'Everyone knows, Mother.'

'Well, you don't have to shout about it,' Amani said, despite the fact she was choking back tears from stifling her desire to laugh.

'Now, for his love-making skills! He has so much of everything else, from a big head to huge lips to bushy brows, where did his important equipment hide when the size large was offered?'

'Stop it, Dalal, you are killing me,' Maha shouted.

Dalal's savage indictment of her husband created such a riot of hilarity that ten or eleven of our female servants rushed into the courtyard to see if all was well. 'Madam, we believed there was a revolt.'

'Ladies,' Dalal said, 'there is no revolt here, but there is a revolution! A revolution has begun! Saudi women will no longer linger in bad marriages. Saudi women will kill their abusers. Saudi women are tired of Saudi men! Believe me, ladies, if you saw my husband you would help to start a revolt. A revolt to force the man to wear a mask.'

Maha shouted, 'The Saudi in the iron mask! There should be a movie made about a man so physically repulsive that his wife makes him wear an iron mask!' Maha's comment brought to mind the movie *The Man in the Iron Mask*, which created another round of loud laughter.

Dalal, I decided, was sharing Maha's 'juice' – which was very unwise!

Amani's austere manner was starting to show. 'Please, Dalal, please. He is your husband. You must show respect.'

'Easy for you to say, dear cousin. Your mother found you a very handsome husband who is also intelligent and kind.'

Amani looked at me and smiled. 'Thank you, Mummy.'

Despite Amani's stern ways, when she calls me mummy in her sweet voice I am stricken by love for my youngest child.

'Well,' Dalal continued, 'the most unattractive man in the world is so arrogant and has been raised by his family to believe that he is a gift to the world – he believes that I should be so grateful to share his bed that he insults me at every turn when I try to escape his embraces. He wants me all the time. I want him none of the time. Our marriage has turned into a sham; we have nothing but mutual hatred for each other. I must have a divorce, or I fear I might commit a crime.'

'Dalal, dear,' Sara said, 'you do not have to commit a crime. You will get your divorce. While divorce is often a sad and unhappy process, in this case I believe it is necessary. We will do what we can to assist you in making this happen, Dalal. Meanwhile, you can live in our home and we will protect you.'

'What crime?' Munira asked nervously. 'What crime are you thinking to commit, Dalal?'

Dalal regarded her cousin with true affection. 'You are one of the sweetest women ever to live, Munira. I know what you endured makes my marriage seem a bed of roses. I am sorry to make light of all these problems, but hatred will drive a person to commit a serious crime.'

'You are going to kill him?' Munira asked in a whisper.

With a face blank of emotion, Dalal said, 'No, darling, I am going to trim those eyebrows.'

'That is all right, then.' Munira looked relieved. None of us had the heart to tell her that indeed Dalal was considering physical violence.

By this time Maha was hysterical with laughter.

Dalal and Maha began laughing and plotting with enjoyment, while Sara and Munira were whispering about one thing or another. Amani was watching everyone closely, for she rarely enjoys a foolish evening. My daughter, always serious, truly does not know how to have fun.

I sat quietly and stared, reflecting on each of the women who was my relative and my guest. All were magnificent and courageous women.

Sara had overcome the most brutal marriage to find true love and absolute happiness. With Assad, she has the happiest and soundest relationship of any I have known.

Munira, too, had survived the beatings and abuse of a brutish man. While she would not find true love, for she had intentionally closed the door on that possibility, she was at least happy with her children and grandchildren and with her travels.

Dalal was the unfortunate recipient of an arranged marriage gone bad. But Dalal was going to thrive. With the assistance of her family, she would be granted a divorce. I felt certain that she would be married again one day and would have children. This bushy-browed bully of a man would be reduced to a very unpleasant error and failure in her life, all brought about by the fact that women have no power to choose their own destiny in this land – whether in the relationships they make or the work they do. So much power rests with others. But Dalal would survive.

While my childhood was emotionally abusive due to my father and my brother Ali, I too had survived intact. And my marriage was one to be envied. Although

Kareem and I had had a few rocky years in the beginning, we had healed all wounds and now mainly knew joy in our marriage.

Amani was a happily married girl with a kindly and devoted husband, a man who refused to be the tyrant that I felt Amani believed men should be.

Maha would never marry a man, and over the past year I had come to see that her choices were not the phase of a rebellious girl. She was a woman who preferred women in her life, and thankfully she could make that choice and live the life she wanted in Europe.

How happy I was that neither of my daughters had ever known the pain of abuse. But there were four previously abused women around my table, and all were happy to express their emotions and their misfortunes, yet the evening did not feel burdened with woe or tortured by memories.

The historic events that had affected Saudi women since the beginning of time were suddenly enlivening our lives. We have lived through the turmoil and troubles of our male-dominated society, and we have long contemplated the day when there would be a female revolution – like a volcanic eruption. Still, we love our homes and love many in our families, and we will continue to try to navigate the difficult terrain that sometimes threatens to upset our lives. Like a complex tapestry with many threads, Saudi life and history are still entwined as we move further into the twenty-first century. As our knowledge grows, we will wash away the bad and keep the good.

For me, the courageous and divine women in my garden reminded me of a sprinkling of stars that would light the way for generations of Saudi women to come.

Chapter Nine

Before I Go

T WO WEEKS AFTER THE MOST divine gathering of women in my garden, I was alone without family for one of the few times in my life. Kareem was out of the country for a week, my sister Sara was in Kuwait with Assad visiting a good friend, Maha was in Dubai, Amani was resting in bed with a cold, and Abdullah was at home, refusing to leave Zain for even a moment. Her due date was drawing near, although her physician had warned that when twins were waiting to come into the world, there was no possible way to predict exactly the day and hour of their arrival.

Although alone, I was not lonely because my active mind was good company. There had been some unexpectedly pleasant news, worthy of a second gathering at my home with my friends and family – one that would enable us to celebrate something positive for a change.

With the assistance of Sara and Assad, we heard that Dalal had been granted a very fast divorce and was at last enjoying new-found freedom. Although divorces in

Saudi Arabia are difficult to achieve for the wife, if the husband does not disagree with her request, the divorce can be given in minutes – all the husband has to do is say 'I divorce you' three times in a row, then notify the clerics and courts. If the husband does *not* agree, generally it is a lost cause for the wife, but in this case, when Dalal's husband heard that she was going to broadcast to the entire family her complaints about his character and habits, he quickly agreed to a divorce, saying those greatly desired words, 'I divorce you', three times.

Dalal now had finally escaped from a man few women would desire and was taking a lengthy holiday in California.

Sara had recently informed me that Nona's situation had improved after a true nightmare. Nona had already been divorced by her husband – the poor girl had become so distraught by endless rapes by the stranger she had married that she required psychiatric care. For men who have a brutish and bullying nature, it appears that the power of being able to force a young woman to have sex is a most satisfying experience for them. But as Nona withdrew into a silent world, sitting without eating and staring without speaking, her husband showed that not only was he cruel but also ignorant. Her persecutor truly believed that Nona's mental problems were contagious and he might be in danger of contracting her sickness.

Surprisingly, this is not unusual in the Arab world, for there is little understanding of psychological problems created by traumatic personal circumstances. Fortunately, though, her condition meant that Nona had been divorced. Less fortunate for her, however, her divorce meant that she had to return to her family home, where her father almost instantly resumed his illicit relations with her, his own daughter.

Sabrina told her mother that she had secretly slipped into Nona's home on a day when her father was working and that she did not recognize her friend. Sabrina reported that Nona's lifeless, glassy eyes stared straight ahead. Her once chatty and bubbly personality had been silenced. Her once pretty face was shallow and grey. Her body was so malnourished that Nona seemed lost in her clothes; they merely hung from her frail body.

Hearing this horrific news, Sara and Assad made an unsolicited visit to Nona's mother and found that she was eager to help her daughter. She agreed for Sara and Assad to arrange for Nona to be admitted into a private facility that discreetly treats the mentally traumatized. She would tell her husband that Nona had escaped from the house and could not be found. Aware of her husband's abusive behaviour towards her daughter, she also knew that she would pay for Nona's absence, for her husband would almost certainly blame his wife and beat her severely.

Tearfully Nona's mother explained, 'I have endured many beatings by my husband. I can endure one more if it saves my daughter.' Perhaps most worryingly the physician in charge had not questioned Assad's story that Nona was a victim of rape by her father, who had abandoned the family and wanted no further contact with his daughter. This, of course, was a false story told to keep authorities from getting involved and insisting upon returning Nona to her guardian.

Sara and Assad were also attempting to arrange asylum for Nona in a northern European country where requirements for entry were less strict since Nona's father had once again taken and hidden Nona's passport. So there was hope that Nona might heal and resume her life in far better circumstances.

Despite these positive developments for two very well-deserving women, my mind was in turmoil. Although these days I am as joyful a woman as one can be, awaiting all the promised changes that will improve and enrich the lives of Saudi women, I am as dejected a woman as I can be when it comes to human-rights abuses in my country. Women's rights and human rights are like a hand in a glove in chilly weather – each is necessary for the other to properly function. While women in Saudi Arabia have good reason to feel hope in their hearts that our Crown Prince will keep his promises, the young men and women who have focused their energies on freedom of speech have few hopes of relief from persecution.

All who read about civilization are keenly aware that human advancement is never complete. It is forever ongoing. A confident society encourages and compels its youth to think for themselves. It is the young who replace the old in all things. It is the job of the youth to push aside old laws no longer appropriate for society, creating more fitting regulations for their times and their circumstances. This shifting is as old as time itself.

Saudi Arabia is a kingdom bubbling with the educated. Since the days of King Faisal, education for Saudis has been a top priority and the number of our educated youth proves that our government's efforts to provide education for all Saudis has been successful. Unless fathers forbid it, even girls in small villages have access to education. Therefore, there is hope that most females in my country receive at least a primary education.

In the kingdom, school is free for the first twelve years. Children may attend kindergarten, if the parents so choose, but at age six children are enrolled for six years before graduating from primary school. While these schools are not co-educational, as they are in the West, enrolment for boys is 99 per cent, while for girls it is 96 per cent.

After primary level has been completed, schools for intermediate education are also free and available to all, although only 47 per cent of girls enrol, while 95 per cent of boys attend. Three additional free years of secondary education automatically follow. This is when students are given a choice to continue general education studies or specialize at technical institutes. The gross enrolment for the final three years of free education is 91 per cent.

Seventy per cent of students who graduate from secondary education continue to university within Saudi Arabia, while approximately 5,000 Saudi students are awarded assistance to travel abroad. Most girls are now allowed to study abroad for the first time since King Khalid's reign in the early 1980s, when a law was passed against this.

Once educated, however, many of these young people are unable to find a job.

More and more, this generation do tend to seek greater personal and political freedoms so that they can be involved with important decisions made in this kingdom. But to my growing despair whenever a Saudi citizen pushes for reforms they bring danger to themselves and their loved ones, for our government is now targeting anyone who criticizes the regime, delivering extreme punishments for speaking out.

For the past few years, educated, thinking and compassionate individuals have been quietly appalled as arrest after arrest has occurred of young Saudis who are demanding personal freedoms unknown to most in our kingdom. These young men and women have given up their freedoms after calling for freedom. While some are being held in prison without charges being filed, many have been convicted and sentenced to lengthy prison sentences.

It is these good Saudis – who want nothing more than the freedom to speak what is on their minds – that are now on my mind. It is a major problem and troubles me greatly. I dearly want to help them in some manner, but I am not certain what form that help might take. Meanwhile, I decided to commemorate these courageous ones by thinking about them, talking about them and helping to make the world aware of their plight.

My mind lingered upon a studious-looking Saudi man who has a serious view of life. Nadhir al-Majid is a teacher and a prominent Saudi writer. This unassuming and peaceful man was left in relative peace by the authorities until he expressed his independent view on two important topics that affect all Saudis: politics and human rights. He then dared to participate in peaceful protests over discrimination against Saudi Arabia's minority Shia community. Al-Majid also communicated with various international human-rights organizations and expressed his view in the articles he wrote that Saudi Arabians should be allowed to protest peacefully and that writers should be allowed to express their support for such protests. While none of al-Majid's activities appeared to be worthy of being charged as a crime, for he wants the best for our country, our Saudi government, composed of men who are of my blood, did not share my view. Al-Majid was tried in court on a variety of charges, such as 'failing to obey the ruler', but was not allowed an attorney to represent him – neither was his family allowed to attend his court hearing. After this sham court case was heard, al-Majid found himself facing seven years in a bleak Saudi prison, to be followed by a seven-year ban on travel.

Abdulaziz al-Shubaily is another young Saudi who will spend the most productive years of his life in prison. Looking at a photograph of the smiling and evidently good-natured al-Shubaily, one would never guess the seriousness of his quest to help those being wrongfully imprisoned in my country. Al-Shubaily is a prominent Saudi human-rights advocate who, as a lawyer, used his considerable skills to represent other Saudi men who were held in prison for years without charge. Al-Shubaily sealed his fate and lost his freedom when he publicly called for the release of these detainees. At the same time, he appealed for the right to peaceful assembly. For his views, he was charged with incitement against public order and insulting the judiciary, among others. The court sentenced al-Shubaily to eight years in prison, to be followed by an eight-year travel ban. He was also banned for an additional eight years from using social media.

Then there is Essam Koshak, who was arrested and has been held without charge. His crime? He used the Twitter media site to appeal for human rights in Saudi Arabia. Most likely when he is charged and tried, he will also receive a long prison sentence.

Finally, Ahmed al-Musheikhis, a founding member of a human-rights centre in Saudi Arabia, is yet another man who was harassed, intimidated and arrested for simply helping to create a space for human rights.

Others whose names I feel compelled to mention to the world outside Saudi Arabia are Issa al-Nukheifi, Fowzan al-Harbi, Saleh al-Ashwan, Alaa Brinji, Abdulkareem al-Khodr, Sulaiman al-Rashoodi, Fadhil al-Manasif, Waleed Abu-al-Khair and Mohammed al-Qahtani. So many young people seeking justice – and of course there are many others. Regrettably, by the time you are reading this, I feel certain that many more young Saudis will be languishing in prison for nothing more than communicating their opinions on social media.

And never can I forget the young man who first caught my interest regarding the perils facing young, educated Saudis who push for the personal freedom to speak and write their opinions of the limitations Saudi citizens are experiencing. That young man is Raif Badawi.

In the fifth book about my life, *Princess: Secrets to Share*, his full story was told. Raif is a Saudi writer and activist, and the creator of the website Free Saudi Liberals. Raif was arrested and charged with 'insulting Islam through electronic channels' and was convicted and sentenced to seven years and 600 lashes in 2014. After his wife Ensaf Haidar and others broadcast the injustice against Raif, my government took revenge and increased his prison sentence to ten years. The Saudi government also increased the number of lashes he must endure to a total of 1,000. That number of lashes will kill the strongest man, and Raif Badawi is frail with health issues, suffering from diabetes. He has survived the first fifty, but his health is declining and his wife fears he will not survive the full 1,000 lashes.

My mind is in turmoil, wondering what will become of these young men. How will it end? Will their lives be an endless horror of imprisonment and torture? Will they die in prison, forgotten by all outside their immediate family? Will the world ever hear their stories and know of their pain and suffering?

How can the men I love and call my family squander the hearts and minds of the young people of Saudi Arabia? All these thinking, educated men and the women who support them should be brought into the government to join hands with our leaders so that our country will become what its people deserve: a compassionate and caring nation where all can reach their zenith.

As surely as there is Saudi sand beneath my feet, I keenly feel that the men of my family will one day recognize the error of their decisions and will most certainly regret arresting, torturing and condemning the young men and women who love their country and desire freedom and prosperity for all.

*   *   *

After a fitful nap I awoke with the nagging problem of publicizing my disapproving opinion regarding human-rights abuses in Saudi Arabia through the pages of a book. For sure I knew that when my husband discovered that I had publicly criticized those uncles and cousins who hold the highest positions in our Saudi government I would meet with strong resistance and there would perhaps follow a fierce argument with the man I love. But my husband knows that I find it impossible to remain silent when innocent young men and women are arrested and tried as criminals in court and then sentenced to many years of imprisonment for nothing more than attempting to participate in the social and political changes that are most certainly coming to Saudi Arabia.

It is my belief that all human beings should be allowed an opinion about all aspects of life without suffering dire punishments.

Although I did not relish the prospect of doing battle with Kareem, for I love and respect my husband, I would not allow the prospect of a spousal disagreement to close my mind and still my tongue.

Just when I was considering how I might present and win my case with Kareem, I was startled by the ringing of my telephone. I smiled with relief when the caller ID identified Dr Meena, one of my dearest friends, who is as kind, good and wise a woman as I have ever known.

I was privileged to first meet Dr Meena in 2012, when I attended a conference about education for girls in my home city of Riyadh. I immediately said yes to the invitation when I saw that the conference focused on reaching out to teenage Saudi girls, encouraging them to consider the medical field as their choice of a career. Befittingly, the conference was held at a hospital in Riyadh.

Although I have used my abilities and my wealth to help many girls and women to escape abusive relationships, over the years I have seen that education is an appropriate tool with which to battle marital abuse. Thus, I have slanted my charities to favouring educating girls, as I believe the greatest of all riches is education. No one can take a degree or the knowledge that comes with it from a woman who has earned it. A solid education is an instrument that will help to ensure independence for life. It will help to ensure that a woman's children also become educated. Those who have children but lack money find themselves totally helpless and dependent upon a husband for all things.

Dr Meena was the main speaker at that educational conference. Never shall I forget my first impression. She was a slight figure, dressed in a doctor's white coat. She was an attractive woman but totally natural, as she did not adorn herself or make use of any beauty products – she wore no jewellery other than a simple watch. Unlike most Saudi women, her hair was cut in a short bob.

When I was first introduced to Dr Meena, I soon realized that she was not impressed by the fact I was a princess. If anything, she was almost indifferent to my status, which is a reaction I rarely see, for most people in the world are entranced by royalty. They really should not be, for royal titles tend to be unearned and most who are royal have inherited their title and the enormous wealth that goes along with it without lifting a finger. I would prefer people to be impressed with those who have earned their just rewards – or who have used their education to enhance the lives of the less fortunate in our society.

While I did not know enough about Dr Meena to have an opinion, once she began speaking I was immediately impressed by her knowledge, her common sense and her ability to inspire her audience.

While I expected that a Saudi woman who had earned a medical degree would have been born in a wealthy, professional or business-class Saudi family, with Dr Meena this is not the case. She was born into an extremely deprived family in one of the poorest regions of Saudi Arabia, Al-Kharj. She was the last of four daughters.

In Saudi Arabia, any woman who gives birth only to daughters is scorned by her family and neighbours. This happened to Dr Meena's mother. But their true nightmare began when her father became so enraged by the birth of yet another daughter that he plotted to bury his fourth daughter alive in the nearby sands. That sinister plan was halted when a wise uncle heard that his brother was in danger of murdering all four daughters. That uncle intervened and saved four lives.

That's when Dr Meena's father divorced his wife and decided to abandon the entire family. He delivered his wife and four daughters to his in-laws and left them there to fend for themselves.

There was more bad news when Dr Meena's grandparents actually obstructed the doorway with their bodies; cruel and heartless, they struggled to keep their daughter and four granddaughters from entering their home.

Heartbreakingly, the young mother and her four little girls were unwanted by all.

Only the intervention of Dr Meena's oldest sister saved the situation. The young girl was only six years old but was very clever, and their bleak and difficult life had helped to develop an inflexible resolve in her. While blocked outside the house, and longing to get inside, that young girl remembered the tale she had heard in the village about a camel's willpower. She was told that once the camel's nose is in the tent, the camel is in, for the body will soon follow. The young girl fought with all her strength to get a toe into the house, which she believed was equivalent to the camel's nose in the tent. She wrapped her little body around her grandmother's legs until she was able to pass through beneath her grandmother and collapse on the sand floor. That's the moment when Dr Meena's mother used her last bit of strength to hold tight to her small children and newly born infant and rush in behind her oldest daughter. Once inside the house, the young mother refused to leave.

Over time everything was sorted out, but there was always misery in that home where the parents were so selfish that they felt no responsibility to save their own flesh and blood. After the grandmother died of natural causes, the grandfather became more amiable because he knew, selfishly, that he would need his daughter and granddaughters to take care of his needs in his old age.

Although Dr Meena was born poor when it came to possessions, she was born with an extremely high IQ and had immense common sense, which for me is an important treasure that will take most people much further in life than a bulging bank account. The combination of these two mental attributes won the young Dr Meena many awards and even earned her a scholarship to college and medical school. She was top-ranked in her field. Despite endless obstacles, Dr Meena triumphed over most women who are born with every resource.

Once she was in a solid financial situation, she used all the funds she earned above what were necessary for her upkeep to help other girls born into poverty. She is an unselfish and enlightened young woman.

From that day, I sought a friendship with Dr Meena. She was less keen to be friends with a princess and it took some time before she discovered the work that I do in order to help young women pursue their educational goals. However, once she came to know the real Princess Sultana, she accepted my extended hand of friendship. And from that time we have combined our resources to assist many young women in need of escape from abusive situations and have helped them to gain an education.

Today, I was excited to be hearing from Dr Meena. I quickly answered my phone to learn that she was reading a Reuters article printed in one of the British newspapers delivered to her in the kingdom by a close friend. Much to her despair, the article was reporting on the numerous protests against our beloved Crown Prince Muhammad regarding the war in Yemen and the rise in arrests in the kingdom for human-rights abuses, the very subject I had been mulling over all morning.

Dr Meena is a huge fan of our king-to-be. As she frequently says, 'He is the first man to make the rights of women a priority.' She can forgive all other things, if Crown Prince Muhammad keeps his promises. No one outside the kingdom could possibly understand how dear this man is to the women of my country, for he is the only man in a position of power who appears willing to risk all to elevate our status. We have waited so long for such a man and now we will forgive him almost anything if only he will help us.

'I am so distressed,' Dr Meena told me. 'Listen, please allow me to read a few bits of this article to you, Princess.'

'Yes, please do,' I told her. 'I have heard something about these protests.' Truthfully, I had read all the reporting that I could find, as I have the keenest interest in our Crown Prince and the various moves he is making in our country.

'Listen to this. Here it says that during his high-profile meeting with Queen Elizabeth, there were protests over his human-rights record. Listen to this, Princess, there was discord even in the British Parliament. How dare they?' she muttered angrily.

I grunted slightly but said nothing. I had been in England when Crown Prince Muhammad was there and I had watched these events on my hotel television. I said nothing, for Kareem did not want me to tell others that I had been out of the country and at many of the same places our Crown Prince's travels had taken him.

'And now, listen to this, Princess. "Demonstrators gathered outside [Prime Minister] May's office amid a heavy police presence to protest at both countries' role in Yemen, where war has killed around 10,000 people. A Saudi-led coalition intervened militarily in Yemen in 2014 and critics say that Riyadh has been using British-supplied weapons in devastating strikes." '

'I guess the world wants us to sit still while Yemen fills up with the Iran-allied Houthi terrorists,' I puffed. 'Once they have killed all who oppose them in Yemen, those Houthis will cross the border and try to kill us.' There was a trace of disbelief in my voice. Few people in the world really know the tangled complications that make up the political scene in Yemen. But the current group of power-hungry Houthis are killing more Yemenis than the bombs falling from the Saudi-led coalition.

My thoughts were interrupted by Dr Meena's continuing outrage. 'Princess, listen to this! A man threw an egg at our prince!' She was provoked by the image in her mind of anyone daring to throw something at our Crown Prince. 'But they arrested that criminal,' she said with satisfaction.

'Now, Princess, listen to this!'

I lightly interrupted. 'Dr Meena, please save that article and bring it over. I wonder if you are free this evening. If so, please do come for dinner so that we can discuss the humanitarian issues in Saudi Arabia that have caught the attention of the world press. Is that possible?'

'Of course, Princess. In fact, I already had an urge to discuss that very topic with you.'

*   *   *

Suddenly, I was glad that my entire family was unavailable, as I felt a strong urge to confide in a friend. I took a second nap prior to Dr Meena's arrival and was fresh and rested when she appeared for a quiet dinner prepared for just the two of us.

I have a small dining room adjacent to my living quarters and that is where our meal was served. Although Dr Meena is a woman who has always watched her health carefully, she does enjoy a tender and juicy steak on occasion, so I had some Australian fillets prepared along with baked potatoes and a delicious vegetable stew. Thankfully, Dr Meena does not drink alcohol, not even wine. Having given it up myself ten years ago, I prefer not to see or even smell alcohol, as it had created many problems between Kareem and me. Once when my personal life was troubled, I became addicted to alcohol, but thankfully with the help of my husband that phase of my life ended quickly. Now I cannot imagine how I ever felt pleasure drinking a substance that caused me to lose control of my senses. I learned through my own mistake that addiction is a very powerful enemy!

'Dr Meena, we are living in interesting times,' I said.

'Yes, Princess. As difficult as life was for me as a child, I would not trade being a Saudi woman for any other life. I have never known a dull moment. Have you?' she asked, with a wide smile.

Never had I considered such a question, but suddenly I knew Dr Meena was correct. Although we Saudi women have faced far too many challenges, our lives are not uninteresting – at least not the Saudi women of our age.

'Well, no. I have never known a dull moment,' I said with a hint of surprise in my voice. 'I am sure that life for some Saudi women in the past was incredibly so. Think about the women kept in purdah, when they were not allowed to leave the interior of their homes even to go to the market. But you are so right, Dr Meena, life for women currently alive in Saudi Arabia is never dull, although much of our excitement comes from doing battle to achieve even the most basic human rights. But I see what you mean, to live in a time where one must push for freedom is actually quite interesting.'

'See. I knew you would agree with me. Being a Saudi woman is much more challenging than, say, being a woman from Canada, where everything necessary for life appears to work so well. I wonder what excites those women in Canada,' she said jokingly. 'As for me, every day of my life I have the ability to help someone in need. In fact, my life is filled with people who need me. That is never dull. Every day of my life I have the opportunity to converse with like-minded women, such as yourself, Princess. That is never dull. Every day I read about my country in news reports from all over the world. While that can be maddening because very few journalists know anything about Saudi Arabia – they just regurgitate what they hear or read. However, it is never dull to see that everything happening in one's own country is of interest around the world.'

After we finished our pleasant dinner, Dr Meena and I settled in with cold juice and sweets, although I noticed Dr Meena barely nibbled on the little treats before her. But Dr Meena did lift her glass of juice.

'Here, dear princess, here is to the excitement that keeps our lives from being dull!'

'Hear! Hear!' I said, laughing.

'You wanted to talk, Princess?'

I did not hesitate to tell her all that was on my mind. 'My heart is full and heavy – full of anguish for all the young people who have been arrested and now jailed for speaking their mind, for expressing their ideas, for having opinions of their own. What are the men of my family so afraid of, why are they so obstinate?'

Dr Meena did not appear to be surprised by my outburst. 'Go on,' she said.

'I have been researching all the young lives being ruined by our government's eagerness to arrest any and all who simply express an opinion on social media.' I looked directly into Dr Meena's expressive brown eyes. 'Why do you believe that our government is so adamant that no Saudi shall be allowed to make the mildest criticism of our country?'

My good friend sat back, inhaling and exhaling several times before speaking. 'Well, Princess, I will tell you what I think. I, too, have been disturbed by the intimidation and arrests of these young people. But if you look back at history you will find that when a country undergoes great change, there seems to be a lack of confidence in the leaders and rulers that they can successfully create a new society if they allow the masses to become involved – in their defence, it does get so much more messy when there are thousands of voices spouting their thoughts and ideas versus, say, ten or twenty who make the actual decisions and laws. I believe that the rulers of Saudi Arabia are the same in this respect as every other country when change is needed, and in our case, as you know so well, change is urgently needed.'

I nodded, listening to this smart woman.

'Just think about the Western nations, when only one simple decision had to be made: would women be allowed to vote or not? Entire nations were burning, hundreds if not thousands of women were being intimidated, beaten, arrested and put in prison. It caused outrage for years and many suffered in this fight for equality.

'Saudi Arabia has a much more complicated set-up when it comes to social change. Almost every custom and law in this country to do with women needs to go into the history books and stay there. For centuries, we have not been allowed to do anything of any importance. And our laws or customs, which forbid practically everything of normal life for women, and for men, have created a society like no other. In America and Europe they simply trimmed the trees in the forests to make change – in this country, they must rip up the entire forest: dig up the roots, throw them away and start anew.'

I could not help but laugh at Dr Meena's passion and excitement, although we were discussing a very serious subject.

'Yes, I see what you mean.' I leaned forward and spoke in a low voice, as I did not want any of our servants to hear what I was about to say. 'Yet I feel great disappointment, even anger, when I read about a young man or a young woman whose life is ruined only because they are asking to be free to discuss politics or issues to do with personal freedom. If our leaders feel it is too dangerous for Saudi citizens to be involved, why can't they take a softer, more humane approach? Why can't they take away the computers and phones when they feel someone has overstepped the boundaries during this very risky time? Why do they have to put these young people in jail, ruin their lives, flog them? Why does the punishment for what I see as the most minor of offences have to be so extreme?'

'You are asking me a question that I do not have an answer to, Princess. There are many possibilities. Perhaps our prince does not want these voices exclaiming to the world what they desire because he believes that he, and they, are competing for the same applause.

'But then again, I believe that our Crown Prince cannot allow anyone to interfere in his plans to free up this entire nation. You and I both know that a tidal wave of social change cannot occur at once. The kind of changes our prince is planning will have to be done deliberately and slowly. He is only thirty-two years of age. I predict that he will be at least fifty-two years old when he will feel he has accomplished what he set out to do.'

'*That long?*'

'Yes, you will see, it will be at least twenty years before all our dreams come true.'

'May we live that long,' I said with conviction. I had not yet told Dr Meena about my health scare, and probably would not on this night, as it would take over the evening's conversation. 'Tell me, do you believe it will be necessary for our government to continue arresting people who simply give an opinion?'

'Most likely – at least for a time. Think about this. Our Crown Prince is not yet the leader he will be. He is young. He is brash. When he becomes king, he will be a king like no other. Brace yourself for a whirlwind of a king, for he is in a hurry, but he will find that to move an entire nation of people from the twelfth century to the twenty-first century will be a challenge like no other. And although it will be a challenge for him, it will be a thrill for the rest of us.'

'A thrill? Really?'

Dr Meena looked at me with a twinkle in her eyes. 'Princess, I am so glad to be alive during this time. I like a whirlwind and one is coming.'

'Well, there is a lot on his young shoulders,' I said, thinking about the various things Kareem had told me, conversations I dared not share with anyone. I grimaced. 'I believe that everyone is turning with hope, and with doubt, to this young man. I hope he can survive the enormous scrutiny he will undergo. I hope he is able to withstand the immense responsibility.'

Dr Meena laughed again. 'His shoulders are very broad, Princess. He can succeed when no one else would be able to pull it off. However, not everyone is a strong supporter. One of my brightest students is wary, although I assured her that we need this man – we need this strong personality – otherwise Saudi Arabia will continue to stew in the past. It will truly be left behind in the world.'

Dr Meena took a sip of her juice before continuing. 'After my watchful student read that our Crown Prince now owns the most expensive home in the world – the French chateau he purchased for over $300 million – and then quickly followed that purchase by another extravagant acquisition – $450 million for a Leonardo da Vinci painting of Jesus Christ – my student wrote me a note that said, "This man desires everything, envies everything, and wishes to seize everything." '

I winced. I have personally observed the lavish life-styles of most of my royal cousins but could understand how the back-to-back purchases of the chateau and the painting would provide the opposition to our Crown Prince with significant information to attack him personally. But few in the world realize that most royals in oil-rich countries have so much ready cash that such purchases are not considered to be worthy of a discussion.

'Yes, I had just as soon those purchases were kept confidential, but there is nothing to be done.' I grimaced. 'Please do destroy that student's note. I do not wish to visit you in prison!'

'Oh, I kept it. But there is no name on the note and the prince is not named. But do not worry, it is in the safest place that no policeman would look.'

'Dare I ask where?'

'No, it is best not to enquire,' she said with a big smile.

The evening ended far too soon, but Dr Meena had early appointments with her patients so I did not protest, although she and I agreed to meet the following week to review the information we might find on the many imprisoned young Saudis who are languishing in prison for speaking their minds. She and I decided I would provide funds to help the families of the imprisoned to meet their financial needs and also to pay for the services of lawyers to plead their cases. It would be good to help those men, in whatever capacity we might find to do so.

After Dr Meena departed, I felt much more relaxed. For the first time, I fully understood and truly believed that our prince was undertaking the most enormous challenge of any leader of any nation in the world. He was soon to be king of the most unique land – a nation which was desperately in need of sweeping changes that only he could make.

It is against a dark background of an ancient desert kingdom that he must shine a light of change. I knew on that night that his was truly a struggle to remake a nation, and all the results he would reap would be with us for centuries to come.

I was grateful to Dr Meena for bringing me a degree of hope, for I now believed that the best was being done for my country.

That evening I said a prayer of thankfulness that I was born a Saudi woman and that I was still with the living in the year 2018 to witness the exciting human advancement that I knew was coming to my beloved kingdom.

The stage is now set for years of excitement.

It is my hope and prayer that before I go, I live to witness, feel and celebrate the thrill of this excitement.

Chapter Ten

Once Upon a Time

WITHIN A FEW WEEKS I was overwhelmed with more excitement than I desired. Unfortunately, this excitement had nothing to do with the advancement and changes Dr Meena and I were enthusiastically expecting to come to Saudi women. This excitement was to do with twins who were coming into the world nearly two months early.

Kareem had nearly caused me to have a heart attack when he bounded into my private quarters in the early hours of the morning loudly exclaiming, 'Sultana! *Get up!* Sultana! Abdullah wants us at the hospital. Zain is unwell – she has gone into early labour.'

'What?' I asked, quickly pushing the bedcovers off my chest and raising myself to a sitting position.

'*Get up! Get up now!* There is a crisis, sweetheart. Zain and the babies are in danger.'

With those alarming words, I was instantly awake. I, too, sprang into action and was out of bed and standing upright in a split second, my hand at my throat, staring at my husband, who was visibly alarmed, an emotion rarely displayed by Kareem.

'I will go and arrange the car. Meet me at the back, at the circular drive.' Kareem was unquestionably worried.

That's when I began to nervously wonder what he had not told me.

'Yes, all right, I will meet you there.' Then I haltingly asked, 'Kareem, is everyone still alive?'

'Hurry!' he said as he ran out of the room, failing to answer me.

I steadied myself by leaning against the wall and taking several deep breaths. Zain and the babies must be all right! My son would never recover if he lost his wife or the babies.

I felt tears forming in my eyes, but pushed back to keep from collapsing, steeling myself for the coming crisis before rushing to get ready. I quickly selected a comfortable dress with long sleeves and a hem that reached my ankles. I knew the dress was suitable to wear at the hospital, where we were sure to see Zain's family. I hurriedly washed my face and combed my hair, twisting my tangled curls into a big bun at the nape of my neck. At the last minute, I remembered to stuff an abaaya and scarf in my large black bag, thinking that I would throw them over my clothes once we arrived at the hospital.

As I hastily made my way out of the palace, I could not help but wonder whether perhaps I could soon forget about ever again wearing the hated black robe. My cousin the Crown Prince and Sheikh Abdullah al-Mutlaq, a cleric who is a member of the Council of Senior Scholars, both recently announced that Saudi women no longer had to wear the abaaya robe. Sheikh al-Mutlaq expanded his comments when he said, 'More than 90 per cent of pious Muslim women in the Muslim world do not wear an abaaya. So we should not force women to wear it, although all Saudi women should dress modestly.'

However, there is a law that requires the abaaya for women in my country and until that law is rescinded many women – particularly in Riyadh – will not feel comfortable tossing their abaaya. Our city has always been the most conservative of the large cities in the kingdom. Even now there are still many very active clerics roaming the souks and streets of our capital, looking for what they believe are wayward women to verbally, or even physically, assault. The stern faces and laser stares emanating from the black eyes of Riyadh-based clerics have long reflected their unyielding and hard hearts, for most truly believe that women are the source of all evil and the cause for all the problems of the world.

We know that the radical clerics are boiling with anger by all the high-spirited conversations about women being allowed to drive and women discarding their abaaya, so our female common sense has nudged our behaviour.

Truthfully, Saudi women will most likely always dress modestly because it is an ingrained part of our culture. Still, most will be pleased to stop veiling themselves and will put these items and the black robes in the back of the closet, perhaps to bring them out in our old age and show our grandchildren what grandmother was once forced to wear!

I felt a touch of envy for the women who live in Jeddah, for I had heard that in that more modern-minded coastal city brave women are burning their veils and the hated black robe in their garbage bins and taunting the clerics who dare question them about their hair and bodies not being covered by the usual black attire.

But for now, my mind must be focused on my son and his family. While walking rapidly down the long hallway to the back entrance to our palace, I replayed in my mind what Abdullah had confided the week before when I had invited his family over for a barbecue party by the pool.

'Mother, I wish that I could say yes, but we cannot. Zain has gained an unusual amount of weight this past month. With the babies due in a little less than two months, her physician says she should get a lot of bed rest.'

'Of course!' I said with a loud voice. 'Of course she will have substantial weight gain, son! Your wife is carrying two babies at once!'

Abdullah shrugged. 'Mother, the doctor appeared to be worried. He mentioned the swelling of her ankles – he is concerned about the possibility of uremic poisoning.'

I gasped, for like most women who have borne children, I had been told to be alert for any unusual weight gain during the last three months of my pregnancies. Uremic poisoning, I knew, could threaten the lives of Zain and both babies. Now I was wondering if this emergency two months prior to Zain's due date was connected to uremic poisoning.

Kareem ordered our driver to go as fast as the speed limit, but no faster. He knew that if we were pulled over, the officer would begin to flatter and fawn once he understood that he had stopped a member of the royal family. This kind of behaviour would only delay us. I suppose that some royals have received speeding tickets in the kingdom, but I have yet to hear of such a case.

The journey to the hospital generally takes thirty minutes in the daylight hours when traffic is heavy, but we arrived at the hospital in only twenty minutes due to the early morning hour, when there were fewer vehicles on the road. However, that short period of time felt like hours to me, as I anxiously willed myself to be beside my child and his wife.

Finally, we were pulling into the hospital grounds. 'I feel as though I just left this place, Kareem,' I said with a despairing tone.

Kareem stroked my hand. 'Thanks be to God that you are no longer a patient, that you are now healthy. Our son is going to need us.'

Our driver pulled in at the entranceway to the building that housed the obstetrics and gynaecology department. Abdullah had arranged for one of the hospital administrators to be waiting at the front door for our arrival. Abdullah's attention to the matter saved us many minutes, for the hospital is huge and we are not that familiar with the area where babies are born.

The administrator timidly identified himself and told us that he was from Alexandria, Egypt. He could not answer any of our many questions about our daughter-in-law, but told us that Maternal Fetal Medicine was in charge of Zain's case. 'The department is excellent,' he reassured us. 'They have much success with this type of high-risk pregnancy.'

'High risk?' I asked. 'I was unaware that Zain's pregnancy was high risk. Were you aware of this, Kareem?' I would be very angry with my husband if he had been forewarned of possible danger and had failed to share that information with me.

'No. No, of course not,' he said, while shaking his head. 'I believe that this emergency occurred only a few hours ago.'

The Egyptian administrator became even more uneasy at my sharp tone. Not many men in the Middle East are accustomed to assertive women. The man had just then developed a facial tic and his voice grew high-pitched. He spoke to my husband, telling him, 'I just arrived in Riyadh, Your Highness, and this is my first month in this position. Please do let me know if I satisfy your needs.'

'You are fine,' Kareem assured him. 'Just get me to my son as soon as possible.'

'Yes, Your Highness.'

'Just call me Prince Kareem.'

'Yes, Your Highness.'

'Just call me Prince, then.'

'Yes, Your Highness prince.'

Slightly exasperated, Kareem raised his eyebrows and exhaled, but said nothing more.

I would have laughed, but under the circumstances nothing was quite amusing enough to generate such gaiety from me. In our country, only the king is referred to as 'Your Highness', but the poor man was so tense being around a member of the royal family that Kareem's instructions did not transmit effectively to his brain.

After walking down some long corridors, we finally saw our son, who was sitting in the waiting area designated for members of the royal family. My heart fluttered when I realized that Abdullah was cupping his face in his hands. Was my son weeping? Had we lost Zain, or the babies?

I hurried to my son, happy that I had forgotten my abaaya in the car, for surely I would have tripped over, with that flowing gown floating around my feet.

'Abdullah! Son! We are here.'

Abdullah looked up. My son looked dazed. 'Mother. Father. I am glad you are here. Zain is in trouble. The babies are in trouble.' He stood and hugged us both. 'The doctors are with Zain now. I do not know what is actually occurring at this moment. It is all so confusing!'

'What did the doctor tell you was happening when you last spoke with him, Abdullah?' Kareem asked.

'I wrote it down.' Abdullah pulled a small notepad out of his pocket. I saw that my son's fingers were trembling, as he fumbled with the pad. He cleared his throat. 'Eclampsia. They said she has eclampsia. Something to do with uremic poisoning. The doctor says that some women do have this problem, and that it can be a true crisis unless diagnosed quickly.'

My son's voice broke. 'Because they started treatment quickly, Zain is going to be all right.' Abdullah exhaled, and once again his voice cracked. 'She *has* to be all right.'

With Kareem on one side and me on the other, we encouraged Abdullah to sit once again. The three of us huddled in a corner, waiting, praying that all would be well. We were alone. Abdullah told us that Zain's entire family was on holiday in France. They had taken their holiday early so as to be in the kingdom when the twins were expected to arrive. Now they were in France, frantically booking flights to return home.

The next twenty-four hours were the most harrowing of our lives. We were helpless and could do nothing more than anxiously wait for medical updates. First, we were told that Zain and the twins were all in a precarious situation and that it would be hours before we would know the outcome. Later an assistant physician gave us the welcome news that Zain appeared to be out of danger and that the twins had been born, although the distressing news was that there were no guarantees that either baby could be saved. The emotional rollercoaster threatened to weaken my already depleted reserves of strength and energy. If I did not take care, I might find myself back in the hospital.

I noticed Kareem studying my face. 'Sultana, your eyes are barely open. You are not yet fully recovered from your own health issues. Sweetheart, I will stay with Abdullah. I believe it best for you to go home and rest. You will need your energy once we can see Zain and the twins.' Optimistic as ever, my husband refused to acknowledge that we might lose either of the babies.

'Never. Never. I will not leave. Do you think I could go home and sleep? No. Never.'

Kareem nodded with understanding. He knew that he could never convince me to leave my son before we had the news that his wife and newborn babies were going to survive this nightmarish health emergency.

'All right. I will find more comfortable quarters for us.'

And that is what my husband did. Soon I was attempting to relax in a comfortable easy chair, with Kareem and Abdullah within arm's reach. Suddenly my eyes popped open as I realized we had failed to question the physician on the sex of the twins. Were the babies boys? Girls? One of each?

'Son, did the doctor say whether you are the father of twin boys or twin girls?'

'Mother, I forgot to ask,' Abdullah said with a shrug, indicating his indifference as to the sex of the twins. 'I do not care if the babies are girls or boys. I only pray that they will live.'

'You are right, son. You are right. We only want them to live, nothing more.'

Abdullah shook his head sadly. 'Yes, I will be the happiest man in the world if only they can live, Mother.'

I stroked my son's arms and shoulder, but he did not react.

'Try to sleep for a while, Sultana,' Kareem urged.

Although it was impossible to sleep, I restlessly stretched out, closed my eyes and hoped that my strength might return in order to help my son through this ordeal.

*   *   *

Five weeks later I felt a most unusual sensation. I was no longer secured to the earth by gravity, but instead I was floating off the crust of planet earth and into the atmosphere. I felt no fear. I was instead happy to be leaving my earthly home. Very soon I was calm and not frightened at all when I found myself in the most beautiful place – a place that all who are religiously devout dream about. I was in Paradise.

And that is when I discovered my greatest reward: there were Abdullah's twin girls – their bright brown-green eyes found mine and their little heads and faces glowed, as though someone had lit a soft shimmering candle within the crown of their skulls. The two girls were not identical and so their appearances did not match. One baby was fair-skinned, with a delicate and elegant face, the other baby had a luscious bronze complexion, with a full face that was twisted by a very wide smile. The delicate baby appeared to be a teeny doll and was so serene, while the more vigorous baby was kicking her heels high and laughing with every jolt – one would think that there was a little sandstorm in her bassinet. Her covers were soon pushed to the side and her fat little legs were active; as I tried to cover her tiny body, she kicked and laughed as though she understood my thoughts and that the joke was on her *jadda*.

I felt myself floating in the air, close to those precious bundles of joy. I leaned over their small cribs, both pale pink, elegantly carved bassinets decorated with frilly pastel yellow bedcovers. With one hand I touched the miniature fingers of one baby, and with my other hand I sought the touch of the second. Those little fingers grasped mine and felt strong, holding on tightly. Abdullah and Zain's babies knew that their grandmother needed comfort – that it was vital for her to feel joy. I knew then that I must remain with these granddaughters of mine; even after my passing, I would watch over them for ever in Paradise.

That's when I began to hum a little lullaby I had recently heard my daughter Amani singing to her toddler, Faisal. Although I could not recall the words, I did remember the music. It was a song composed by Marcel Khalife, a famous Lebanese composer and singer. While humming, I stroked their tiny little heads and hands. Overcome by the immense love that filled my entire body, I knelt in between the two bassinets, as there was just enough room for me to squeeze in that tight space.

'Ah, you are golden babies,' I whispered. 'Perfect in every way.' I moved closer and took turns covering their sweet little faces with kisses. My little sandstorm baby was pushing for all the attention, but I forced myself not to give into the temptation and to love each granddaughter equally. I looked into the eyes of what would for ever be known as my sandstorm baby and told her, 'My love for you is greater than the strongest wind ever recorded in a Saudi sandstorm. I am here for you, always.'

That's when I saw a double-width rocking chair sitting in a corner of the spacious nursery. I was suddenly so physically powerful that I easily lifted both babies, one in each arm, settling into the chair, cuddling them both equally. My granddaughters were the purest perfection – now I felt a powerful urge to tell them both the most wonderful fairy tale.

My words were spoken in a low, soft voice, as I had no information as to the guidelines of the nursery in Paradise, and I had no desire to disturb anyone – but both babies gazed into my eyes as though in a pleasant trance and I was sure that, despite the fact they were infants, they understood every word their grandmother spoke.

'Little darlings, *Jadda* is going to tell you a fairy tale like no other, so relax in my arms and hear the history of your desert kingdom on earth.'

*　　*　　*

I smiled contentedly at my sweet granddaughters, happy to reveal the history of the land where they were born. They would never know the experience of how it felt to live and love, nor what it was like to be a Saudi princess. I smiled – I could have sworn that both babies returned my smile with smiles of their own.

'Once upon a time there was a land with dark forests and rolling grasslands. The land we now know as Arabia was once lush and fertile. There was rainwater that fell when the monsoon appeared. It was a place where early humans from Africa discovered the lush terrain, thus the Arabian countryside drew migrants from Africa. Most scientists believe that early humans followed the coastline of Arabia and eventually arrived in southern Asia.

'Our country had a number of periods in history when rain fell abundantly. It was during those periods that Arabia prospered for farmers who tilled the land and hunters who were skilled enough to kill the beasts that roamed the green forests.

'Once upon a time the weather affecting this land called Arabia dramatically changed when the monsoon rains shifted. The once green forests became rolling sand dunes. The sun scorched the earth and, without precious water, most of Arabia became a vast desert.

'After the weather shift destroyed the green trees and dried up the rivers and lakes, Arabia became a place to avoid.

'Once upon a time, very brave but exceptionally quarrelsome men rode camels and slashed their ene-mies with hand-made sharp sticks and swords. These men fought each other over the barest essentials of life: water, camels, dates and women.

'Once upon a time, those born female were treated as inconvenient property, possessions that must be guarded. Many rules were established that meant many women were forced to live as slaves under brutish men who were so ignorant that they knew nothing of kind-ness and patience.

'Once upon a time, many baby girls, baby girls just like you, my darlings, were so despised by their fathers that they took them to the desert and buried them alive.

'Once upon a time, a great Prophet from the holy city of Mecca delivered God's message to those living in Arabia. He guided those men to be better than they had been. This new religion spread over much of the settled world and today is one of the main religions.

'Once upon a time, an exceptionally intelligent and cunning man who had been blessed with a powerfully strong physical figure fought to make his country whole – bringing together all the tribes in the area.'

I looked at my little granddaughters. 'This powerful man was your great-grandfather, my darlings. Your great-grandfather adored children. In his view, he never had enough children, even when the figure rose to forty-five sons and fifty-eight daughters. This is a man who had one hundred and three children who lived, and others not counted who did not.

'Should human beings be able to live long enough to come to know three or four generations of their descendants, he would have bestowed his love upon you during your short time on earth.

'Once upon a time, our ancestors were very poor – so poor that many Saudi Arabians starved to death whenever a drought plagued the area.

'Once upon a time, your great-grandfather was told that a rocky basin lurked under the thin crust of our dusty kingdom – and the greatest riches were found under that crust.

'Once upon a time, your very cunning great-grandfather set the stage for Saudi Arabia to prosper. The great wealth that had been hidden for many centuries was used to build magnificent cities across the kingdom and enrich the people.

'Once upon a time, one of the poorest countries in the world became one of the richest.

'Once upon a time, two little girls who were princesses were born in this rich country, but there was a tragedy when they were lost to a terrible disorder during the time of their birth.

'Once upon a time, their parents and grandparents were so saddened that their grandmother decided that she must join them in Paradise.

'And, my precious darlings, here is your grandmother ... I am here with you, for so long as it is allowed.'

I looked to see that both my precious granddaughters were sleeping soundly. Now I realized that I should look around and find out my place in Paradise. I hoped that I would do nothing more than care for my granddaughters.

At that moment, the brightest light I had ever seen exploded full upon my face. I blinked. I cried out, thinking that I was going to be taken away, denied the right to stay with my grandchildren.

'No! Go away! I want to stay here with my granddaughters.'

'Sultana! What are you doing?' It was Kareem. My husband paused, then asked with a crazed look on his face, 'Where is your nurse? She was supposed to stay with you every minute. I knew if you woke up unattended you might wander around the palace and you are too weak to be up and walking!'

I was confused and puzzled to see Kareem standing above me, but I could tell from his voice that he was very concerned. He turned off the bright light and clicked on a soft, well-shaded lamp. Still convinced that I was no longer alive, I asked Kareem, 'Are you in Paradise, too?'

'Paradise? What you are talking about? You must have been dreaming.'

'Kareem, I believe that we are in Paradise with the babies.'

'You are not in Paradise, Sultana. Let me assure you, you are not in Paradise!'

'Where am I?

'You are in a royal palace in Riyadh – a lot of people might consider this palace Paradise, sweetheart, but we both know that is not the case. In fact, you are in the nursery I had set up for the babies while Zain is recovering. Abdullah and Zain, Little Sultana, Feisal and the twins are staying with us for a few months.'

'Are you sure I am not dead?'

'You are not dead, darling. If you were not holding our granddaughters, I would pinch you and you would understand that you are very much alive, thanks be to God.'

'So I am not dead.'

'No, put that thought out of your mind. Sultana, it has been a little over a month since the babies were born. You suffered a very frightening nervous collapse when told that the babies were not going to live – but then a miracle! Both babies were saved. But by then the physician had been forced to sedate you. You had become hysterical and frightened us all.

'Zain and the babies, and you, remained in the hospital until three days ago. You have continued with the sedatives for weeks, as each time the doctor took you off the pills, you became confused and dangerous to your own safety. But it seems you have regained your mind and your strength.'

'Our granddaughters did not die? I did not die?'

'No, Sultana. Everyone is alive. Zain – the babies – you – all are alive, sweetheart.'

'Paradise and the babies seemed so real to me,' I said in a whisper.

'Well, the babies are real. Thank goodness you did not drop one of them. How did you get both these babies out of their bassinets and with you in this rocking chair?'

'I felt myself a superwoman.'

'Sultana,' Kareem said, 'you are physically weak from being in bed. Do not move. Wait here. Do not try to get up with the babies in your arms. I am going for help.'

'All right. I will not move.'

I stared at the little angels in my arms and was suddenly very glad they were not real angels, and that they would have the opportunity not only to live in the centre of a warm and loving family, but also through the excitement of all that was happening in Saudi Arabia.

'You are alive, my darlings! Alive,' I whispered. Then I smiled, despite the fact I was still in a state of shock to find myself living on earth. The most wonderful news of all had not yet sunk in – my two little granddaughters were alive, Zain was alive, indeed there had been a miracle that all of us lived through the physical and emotional turmoil of that terrifying evening, of which I only remembered a few vague details.

Kareem crept back into the room, now determined not to awaken the babies, who were surprisingly still, sleeping soundly after all the racket my husband had made. Two nurses wearing nightgowns and robes followed him. He started berating them in a whisper, if such a thing is possible. 'Now tell me, how did my wife leave her room, come into the nursery, collect these babies and no one saw her?'

'Sorry, sir. It was not our shift,' one of the nurses explained. 'There are two other American nurses who took over after our shift, but it seems that they have disappeared – we do not know where.'

One of the nurses in the room was a Filipina, the other was British. I have always felt safe in the professional care of the nurses we have hired over the years and was more than surprised that the two Americans had disappeared from their shift. Such a thing was not normal for those who worked in the kingdom's health-care field.

For a moment, I wondered if they had been kidnapped, but I kept that thought to myself as Kareem was already looking at me as though he feared I might mentally snap at any moment. I had no wish to alarm him further. His face had turned so red in anger that I thought he might have his own nervous breakdown. Thankfully, he quickly grasped the fact that the two nurses he had awakened were innocent.

'All right. I am sorry to have to ask you to do this, but I will need you both to work a double shift tonight. You will receive a big bonus, I assure you. Tomorrow those two Americans will be discharged and sent out of the kingdom – they do not take responsibility seriously! I will find someone else to take their positions.'

He glanced at the furnishings in the room. 'There are two reclining chairs in this room. Do take turns sleeping – one sleeps, one watches the babies.'

'Do we need to put on our nursing uniforms, sir?' the Filipina asked.

'No. No, do not worry. Just stay in your night clothes. Be comfortable.'

I knew no one's name, but did not ask at this time – tomorrow would be soon enough for me to discover all that was going on in my home.

That's when the British nurse smiled at me and said, 'Princess, we will each take one of the babies and return them to their bassinets. We promise that we shall not leave them for one second.'

I did not want to give the babies up, but I knew that I could not sit in the rocking chair and hold on to them for ever. Reluctantly, I allowed the nurses to remove the babies from my arms.

'Yes, of course.'

Kareem smiled at me and held out his hand. 'Welcome back, darling. I missed you.'

I could not believe that for weeks I had been unaware of all that was happening. I felt so good now; it was difficult to imagine how my mental capacity had deteriorated when told that the twins were not going to live!

Kareem and I walked arm in arm to my quarters. 'I will be staying with you the remainder of this night, Sultana.'

'I am sorry, husband – sorry that I was not well enough to help you through such a crisis.'

'Do not worry. Maha is home. Little Sultana is out of school. I have a full staff helping those two to keep order.' He leaned in and whispered, 'I would not want to work for Maha! She is strict and puts up with no foolishness.'

I raised my eyebrows, hoping that Maha was not mean to anyone.

'Thank you, Kareem,' I said. Suddenly I was so tired I knew that I would sleep many hours without the assistance of any sedatives. It would be a sleep of pure contentment, but before sleeping I said a prayer of thanks that the babies and I were still living the human life on earth. What fun I was going to have with two new grandchildren!

*   *   *

Three days later I was so well that I felt I had never been incapacitated. Zain had been very ill and was still unable to care for her children alone, although she and Abdullah spent hours in the nursery holding their daughters and delighting in their cute little ways.

Little Sultana was as happy as I have ever seen her – her lovely attitude made me so glad that she had not been stricken with the jealous gene that had contaminated my two girls, most particularly Amani.

Little Prince Feisal was staying with Zain's mother and was being royally spoiled. Zain's entire family has always loved Feisal more than Little Sultana – this stuck like a dagger into all our hearts. They were so set on the sexist theme that boys are good and girls are bad that we had to work doubly hard to reassure Little Sultana, but also balance out Feisal's life, so that he did not become a vain and arrogant man like so many of our royal princes. There were too many men like Dalal's egotistic husband, who would probably never keep a wife happy. I believed that many divorces were in his future, a man so insufferable that no woman would live with him very long. I did not wish that kind of future on my precious little grandson, who was still a sweet boy and as yet had been unaffected by the prejudice shown to him and against his older sister.

Now with twin girls, I was told by Kareem that Zain's mother was furious, accusing Abdullah and Zain of using machines to intentionally have girls just to irritate their family. I would have told them exactly what I thought of their ignorance, but Abdullah said that I was forbidden to get into an argument with them – my son wanted peace – even though he disliked witnessing such favouritism. Kareem was finally beginning to trust me with the babies, although the nurses were told that if I wanted to hold the babies they had to be in the room. I agreed, of course. I wished only the best for the twins.

One day when I wanted to visit with them for a while I asked if Little Sultana might help me rather than a nurse. Kareem and Abdullah both believed me strong enough to visit without any accidents, although I was told to leave the twins in their cribs and to admire them there.

'Little Sultana, I have a story to finish telling your little sisters. Do you want to hear the end of the story?' I asked when we were together in the nursery.

'Yes, *Jadda*. I do,' Little Sultana said with excitement.

She and I settled in chairs after asking the nurses to come and move them closer to the bassinets. By this time, the twins had been named by Little Sultana, who had very carefully researched to find the perfect ones for her twin sisters.

The light-skinned beauty was named Yasmine, meaning jasmine flower, a delicate and most pleasing name for the little princess. The beautiful bronze princess was named Kalila, which means beloved.

'You selected the most wonderful names for your sisters, Little Sultana. I would not have thought of those names but they are perfect for the twins. Little Yasmine looks like a flower, in fact, and Kalila is certainly beloved!'

'I know,' Little Sultana agreed. 'I did wish that they each had a very special name.'

'Well, you succeeded. Now, Little Sultana, I wanted to be alone with you, Yasmine and Kalila. I was telling the girls a story a week ago, when I was interrupted by your grandfather. I will tell you the full story later, but for now I would like to finish what I started. It will give your little sisters something interesting to think about.'

'Tell us,' my granddaughter encouraged, sitting in front of Yasmine and stroking her little cheeks.

Both Yasmine and Kalila were much healthier than the week before – they would probably remain underweight for a time due to their stressful arrival on earth, but with each day they became stronger.

'All right. I was telling them the story titled "Once Upon a Time" so that they might know something of their wonderful heritage, Little Sultana. Now I will finish the story.'

'Yes, please.'

'Girls, here is the ending to "Once Upon a Time . . ."'

'*Jadda*, look, the twins are staring at you – they know you have a story to finish! They are too cute!'

'Once upon a time, there was a very prosperous kingdom. There was more money than many knew how to spend – this made some aspects of life easier, yet there was still a big problem in this kingdom.'

'What was the problem?' Little Sultana had a puzzled expression on her face.

'In this kingdom, men ruled and women obeyed. But no one was happy, not the men and not the women. No human being can find happiness when they are tramping on the rights of others: they might say they are happy, but in reality they are not.

'But once upon a time, a very handsome prince decided to transform the lives of all women – this was a prince who loved his mother, and loved his wife, and loved his daughters. He hated his country's subjugation of women. He refused to allow the kingdom to ignore needed reforms so that women could take their rightful place alongside their husbands.

'Suddenly, as quickly as lightning strikes through the clouds to the earth, women were able to toss aside the ugly black robes and veils that had been worn for too long. Suddenly women were able to drive their own vehicles so that they did not have to wait for a man to take them shopping or to visit their families. Suddenly women were able to choose whatever profession they felt most qualified to study. Suddenly women were able to know their husbands before they married them – women would no longer be crushed under the heels of tyrants. Suddenly women were making decisions alongside their husbands – and, with women making important decisions with their husbands, the Kingdom of Saudi Arabia became a much more desirable kingdom.

'Once upon a time, as all these things changed for women in the kingdom, the youngest generation had no knowledge of what it felt like to be ignored, abused and helpless. These changes made all things possible for them.' I looked at each of my granddaughters in turn, hugging and touching each one when I emphasized their names. 'And that means *you, Princess Sultana*, and *you, Princess Yasmine*, and *you, Princess Kalila*!'

Little Sultana was giggling, and even the twins broke out in sweet smiles.

'And, you know what, girls? One day there will be a queen of Saudi Arabia and I recently had a dream that one of my granddaughters would be that queen – so perhaps it will be *you*, Queen Sultana – or *you*, Queen Yasmine, or *you*, Queen Kalila.'

I could see that Little Sultana was getting very excited because her eyes were sparkling and brilliantly dark. She spoke in a cheeky tone. 'I really believe that I should be queen, *Jadda* – I am the oldest.'

'Darling, whoever of the three of you will be queen will be the best queen in the world, doing nothing but positive things for all Saudi Arabians.'

'How do you know one of us will be the best queen?'

'Because, Little Sultana, you and your sisters will always speak with one heart and one voice – you girls will support each other, you will never allow jealousy or anger to create problems. You three little princesses will make this world a wonderful place for other women – and it does not matter who is queen because all three of you will work together to do the best for your country and the women of our country. Everything that was once new can begin again, and everything will advance once women are playing a role in the decisions made by those who lead our country.

'Remember this after your grandmother is no longer able to sit and talk with you: I would want my granddaughters to help Saudi Arabia to be known as a brilliant desert kingdom that did not end in tragedy because the men of the country discovered a world view too late.'

With a big smile, I said, 'It is up to you, girls!' I was as happy as I could remember being in a long time. 'It's up to you! I know that the new generation of young girls can successfully change and challenge the world's view of Saudi Arabia. Where once we were considered a joke – a backward kingdom where women were treated like children for their entire lives – you girls can show the world what Saudi Arabia can accomplish. I feel in my heart that with young women like my three granddaughters the day will come when the world will think of Saudi Arabia as the bright morning of civilization.'

A Closing Note from Jean Sasson

ALL KINGS FACE DISSENT. The legacy of how that dissent is handled will live longer than the king.

*   *   *

Earlier in 2017, when Princess Sultana and I decided to write the sixth book in the series of books about her life, both of us felt that the world of women in Saudi Arabia would vastly improve when grandsons of the first king of Saudi Arabia were named as kings. We reasoned that out of the several thousand grandsons of the founder of Saudi Arabia, surely large numbers of those men had the character to be wise rulers.

The forty-five sons of King Abdul Aziz were nearly all dead – in fact, only thirty-six had reached adulthood, and of those, six had become king. The remaining few sons were of an advanced age, far too old to govern. The princess and I both knew that those elderly sons were too set in their ways when it came to the rights of women. We believed that the lives of Saudi women would improve when much younger and more educated members of the al-Saud family took their place in the lineage of kings.

Our hopes were dashed when our dreams did not come true.

Both the princess and I were naive to believe that the grandsons of King Abdul Aziz would be enlightened rulers. Princess Sultana's own son, Abdullah, was raised by his mother to be fair and open-minded, leading us to hope that other grandsons would be similar to Abdullah. We were wrong. We were late in grasping the fact that a large number of the most powerful of the grandsons of King Abdul Aziz are too wilful, too precocious, and too accustomed to being instantly obeyed.

Princess Sultana now sadly admits that most of the royal grandsons have been overindulged since the moment of their births. Such indulgence has created men who react violently when anyone disagrees with their thoughts and ideas. These royals routinely lash out, imprisoning those who dare to express their personal opinions, *if* those opinions are not a mirror image of their own.

With these thoughts fresh in my mind, the princess and I discussed what I am about to write – an account of Saudi Arabia's various kings, and how they responded to dissenters.

We would like for you to know what we know.

*   *   *

I am a student of history and as an adult lived in Saudi Arabia for twelve years. I have read about and observed how dissent has been dealt with across the ages. Since its formation in 1932, Saudi Arabia has had only seven kings; I have personally met four of them.

I believe that I am one of the few Americans who lived in Saudi Arabia as an expatriate who has enjoyed the opportunity to meet the kings who ruled the kingdom. Albeit, the meetings were casual – I confess that I cannot claim to have been a favoured visitor to the palaces of the kings. However, I was in the company of King Khalid on three occasions while I was employed at the royal hospital, and in the company of King Fahd on seven instances, twice while I was still working at the hospital, and on five occasions when I was a guest of a member of the royal family. Through Peter Sasson's business connections, the Englishman I met in Riyadh in 1978 and married in 1981, I briefly met two kings-in-waiting when I was introduced to Abdullah and Salman. When I met Abdullah, he was the feared Saudi Arabian Crown Prince, a quiet and serious man who was said to be demanding. At the event where I met Salman, he was the beloved Governor of Riyadh, a man known for his honesty.

As a woman who has always taken the greatest pleasure studying the history of things, I have spent enormous time researching the kings of Saudi Arabia. My knowledge grew as I interviewed Saudis royals who knew these kings personally, along with extensive reading on the kings.

I would like to share a few details of how all of this came about, as well as revealing how the previous six kings handled dissent. My intention is to compare their actions with the current King Salman and his favoured son, the Crown Prince Mohammad, for this father and son are currently reproached by the western media and western governments for setting records of imprisoning, torturing and murdering Saudi citizens who express the slightest opposition to the lack of personal freedom for Saudi citizens.

*   *   *

I first arrived in Saudi Arabia in September of 1978. That period in Saudi Arabia's history was an exhilarating time of extraordinary change. While most expatriates stayed only a few years in the kingdom, claiming that the authoritarian regulations were a deterrent to enjoyable life, I personally experienced a pleasurable twelve-year residency in Riyadh.

During those busy years of economic and infrastructural growth, expatriates from every continent were streaming into the kingdom. Fortunately, I found Saudi citizens overwhelmingly friendly and welcoming, quickly discovering they were most inquisitive about Americans.

The benevolence I encountered is supposedly no longer displayed to expatriates living and working in Saudi Arabia; therefore, I know that few visitors to the kingdom enjoy the opportunities that were a routine part of my expatriate life. Such opportunities, including meeting four of the seven kings who have ruled the kingdom, affords me a unique vantage point from which to observe how these men reacted when Saudi citizens expressed disagreement with repressive Saudi laws. While there are many interesting aspects to all seven kings, I am concentrating only on one subject in this short note, which is a brief explanation of how each of the seven kings handled dissenters.

*   *   *

I will begin with the first king of Saudi Arabia, a man who passed away when I was only a toddler, unaware of the great importance that the kingdom, and the Saudi people, would have on my future.

I have no knowledge other than what has been told to me or was written about the extraordinary Saudi king, Abdul Aziz.

King Abdul Aziz bin Abdul Rahman was the founder and first king of Saudi Arabia. He ruled from 23 September 1932 until his death on 9 November 1953. King Abdul Aziz was a warrior who cleverly settled the tribal issues of the Arabian peninsula so that he might form a country, which he did with the greatest of success. Without King Abdul Aziz, nothing about Saudi Arabia would be as it is today. And, yes, there were numerous instances of tribal and individual dissent during the turbulent time of tribal battles, and later during his early stages of rule over all the tribes of the Arabian desert that is now known as Saudi Arabia.

No one denies that Abdul Aziz was an impressive presence physically, psychologically, and intellectually. Large-boned and taller than most at 6'4", he was a man not easily forgotten. Tales of his intense bravery, calm demeanour in the face of crisis, and extraordinary wisdom are still celebrated by most Saudis.

King Abdul Aziz was not a man who would accept dissent, and there were troubling disagreements that brought forth his sword to settle issues. Nonetheless, he was a man who often displayed notable wisdom with dissenters, usually convincing the dissenter that the king's way was the best way. He often used Arabian folk tales to persuade the stubborn. No incidences have been recorded of this first king resorting to needless bloodshed. He was a rare warrior king who preferred peace to discord and war.

Thus, King Abdul Aziz, the father of the following six kings, tapped into his common sense, charisma and wisdom to resolve issues without bloodshed whenever possible.

After King Abdul Aziz passed away of a heart attack in 1953, his son, Crown Prince Saud bin Abdul Aziz al-Saud, was acknowledged as the kingdom's second king and new ruler. There is always plentiful dissent when a monarch dies and another is appointed to rule, but by the time Saud inherited the throne the rebellious tribes had been subdued and their voices of dissent silenced.

King Saud was said to be a man of such happy disposition that he rarely created animosity with any man. The second king of Saudi Arabia announced that his main goals were to defeat poverty and disease in the kingdom his father had founded, although his massive personal expenditures made reaching that admirable goal impossible. He was a man who married multiple wives and fathered over one hundred children. Such a huge household depleted the kingdom's reserves, and eventually signs of discord began to show amongst King Saud's royal siblings.

The family disagreements rumbled on until, after eleven years of rule, King Saud was forced to abdicate in 1964, at which time his half-brother Faisal was named king. Yet despite the family disagreements, there were no deaths as a result of this feud, as Saud was not a man with cruelty in his heart. Forced into exile, King Saud, his wives and his children lived in Europe until his death in 1969.

Faisal bin Abdul Aziz al-Saud became the third king of Saudi Arabia. He was best known for being pious and thrifty and was the exact opposite of his brother, Saud. But while Saud faced little dissent, Faisal's plans to limit the powers of the radical clergy, and to bring modernization to the kingdom, created enormous hostility within the religious clergy and those Saudi citizens who reacted negatively to King Faisal after hearing the heated sermons against Faisal's plans for modernization. The danger created by the radical dissenters to the kingdom's progress was so great that Faisal quietly but determinedly fought against this opposition in a manner that would have been unthinkable under his father, or his brother, Saud. Those who fought against the changes King Faisal sought, were imprisoned. Even royal princesses who demanded expanded rights were taken from their homes and cast into dark prisons, where they languished for many years. Members of the al-Saud family nervously whispered stories about journalists, who by attempting to destabilize Faisal's reign by their political writings, were reportedly assassinated in Lebanon and other Middle Eastern countries.

King Faisal was a hard-working king devoted to the country he ruled, who thought only of bringing Saudi

Arabia into the modern age, yet he was not a man who accepted dissent of any kind.

This king who most forcibly fought against dissent was destined to die at the hands of a dissident. It was 25 March 1975 when King Faisal was tragically felled by an assassin's bullet in his own *majlis* (a large room in a palace where men in the Middle East gather to visit and discuss issues of the day). The assassin who shot Faisal was Faisal bin Musaid, a son of King Faisal's own half-brother Musaid. He was avenging the death of his own brother Khalid bin Musaid, who had been killed while violently protesting the launching of television stations in the kingdom, a result of King Faisal's secular reforms.

Although King Faisal had powerfully contained and quieted many dissenters, in the end his policies led to his own violent death. His loss was a great pity because King Faisal was Saudi Arabia's most determined king, who promoted progress in multiple areas in the kingdom.

At King Faisal's death, the most benevolent of all of Saudi Arabia's kings came to power; a man who was often named as the nicest man in the entire kingdom. The fourth king to rule was King Khalid bin Abdul Aziz al-Saud, who was the fifth son of his father, King Abdul Aziz. Khalid was not particularly fond of being king as he had lived a dramatic life astride a fighting camel alongside his father during the tribal wars. When peace finally came after many years of warfare, Khalid relished the serene lifestyle. His main interests in life were his family, horseback riding and falconry. Khalid was the father of ten children, six of whom were daughters.

Royals who knew the family well proclaim that Khalid's daughters are some of the nicest and the most beautiful women in the kingdom.

During Khalid's reign the kingdom rapidly grew in prosperity. Most Saudis were contented with the vast riches that had come to them, and to their country. Indulged populations are not prone to dissent. In fact, Saudi Arabians who had grievances about the continued repression at the hands of the uncompromising clerics and forbidding security officials in Saudi Arabia often told this author that they could not get anyone to dissent during the 'Economic Go-Go years'.

However, there was a dangerous act of rebellion when five hundred religious radical dissidents invaded and occupied the Grand Mosque in November 1979. After the Grand Mosque was retaken by government forces, the rebels were arrested and executed. Although a consistently genial man, King Khalid did not hesitate to sign the death sentences of the dissidents.

When King Khalid died of a heart attack on 13 June 1982 the baton of kingship was passed to Saudi Arabia's fifth king, Fahd bin Abdul Aziz al-Saud.

King Fahd was the eighth son of King Abdul Aziz and physically presented a much more powerful figure than his half-brother Khalid, whom he succeeded as king. King Fahd had lived a playboy life of glamour and to appease the religious figures who were disgruntled at the thought of such an offender of Muslim principles becoming king, he sought their support and approval by strengthening their authority. From the time of King Fahd's reign, radical clerics celebrated having been given authority over the personal lives of

Saudi Arabians. When Saudi reformists protested King Fahd's actions by petition they were harshly punished with long prison terms and the loss of their jobs. King Fahd was decidedly more severe with those who challenged his authority than any former king, save for King Faisal.

At King Fahd's death on 1 August 2005, Saudi Arabia's sixth king, Abdullah bin Abdul Aziz al-Saud, assumed the crown. Abdullah was the thirteenth son of his father, Abdul Aziz. Abdullah was said to be a stern man and Saudis who had supported King Fahd trembled as to what fury might be directed to them. However, King Abdullah pleasantly surprised many Saudi Arabians when he presented himself to be a man who set in motion various developments for the kingdom, such as government educational reforms, rights for Saudi women, and Public Health awareness. The most welcome change happened when King Abdullah set about dismantling the untouchable authority of the religious clerics who often made life miserable for Saudi citizens. Surprisingly, there were few dissenters to voice criticism during Abdullah's reign, although the king did react firmly to silence those who became verbally aggressive against the country through social media.

Few know the exact details, but King Abdullah was said to have severely punished the daughters of one of his thirty wives who fled the kingdom. Those children are supposedly still under house arrest in the kingdom, but no one, not even other royals, knows with certainty the outcome of the human rights violations against his own daughters.

When King Abdullah passed away at age ninety on 23 January 2015 most Saudis expressed genuine sorrow, even those citizens who had dreaded his rule. But history will show that King Abdullah was a seasoned ruler who created much positive change for the country and the people.

At King Abdullah's death, his half-brother Salman assumed leadership of Saudi Arabia. Salman's rule is historic, as he is the last son of the first king who will rule. From Salman, the baton of kingship will pass to the grandsons of King Abdul Aziz, and more specifically to Salman's favoured son, Crown Prince Mohammad bin Salman bin Abdul Aziz al-Saud.

Prior to being appointed Crown Prince, Salman served as Governor of Riyadh for forty-eight years, from 1963 until 2011. While Salman was known as an experienced and successful administrator during the lengthy time he served as Riyadh's governor, his abilities had diminished by the time he became King of Saudi Arabia. Many people in the royal family whisper that Salman has lost his mental sharpness due to the ageing process. If this is the case, perhaps that explains how a genial man who was known to be the second nicest royal (after King Khalid) suddenly became a hard-edged ruler, approving arrest warrants, imprisonment, torture and public floggings for young Saudis who expressed mild criticisms of many of Saudi Arabia's repressive policies on various media sites. Other Saudi royals say that the King is under the complete influence of his chosen son, Crown Prince Mohammad, the man the CIA claim ordered the murder of the late Jamal Khashoggi, the *Washington Post* reporter viciously killed in the Saudi Embassy in Turkey in October 2018.

*   *   *

I have shared how dissent in Saudi Arabia has been dealt with over the years under each of the seven kings of the kingdom.

The future now holds all of Saudi Arabia in the grip of one young man, Crown Prince Mohammad bin Salman bin Abdul Aziz al-Saud.

With this new king-in-waiting, great hope arose with the desert sun. But that light of hope quickly faded into the darkness of despair.

No matter how long his reign, no matter what good he does, a record of torture, human abuse, and of murder written by his own hand, cannot be erased.

Epilogue

Final thoughts from
Princess Sultana al-Sa'ud

Written on 10 November 2018

A LTHOUGH I AM A PRINCESS who has lived a life
of excitement and adventure, the last year of my
life in Saudi Arabia has been a tempestuous mix of joy,
hope, fear and anger. In the beginning, the joy in my
heart created a song on my lips for my hope was as high
as the highest mountain peak on earth. I was the happiest princess in Saudi Arabia when my cousin,
Mohammad bin Salman bin Abdul Aziz Al-Saud,
soared past the ranks of various royal princes who were
vying for an opportunity to be called King of Saudi
Arabia. Yes, he was young. Yes, he was not as experienced as many other sons of the fathers who had been
guiding the kingdom since King Abdul Aziz, our grandfather, founder of our nation, and the first king of our
country passed from this earth, before the Crown
Prince was even born. Yes, there was talk in our family
that our young cousin had not yet reached a mature

place in his mind so that he might successfully lead a nation.

But I did not agree or care about the irksome opinions of my royal cousins and friends, because this cousin of mine perfectly articulated the hopes and dreams of Saudi women. His passionate words on our behalf felt as though he had the heart of a woman who had fought and longed for total freedom for too many years to count. When his mouth opened, he said the words that were in our hearts and minds. He assured us that the kingdom was moving forward, and that his top priority was to elevate the status of women – that women would take their places beside their men in building our country until we surpassed all others. He, as I, appeared appalled that ours was the only country on earth where women were forbidden to drive.

This cousin of mine was going to change our female world in a most magnificent way.

And, he did.

At least for a time.

After his announcements, we believed that we were the luckiest of all women to have such a man professing his determination to right all the wrongs we had endured for too many years.

How we celebrated his promises and ideas for our future!

How we partied, with Saudi women from every corner of our kingdom taking turns quoting his words from memory, our own tongues licking our lips in pleasure that such great and unexpected freedoms were waiting for his single command.

In our dreams, all our problems were going to vanish.

Our joy soon receded for the nightmares returned when we learned the new reality that every promise was topped by a threat, and that every pledge hid a bitter pill that all Saudi women were forced to swallow.

Our hopes dwindled until our balloon of expectation burst.

Our festivities ended.

How devastated we became when we realized that we had been embarrassingly naive to unquestioningly believe all that was promised.

The courageous women who most deserved the chance to steer an automobile around the cities and towns of our country will never know the pleasure of an open window allowing a breeze to blow through their hair. Those fearless women who led the battle to drive have not experienced the marvellous feeling of driving their cars to work or school or shopping. Why? Because those resolute women who displayed pluck and audacity are now behind bars in a dark and damp prison, sitting alone every day, dreaming lonely dreams of what might have been. They are truly isolated, for their families are too terrified to speak on their behalf for they now see the truth, that Saudi Arabia is in the strong grip of a powerful man who will ruthlessly silence them if a single independent thought is communicated.

The Saudi women who supported their heroes are wild with rage, but that rage we must contain within our hearts and our angry words must remain silenced, heard only by those whom we love and trust, or we, too, would find ourselves confined in a filthy prison without proper food, and without hope that one day we would be free to return to our families.

Merry talk of lifting the hated guardianship law is no longer heard. Without the termination of that one female-confining law, Saudi women will never be free, for our male guardians hold life or death over our heads.

Many well-meaning, wealthy and prominent Saudis – some of whom are royal cousins – have been arrested and forced to forfeit the bulk of their wealth. Those who dared refused are still in prison.

Royal cousins who defied our Crown Prince have vanished. There are rumours that a number of the wealthiest of our family, and most prominent prior to cousin Mohammed's rise, died during interrogations.

To our surprised horror, royal family members, uncles or cousins to the king-in-waiting, for the first time, have been targeted by the rulers of our land.

While Saudi Arabia needed a strong ruler who would confront and overcome the old thinkers who wished to keep Saudi Arabia in the dark ages, we did not pray for a ruler who would overwhelm the honour in our family. Our grandfather Abdul Aziz left us with honour in our hearts and minds, a man who would have never ordered the arrest and rough interrogation of those of our own blood.

I want to ensure those readers who care about me, and other women in the kingdom, that all you read in this book is true. At the time these stories were revealed, there was the greatest hope and affection in our newly appointed Crown Prince. Yes, there were female parties of celebration. Yes, we were guileless, for we believed the comforting words that were spoken and the joyful promises that were given.

While I cannot change the past, I can change my future. While I do not have the power to go back in time and transform my trusting manner of thinking, I can assure readers who care enough to continue reading my story, that while this is a disheartening setback for the women of Saudi Arabia, it is not the end of the story. While I had believed that I could lay aside my battle armour and apply all my resources in building the female power base, I now know that I once more I must pull my heavy breastplate onto my body and prepare once more for battle.

Yes, the king-in-waiting is my cousin.

Yes, I felt the greatest affection for his words and promises.

Yes, my heart is broken.

Yes, my anger is building.

But no, I will never give in.

Do not forget us, for we are your sisters of another land, one where our bitter disappointments spur us on to take great chances risking our freedom and, in this case, even our lives, for I have no doubt that this cousin would enthusiastically put me to death if he could discover my identity.

Prayers to God are very powerful.

Remember me and all the other women of Saudi Arabia in your prayers.

Appendices

Appendices

Appendix One

King Abdul Aziz al-Sa'ud

King Abdul Aziz al-Sa'ud is the grandfather of
    Princess Sultana.
Born: 15 January 1876 in Riyadh, Emirate of Nejd

Family

His father, Abdul Rahman bin Faisal, was the last
ruler of the second Saudi state. His mother was Sarah
al-Sudairi. His closest sibling was his sister, Noura
bint Abdul Rahman al-Sa'ud, and the two remained
close for their entire lives. His family, the House of
al-Sa'ud, had been a major power in the centre of
Arabia for more than a hundred years at the time of
his birth.

Significant Events in His Life

The al-Rashid tribe were the main rivals of the House
of al-Sa'ud. The al-Rashids conquered Riyadh in 1890
and Abdul Aziz's family fled their homeland. The

family sought refuge in a Bedouin tribe in the southern desert of Arabia before moving to Bahrain for a short stay. The family then travelled to Kuwait, where they were in exile for nearly ten years.

Abdul Aziz al-Sa'ud grew up to be a physical giant of a man, with a passion for regaining his homeland. This he did in the year 1902. He continued to fight the Arabian tribes until he finally consolidated his dominions into the Kingdom of Saudi Arabia. He became the King of Saudi Arabia on 23 September 1932.

After consolidating his rule, he moved his court from the Masmak Fort to the Murabba Palace in 1938. He lived in the Murabba Palace for the rest of his life.

Wives and Children

Abdul Aziz al-Sa'ud married numerous women, partly in order to consolidate the tribes. No one knows for certain how many women he married, but it is thought that the number is close to one hundred. The most well known of his wives was Hassa al-Sudairi, the mother of the famous seven Sudairi brothers, most of whom held high positions in the government, with Fahd and Salman becoming king, and Naif and Sultan becoming Crown Prince.

Abdul Aziz fathered many children, including forty-five sons and fifty-eight daughters. The most famous of his sons are King Saud, King Faisal, King Khalid, King Fahd, King Abdullah, King Salman and Prince Turki of the Najd. His most famous grandson is Crown Prince Muhammad.

Death

A victim of heart problems, Abdul Aziz became seriously ill in late 1953. He suffered a heart attack on 9 November and died in Taif. He is buried in Riyadh at the Al Oud Cemetery.

Appendix Two

_____

Saudi Arabia Timeline

570	*19 January*. Prophet Mohammed, the founder of Islam, is born in Mecca.
632	*8 June*. Prophet Mohammed dies in Medina. After his death, his companions compile his words and deeds in a work called the Sunna, which contains the rules for Islam. The most basic are the Five Pillars of Islam, which are 1) profession of faith 2) daily prayer 3) giving alms 4) ritual fast during Ramadan 5) hajj, the pilgrimage to Mecca.
1400s	The Sa'ud dynasty is founded near Riyadh.
1703	Muhammad bin Abd al-Wahhab (d.1792), Islamic theologian and founder of Wahhabism, is born in Arabia.
1710	Muhammad bin al-Sa'ud is born.
1742–65	Muhammad bin al-Sa'ud joins the Wahhabists.

1744	Muhammad bin al-Sa'ud forges a political and family alliance with Muslim scholar and reformer Muhammad bin Abd al-Wahhab. The son of bin Sa'ud marries the daughter of Imam Muhammad.
1804	The Wahhabis capture Medina.
1811	Egyptian ruler Muhammad Ali overthrows the Wahhabis and reinstates Ottoman sovereignty in Arabia.
1813	The Wahhabis are driven from Mecca.
1824	The al-Sa'ud family establishes a new capital at Riyadh.
1876	Sultana's grandfather, Abdul Aziz al-Sa'ud, founder of the kingdom, is born.
1883	*20 May*. Faisal bin Hussein is born in Mecca. He later becomes the first king of Syria (1920) and Iraq (1921).
1890	Muhammad bin Rashid captures Riyadh, forcing the al-Sa'ud family out of the area.
1890–1902	The al-Sa'ud family leave the area to live in exile (from Qatar to Bahrain and finally to Kuwait) until 1902, when they regain control of Riyadh.
1901	Abdul Aziz leaves Kuwait to return to Arabia with family and friends, with plans to attack Riyadh.

1902	*January*. Abdul Aziz attacks Mismaak fort and recaptures Riyadh.
	Saud bin Abdul Aziz, son of Abdul Aziz, is born. At his father's death, he will rule Saudi Arabia from 1953 to 1964.
1904	Faisal bin Abdul Aziz, who one day will be a king of Saudi Arabia, is born.
1906	Abdul Aziz al-Sa'ud regains total control of the Nejd region.
1906–26	Abdul Aziz al-Sa'ud and his forces capture vast areas and unify much of Arabia.
1916	Mecca, under control of the Turks, falls to the Arabs during the Great Arab Revolt.
	British officer T. E. Lawrence (Lawrence of Arabia) meets Faisal Hussein, forging a friendship.
	T. E. Lawrence is assigned as the British liaison to Arab Prince Faisal Hussein.
1917	*6 July*. Arab forces led by T. E. Lawrence and Abu Tayi capture the port of Aqaba from the Turks.
1918	*1 October*. Prince Faisal takes control of Syria when the main Arab force enters Damascus.
	Lawrence of Arabia blows up the Hejaz railway line in Saudi Arabia.

1921	At the Cairo Conference, Britain and France carve up Arabia and create Jordan and Iraq, making brothers Faisal and Abdullah kings. France is given influence over what is now Syria and Lebanon.
1923	Abdul Aziz's son Fahd is born in Riyadh. He will one day reign as King of Saudi Arabia.
1924	Bin Saud, King of the Nejd, conquers Hussein's Kingdom of Hejaz. He rules over Saudi Arabia, later taking Mecca and Medina.
1926	*January*. Abdul Aziz is declared King of Hejaz and the Sultan of Nejd.
1927	Saudi Arabia signs the Treaty of Jeddah and becomes independent of Great Britain.
1927–28	King Abdul Aziz crushes the fanatical Islamist tribes of central Arabia.
1931	Muhammad bin Laden (who one day will be father of Osama bin Laden) emigrates to Saudi Arabia from Yemen. He works hard to establish his business, later building a close relationship with King Abdul Aziz and King Faisal.
1932	The kingdoms of Nejd and Hejaz are unified to create the Kingdom of Saudi Arabia under King Abdul Aziz bin al-Sa'ud. Saudi Arabia was named after

King bin al-Sa'ud, founder of the Saudi dynasty, a man who fathered forty-four sons and who continue to rule the oil-rich kingdom.

1933   Saudi Arabia gives Standard Oil of California exclusive rights to explore for oil.

1938   Standard Oil of California strikes oil at Dammam #7.

1945   *14 February.* Saudi King Abdul Aziz and American President Franklin D. Roosevelt meet on a ship in the Suez Canal, where they reach an understanding whereby the US will protect the Saudi royal family in return for access to Saudi oil.

        22 March. The Arab League is formed in Cairo, Egypt. Saudi Arabia becomes a founding member of the UN and the Arab League.

1953   King Abdul Aziz, Sultana's grandfather, dies, age seventy-seven. He is succeeded by his son, Saud.

1953–64   King Saud rules.

1962   Saudi Arabia abolishes slavery.

1964   *2 November.* Faisal bin Abdul Aziz al-Sa'ud (1904–75) succeeds his older brother, Saud bin Abdul Aziz, as King of Saudi Arabia.

1964–75	King Faisal rules.
1965	King Faisal defies Islamist opposition when he introduces television and later women's education. Riots ensue. Later senior clerics are convinced by the government that television could be used to promote the faith.
1967	*6 June.* An Arab oil embargo is put into effect after the beginning of the Arab–Israeli Six Day War.
	3 September. Muhammad bin Laden, the wealthy father of Osama bin Laden, dies in a plane crash, leaving the well-being of his children to King Faisal.
1973	An embargo against Western nations is announced, lasting until 1974. Petrol prices soar from 25 cents per gallon to $1. As a result, the New York stock market falls.
1975	*25 March.* King Faisal of Saudi Arabia is assassinated by his nephew.
	18 June. Saudi Prince Faisal bin Musaid is beheaded in Riyadh for killing his uncle, King Faisal. Crown Prince Khalid is declared king.
	November. Armed men and women seize the Grand Mosque in Mecca. They denounce the al-Sa'ud rulers, demanding an end to foreign ways. The radicals are

led by Saudi preacher Juhayman al-Utaybi. The siege goes on until French special forces are flown to Mecca to assist. The extremists are shot and killed or captured, later to be beheaded.

1980   Saudi Arabia executes the remaining radicals for the siege of the Grand Mosque. The radicals are beheaded in various towns across the country.

1982   *13 June*. King Khalid dies. He is succeeded by his half-brother, Crown Prince Fahd.

1983–2005   Prince Bandar bin Sultan al-Sa'ud, one of King Fahd's favourite nephews, serves as Saudi Arabia's Ambassador to Washington.

1985   Great Britain signs an $80 billion contract with Saudi Arabia to provide 120 fighter jets and other military equipment over a period of twenty years.

1987   *31 July*. Iranian pilgrims and riot police clash in the holy city of Mecca. The Iranians are blamed for the deaths of 402 people.

1990   *July*. The worst tragedy of modern times occurs at the hajj in Mecca, when 1,402 Muslim pilgrims are killed in a stampede inside a pedestrian tunnel.

6 November. A group of Saudi women drive cars in the streets of Riyadh in defiance of a government ban. The protest creates enormous problems for the women drivers: they are arrested and fired from their jobs, banned from travelling and named as prostitutes. This event leads to a formal ban on driving for women.

Saudi Arabia and Kuwait expel a million Yemeni workers as the government of Yemen sides with Saddam in the First Gulf War.

1991   *January.* US-led forces attack the Iraqi military in Kuwait. The ground war begins between Iraq and the Coalition forces. Iraqi forces are routed from Kuwait and are no longer a danger to Saudi Arabia.

1992   King Fahd outlines an institutional structure for the country. A law is passed that allows the king to name his brothers or nephews as successors and to replace his successor at will.

1994   *23 May.* 270 pilgrims are killed in a stampede in Mecca, as worshippers gather for the symbolic ritual of 'stoning the devil'.

1995   192 people are beheaded in Saudi Arabia over the year – a record number.

1996   An ailing King Fahd cedes power to his half-brother, Crown Prince Abdullah.

1997   343 Muslim pilgrims die in a fire outside the holy city of Mecca. More than a thousand others are injured.

1998   150 pilgrims die at the 'stoning of the devil' ritual during a stampede that occurs on the last day of the annual pilgrimage to the holy city of Mecca.

1999   The Saudi Arabian government claims it will issue travel visas into the kingdom to upscale travel groups.

2001   *26 January.* A UN panel angers the Saudi government and citizens when it criticizes Saudi Arabia for discriminating against women, harassing minors and for punishments that include flogging and stoning.

     5 March. Thirty-five Muslim pilgrims suffocate to death during the 'stoning of the devil' ritual at the annual hajj in Mecca.

     March. The Higher Committee for Scientific Research and Islamic Law in Saudi Arabia says that Pokémon games and cards have 'possessed the minds' of Saudi children.

     September. After 9/11, six chartered flights carrying Saudi nationals depart from the USA. A few days later, another chartered flight carrying twenty-six members of the bin Laden family leave the USA.

2002   *17 February*. Saudi Crown Prince Abdullah presents a Middle East peace plan to *New York Times* columnist Thomas Friedman. The plan includes Arab recognition of Israel's right to exist if Israel pulls back from lands that were once part of Jordan, including East Jerusalem and the West Bank.

March. There is a fire at a girls' school in Mecca, but the police block the girls from fleeing the building because they are not wearing the veil. A surge of anger spreads across Saudi Arabia when fifteen students burn to death.

13 April. Saudi Arabian poet Ghazi al-Gosaibi, Saudi Ambassador to Britain, publishes the poem 'The Martyrs' in the Saudi daily *Al Hayat*, praising a Palestinian suicide bomber.

25 April. American President George Bush meets with Saudi Crown Prince Abdullah. Crown Prince Abdullah tells the American president that the country must reconsider its total support of Israel. Abdullah gives Bush his eight-point proposal for Middle East peace.

April. The Saudi Arabian government close several factories that produce women's veils and abaayas that are said to violate religious rules. Some of the cloaks are considered too luxurious, with jewels sewn on the shoulders.

May. There is a disagreement between Saudi diplomats and members of the UN Committee Against Torture over whether flogging and the amputation of limbs are violations of the 1987 Convention Against Torture.

December. Saudi dissidents report the launch of a new radio station, Sawt al-Islah (the Voice of Reform), broadcasting from Europe. The new station is formed with the express purpose of pushing for reforms in Saudi Arabia.

2003   *February.* Mina, Saudi Arabia: fourteen Muslim pilgrims are trampled to death when a worshipper trips during the annual hajj pilgrimage.

29 April. The United States government announces the withdrawal of all combat forces from Saudi Arabia.

12 May. Multiple and simultaneous suicide car bombings at three foreign compounds in Riyadh kill twenty-six people, including nine US citizens.

14 October. Hundreds of Saudi Arabians take to the streets, demanding reform. This is the first large-scale protest in the country, as demonstrations are illegal.

2004   It is discovered that Libya planned a covert operation to assassinate Crown Prince Abdullah the previous year (2003).

1 February. During the hajj, 251 Muslim worshippers die in a stampede.

10 April. Popular Saudi Arabian TV host Rania al-Baz is severely beaten by her husband, who thought he had killed her. She survived, suffering severe facial fractures that required twelve operations. She allowed photos to be broadcast and opened discussions of ongoing violence against women in Saudi Arabia. She travelled to France, where she wrote her story. It was reported that she lost custody of her children after her book was published.

May. In Yanbu, Saudi Arabia, suspected militants spray gunfire inside the offices of an oil contractor, the Houston-based ABB Ltd. Six people are killed. Many are wounded. Police kill four brothers in a shoot-out after a car chase in which the attackers reportedly dragged the naked body of one victim behind their getaway car.

6 June. Simon Chambers, an Irish cameraman working for the BBC, is killed in a shooting in Riyadh. A BBC correspondent is injured.

8 June. An American citizen working for a US defence contractor is shot and killed in Riyadh.

12 June. An American is kidnapped in Riyadh. Al-Qaeda post the man's picture on an Islamic website. He is identified as businessman Paul M. Johnson Jr. Islamic militants shoot and kill American Kenneth Scroggs in his garage in Riyadh.

13 June. Saudi Arabia holds a three-day 'national dialogue' in Medina on how women's lives could be improved and the recommendations are passed to Crown Prince Abdullah.

15 June. Al-Qaeda threatens to execute Paul M. Johnson Jr within seventy-two hours unless fellow jihadists are released from Saudi prisons.

18 June. Al-Qaeda claim to have killed American hostage Paul M. Johnson Jr. They post photos on the internet showing his body and severed head.

June. The Saudi parliament pass legislation overturning a law banning girls and women from participating in physical education and sports. In August, the Ministry of Education announces that it will not honour the legislation.

20 July. The head of slain American hostage Paul M. Johnson Jr is found during a raid by Saudi security forces.

30 July. In the United States, in a Virginia court, Abdurahman Alamoudi pleads guilty to moving cash from Libya to pay expenses in the plot to assassinate Saudi Prince Abdullah.

28 September. The use of mobile phones with built-in cameras is banned by Saudi Arabia's highest religious authority. The edict claims that the phones are 'spreading obscenity' throughout Saudi Arabia.

6 December. Nine people are killed at the US Consulate in Jeddah when Islamic militants throw explosives at the gate of the heavily guarded building. They force their way into the building and a gun battle ensues.

2005   *13 January.* Saudi judicial officials say a religious court has sentenced fifteen Saudis, including a woman, to as many as 250 lashes each and up to six months in prison for participating in a protest against the monarchy.

10 February. While women are banned from casting ballots, Saudi male voters converge at polling stations in the Riyadh region to participate in city elections. This is the first time in the country's history that Saudis are taking part in a vote that conforms to international standards.

3 March. Men in eastern and southern Saudi Arabia turn out in their thousands to vote in municipal elections. It is their first opportunity to have their say in decision making in Saudi's absolute monarchy.

1 April. Saudi Arabia beheads three men in public in the northern city of Al-Jawf; in 2003 the three men killed a deputy governor, a religious court judge and a police lieutenant.

15 May. Three reform advocates are sentenced to terms ranging from six to nine years in prison. Human-rights activists call the trial 'a farce'.

Saudi author and poet Ali al-Dimeeni is sentenced to nine years in prison for sowing dissent, disobeying his rulers and sedition. His 1998 novel *A Gray Cloud* tells the story of a dissident jailed for years in a desert nation prison where many others have served time for their political views.

27 May. King Fahd, Saudi Arabia's monarch for twenty-three years, is hospitalized for unspecified reasons.

1 August. King Fahd dies at the King Faisal Specialist Hospital in Riyadh. His half-brother, Crown Prince Abdullah, is named to replace him.

8 August. Hope rises in Saudi Arabia after the new king, Abdullah, pardons four prominent activists who were jailed after criticizing the strict religious environment and the slow pace of democratic reform.

15 September. The Saudi government orders a Jeddah chamber of commerce to allow female voters and candidates.

21 September. Two men are beheaded in Riyadh after being convicted of kidnapping and raping a woman.

17 November. A Saudi high-school chemistry teacher, accused of discussing religion with his students, is sentenced to 750 lashes and forty months in prison for blasphemy following a trial on 12 November.

27 November. To the delight of Saudi women, two females are elected to a chamber of commerce in Jeddah. This is the first occasion when women have won any such post in the country, as they are largely barred from political life.

8 December. Leaders from fifty Muslim countries promise to fight extremist ideology. The leaders say they will reform textbooks, restrict religious edicts and crack down on terror financing.

Saudi Arabia enacts a law that bans state employees from making any statements in public that conflict with official policy.

2006   *12 January.* Thousands of Muslim pilgrims trip over luggage during the hajj, causing a crush in which 363 people are killed.

26 January. Saudi Arabia recalls its Ambassador to Denmark in protest at a series of caricatures of the Prophet Mohammed published in the Danish *Jyllands-Posten* newspaper. Discontent spreads across the Muslim world for weeks, resulting in dozens of deaths.

19 February. Following the publication of the twelve cartoons of the Prophet – highlighting what it described as self-censorship – the *Jyllands-Posten* newspaper prints a full-page apology in a Saudi-owned newspaper.

6 April. Cheese and butter from the Danish company Arla are returned to Saudi Arabian supermarket shelves following a boycott sparked by the country's publication of offensive cartoons.

April. The Saudi Arabian government announces plans to build an electrified fence along its 560-mile border with Iraq.

16 May. Newspapers in Saudi Arabia report that they have received an order from King Abdullah telling editors to stop publishing pictures of women. The king claims that such photographs will make young Saudi men go astray.

18 August. According to the *Financial Times*, Great Britain has agreed to a multi-billion-dollar defence deal to supply seventy-two Eurofighter Typhoon aircraft to Saudi Arabia.

20 October. In an attempt to defuse internal power struggles, King Abdullah gives new powers to his brothers and nephews. In the future, a council of thirty princes will meet to choose the Crown Prince.

2007   *4 February.* A Saudi Arabian judge sentences twenty foreigners to receive lashes and prison terms after convicting them of attending a mixed party where alcohol was served and men and women danced.

17 February. A report published by a US human-rights group reveals the Saudi government detains thousands of prisoners in jail without charge, sentences children to death and oppresses women.

19 February. A Saudi court orders the bodies of four Sri Lankans to be displayed in a public square after being beheaded for armed robbery.

26 February. Four Frenchmen are killed by gunmen on the side of a desert road leading to the holy city of Medina in an area restricted to Muslims only.

February. Ten Saudi intellectuals are arrested for signing a polite petition suggesting it is time for the kingdom to consider a transition to constitutional monarchy.

27 April. In one of the largest sweeps against terror cells in Saudi Arabia, the Interior Ministry says police arrested 172 Islamic militants. The militants had trained abroad as pilots so they could duplicate 9/11 and fly aircraft in attacks on Saudi Arabia's oil fields.

5 May. Prince Abdul-Majid bin Abdul-Aziz, the governor of Mecca, dies, aged sixty-five, after a long illness.

9 May. An Ethiopian woman convicted of killing an Egyptian man over a dispute is beheaded. Khadija Bint Ibrahim Moussa is the second woman to be executed this year.

23 June. A Saudi judge postpones the trial of three members of the religious police for their involvement in the death of a man arrested after being seen with a woman who was not his relative.

9 November. Saudi authorities behead Saudi citizen Khalaf al-Anzi in Riyadh for kidnapping and raping a teenager.

Saudi authorities behead a Pakistani for drug trafficking. This execution brings to 131 the number of people beheaded in the kingdom in 2007.

14 November. A Saudi court sentences a nine-year-old girl who had been gang raped to six months in jail and 200 lashes. The court also bans a lawyer from defending her, confiscating his licence to practise law and summoning him to a disciplinary hearing. (The following month she is pardoned by the Saudi king after the case sparks rare criticism from the United States.)

2008   *21 January.* The newspaper *Al-Watan*
reports that the Interior Ministry issued
a circular to hotels asking them to accept
lone women as long as their information
was sent to a local police station.

14 February. A leading human-rights
group appeals to Saudi Arabia's King
Abdullah to stop the execution of a
woman accused of witchcraft and
performing supernatural acts.

19 May. Teacher Matrook al-Faleh is
arrested at King Saud University in
Riyadh after he publicly criticized
conditions in a prison where two other
human-rights activists are serving jail
terms.

24 May. Saudi authorities behead a local
man convicted of armed robbery and
raping a woman. The execution brings
the number of people beheaded in 2008
to fifty-five.

20 June. Religious police arrest twenty-
one allegedly homosexual men and
confiscate large amounts of alcohol at a
gathering of young men at a rest house in
Qatif.

8 July. A human-rights group says
domestic workers in Saudi Arabia often
suffer abuse that in some cases amounts
to slavery, as well as sexual violence and

lashings for spurious allegations of theft or witchcraft.

30 July. The country's Islamic religious police ban the sale of dogs and cats as pets. They also ban owners from walking their pets in public because men use cats and dogs to make passes at women.

11 September. Sheik Saleh al-Lihedan, Saudi Arabia's top judiciary official, issues a religious decree saying it is permissible to kill the owners of satellite TV networks who broadcast immoral content. He later adjusts his comments, saying owners who broadcast immoral content should be brought to trial and sentenced to death if other penalties do not deter them.

November. A US diplomatic cable says donors in Saudi Arabia and the United Arab Emirates send an estimated $100 million annually to radical Islamic schools in Pakistan that back militancy.

10 December. The European Commission awards the first Chaillot Prize to the Al-Nahda Philanthropic Society for Women, a Saudi charity that helps divorced and underprivileged women.

2009

14 January. Saudi Arabia's most senior cleric is quoted as saying it is permissible for ten-year-old girls to marry. He adds that anyone who thinks ten-year-old girls are too young to marry is doing those girls an injustice.

14 February. King Abdullah dismisses Sheik Saleh al-Lihedan. King Abdullah also appoints Nora al-Fayez as deputy minister of women's education, the first female in the history of Saudi Arabia to hold a ministerial post.

3 March. Khamisa Sawadi, a seventy-five-year-old widow, is sentenced to forty lashes and four months in jail for talking with two young men who are not close relatives.

22 March. A group of Saudi clerics urges the kingdom's new information minister to ban women from appearing on TV.

27 March. King Abdullah appoints his half-brother, Prince Naif, as his second deputy prime minister.

30 April. An eight-year-old girl divorces her middle-aged husband after her father forces her to marry him in exchange for $13,000. Saudi Arabia permits such child marriages.

29 May. A man is beheaded and crucified for slaying an eleven-year-old boy and his father.

6 June. The Saudi film *Menahi* is screened in Riyadh more than thirty years after the government began shutting down cinemas. No women were allowed, only men and children, including girls up to ten.

15 July. Saudi citizen Mazen Abdul-Jawad appears on Lebanon's LBC satellite TV station's *Bold Red Line* programme and shocks Saudis by publicly confessing to sexual exploits. More than 200 Saudi Arabians file legal complaints against Abdul-Jawad, dubbed a 'sex braggart' by the media, and many Saudis say he should be severely punished. Abdul-Jawad is convicted by a Saudi court in October 2009 and sentenced to five years in jail and 1,000 lashes.

9 August. Italian news agencies report that burglars have stolen jewels and cash worth 11 million euros from the hotel room of a Saudi princess in Sardinia, sparking a diplomatic incident.

27 August. A suicide bomber targets the assistant interior minister Prince Mohammed bin Naif and blows himself up just before going into a gathering of well-wishers for the Muslim holy month of Ramadan in Jeddah. His target, Prince Mohammed, is only slightly wounded.

23 September. A new multi-billion-dollar co-ed university opens outside the coastal city of Jeddah. The King Abdullah Science and Technology University, or KAUST, boasts state-of-the-art labs, at the time the world's 14th fastest supercomputer and one of the biggest endowments worldwide.

24 October. Rozanna al-Yami, aged twenty-two, is tried and convicted for her involvement in the *Bold Red Line* programme featuring Abdul-Jawad. She is sentenced to sixty lashes and is thought to be the first female Saudi journalist to be given such a punishment. King Abdullah waived the flogging sentence, the second such pardon in a high-profile case by the monarch in recent years. He ordered al-Yami's case to be referred to a committee in the ministry.

9 November. A Lebanese psychic, Ali Sibat, who made predictions on a satellite TV channel from his home in Beirut, is sentenced to death for practising witchcraft. When he travelled to Medina for a pilgrimage in May 2008, he was arrested and threatened with beheading. The following year a three-judge panel said that there was not enough evidence that Sibat's actions had harmed others. They ordered the case to be retried in a Medina court and recommended that the sentence be commuted and that Sibat be deported.

2010   *19 January*. A thirteen-year-old girl is sentenced to a ninety-lash flogging and two months in prison as punishment for assaulting a teacher who tried to take the girl's mobile phone away from her.

11 February. Religious police launch a nationwide crackdown on shops selling items that are red, as they say the colour alludes to the banned celebration of Valentine's Day.

6 March. The Saudi Civil and Political Rights Association says that Saudi security officers stormed a book stall at the Riyadh International Book Fair and confiscated all work by Abdellah al-Hamid, a well-known reformer and critic of the royal family.

20 April. When a member of Saudi's 'religious police', Ahmed bin Qassin al-Ghamidi, suggests that men and women should be allowed to mingle freely, the head of the powerful religious police has him fired.

10 June. After a Saudi man kisses a woman in a mall, he is arrested, convicted and sentenced to four months in prison and ninety lashes.

22 June. Four women and eleven men are arrested, tried and convicted for mixing at a party. They are sentenced to flogging and prison terms.

15 August. Ghazi al-Gosaibi, a Saudi statesman and poet, dies from colon cancer after a long illness. Al-Gosaibi was close to the ruling family, although his writings were banned in the kingdom for most of his life. The Saudi Culture Ministry lifted the ban on his writings the month before his death, citing his contribution to the nation.

26 August. T. Ariyawathi, a housemaid from Sri Lanka working in Saudi Arabia, is admitted to hospital for surgery to remove twenty-four nails embedded in her body. Her Saudi employer hammered the nails into her as punishment.

17 November. King Abdullah steps down as head of the country's National Guard. His son assumes the position.

20 November. A young woman in her twenties defies the kingdom's driving ban and accidentally overturns her car. She dies, along with three female friends who were passengers.

22 November. King Abdullah visits New York for medical treatment and temporarily hands control to Crown Prince Sultan, his half-brother.

23 November. Saudi media announces that a Saudi woman accused of torturing her Indonesian maid has been sent to jail, while the maid, Sumiati Binti Salan Mustapa, is receiving hospital treatment for burns and broken bones.

An estimated four million Saudi women over the age of twenty are unmarried in a country of 24.6 million. It is reported that some male guardians forcibly keep women single, a practice known as *adhl*. The guardians have the right to keep the salaries of the women for themselves. Saudi feminist Wajeha al-Huwaider describes male guardianship as 'a form of slavery'.

2011   *16 January.* A group of Saudi activists launches 'My Country', a campaign to push the kingdom to allow women to run in municipal elections scheduled for spring 2011.

24 January. New York-based Human Rights Watch says in its World Report 2011 that Saudi Arabia's government is harassing and jailing activists, often without trial, for speaking out in favour of expanding religious tolerance and that new restrictions on electronic communication in the kingdom are severe.

9 February. Ten moderate Saudi scholars ask the king for recognition of their Uma Islamic Party, the kingdom's first political party.

15 February. The Education Ministry says the kingdom plans to remove books that encourage terrorism or defame religion from school libraries.

24 February. Influential intellectuals say in a statement that Arab rulers should derive a lesson from the uprisings in Tunisia, Egypt and Libya, and listen to the voice of disenchanted young people.

5 March. Saudi Arabia's Interior Ministry says demonstrations won't be tolerated and its security forces will act against anyone taking part in them.

11 March. Hundreds of police are deployed in the capital to prevent protests calling for democratic reforms inspired by the wave of unrest sweeping the Arab world.

18 March. King Abdullah promises Saudi citizens a multi-billion-dollar package of reforms, wage rises, cash, loans and apartments in what appears to be the Arab world's most expensive attempt to appease residents inspired by the unrest that has swept two regional leaders from power.

22 May. Saudi authorities rearrest activist Manal al-Sharif, who defied a ban on female drivers. She had been detained for several hours by the country's religious police and released after she'd signed a pledge agreeing not to drive. Saudi Arabia is the only country in the world that bans women, both Saudi and foreign, from driving.

18 June. Ruyati binti Satubi, an Indonesian grandmother, is beheaded for killing an allegedly abusive Saudi employer.

28 June. Saudi police detain one woman for driving in Jeddah. Four other women accused of driving are later detained in the city.

25 September. King Abdullah announces that the nation's women will gain the right to vote and run as candidates in local elections to be held in 2015 in a major advance for the rights of women.

27 September. Saudi female Shaima Jastaina is sentenced to be lashed ten times for defying the kingdom's prohibition on driving. King Abdullah quickly overturns the court ruling.

29 September. Saudi Arabian men cast ballots in local council elections, the second-ever nationwide vote. Women are not allowed to vote. The councils are one of the few elected bodies in the country, but have no real power, mandated to offer advice to provincial authorities.

Manssor Arbabsiar, a US citizen holding an Iranian passport, is arrested when he arrives at New York's Kennedy International Airport. Mexico worked closely with US authorities to help foil an alleged $1.5 million plot to kill the Saudi Arabian Ambassador to Washington. On 11 October, Arbabsiar is charged in the US District Court in New York with conspiring to kill Saudi diplomat Adel al-Jubeir.

22 October. Saudi Crown Prince Sultan bin Abdul Aziz, heir to the Saudi throne, dies in the United States. He had been receiving treatment for colon cancer, first diagnosed in 2009.

27 October. Saudi Arabia's powerful interior minister, Prince Naif bin Abdul Aziz, is named the new heir to the throne in a royal decree read out on Saudi state television.

30 November. Amnesty International publishes a new report accusing Saudi Arabia of conducting a campaign of repression against protesters and reformists since the Arab Spring erupted.

6 December. Saudi Arabia sentences an Australian man to 500 lashes and a year in jail after being found guilty of blasphemy. Mansor Almaribe was detained in Medina on 14 November while making the hajj pilgrimage and accused of insulting companions of the Prophet Mohammed.

10 December. Saudi Arabia's *Okaz* newspaper reports that a man convicted of raping his daughter has been sentenced to receive 2,080 lashes over the course of a thirteen-year prison term. A court in Mecca found the man guilty of raping his teenage daughter for seven years while under the influence of drugs.

12 December. Saudi authorities execute a woman convicted of practising magic and sorcery. Court records state that she had tricked people into thinking she could treat illnesses, charging them $800 per session.

15 December. Police raid a private prayer gathering, arresting thirty-five Ethiopian

Christians, twenty-nine of them women. They later face deportation for 'illicit mingling'.

Seventy-six death row inmates are executed in Saudi Arabia in 2011.

Indonesian maid Satinah Binti Jumad Ahmad is sentenced to death for murdering her employer's wife in 2007 and stealing money. In 2014, the Indonesian government agree to pay $1.8 million to free Satinah.

2012   *2 January.* Saudi Arabia announces that on 5 December it will begin enforcing a law that allows female workers only in women's lingerie and apparel stores.

12 February. Malaysian authorities deport Hamza Kashgari, a young Saudi journalist wanted in his home country over a Twitter post about the Prophet Mohammed, defying pleas from human-rights groups who say he faces execution. His tweet read: 'I have loved things about you and I have hated things about you and there is a lot I don't understand about you.'

February. A royal order stipulates that women who drive should not be prosecuted by the courts.

22 March. Saudi Arabia media reports say single men in Riyadh will be able to visit shopping malls during peak hours after restrictions aimed at stopping harassment of women are eased.

4 April. A Saudi official reiterates that Saudi Arabia will be fielding only male athletes at the London Olympics. However, Prince Nawaf bin Faisal announces that Saudi women taking part on their own are free to do so but the kingdom's Olympic authority would 'only help in ensuring that their participation does not violate the Islamic sharia law'.

A man found guilty of shooting dead a fellow Saudi is beheaded. His execution in Riyadh brings the total number of beheadings to seventeen for 2012.

23 May. An outspoken and brave Saudi woman defies orders by the notorious religious police to leave a mall because she is wearing nail polish and records the interaction on her camera. Her video goes viral, attracting more than a million hits in just five days.

16 June. Saudi Crown Prince Naif bin Abdul-Aziz, a half-brother of King Abdullah, dies. Naif is the second Crown Prince to die under King Abdullah's rule.

18 June. Saudi Arabia's defence minister, Prince Salman bin Abdul-Aziz, a half-brother to the king, is named the country's new Crown Prince.

24 June. In Saudi Arabia, a man dies from severe pneumonia complicated by renal failure. He had arrived at a Jihad hospital eleven days earlier with symptoms similar to a severe case of influenza or SARS. In September, an Egyptian virologist says it was caused by a new coronavirus. Months later the illness is named MERS (Middle Eastern respiratory syndrome).

June. Blogger Raif Badawi is jailed for ridiculing Islamic religious figures.

20 July. Saudi authorities warn non-Muslim expatriates against eating, drinking or smoking in public during Ramadan, or face expulsion.

30 July. Saudi Arabia implements a ban on smoking in government offices and most public places, including restaurants, coffee shops, supermarkets and shopping malls.

2013   *9 January*. Saudi authorities behead a Sri Lankan domestic worker for killing a Saudi baby in her care. Rizana Nafeek was only seventeen at the time of the baby's death and proclaimed her innocence, denying strangling the four-month-old boy. Many agencies and individuals worldwide pleaded with the boy's family, and with the Saudi government, to pardon the girl.

11 January. King Abdullah issues two royal decrees granting women thirty seats on the Shura Council. The council has 150 members. Although the council reviews laws and questions ministers, it does not have legislative powers.

15 January. Dozens of conservative clerics picket the royal court to condemn the recent appointment of thirty women to the 150-member Shura Council.

1 April. A Saudi newspaper reports that the kingdom's religious police are now allowing women to ride motorbikes and bicycles, but only in restricted recreational areas. They also have to be accompanied by a male relative and be dressed in the full Islamic abaaya.

16 May. Riyadh vegetable seller Muhammad Harissi sets himself on fire when police confiscate his goods after he is found to be standing in an unauthorized area. He died the next day.

29 July. Raif Badawi, editor of the Free Saudi Liberals website, is sentenced to seven years in prison and 600 lashes for founding an internet forum that violates Islamic values and propagates liberal thought. Badawi has been held since June 2012 on charges of cyber-crime and disobeying his father.

20 September. US prosecutors drop charges against Meshael Alayban, a Saudi princess accused of enslaving a Kenyan woman as a housemaid, forcing her to work in abusive conditions and withholding her passport. Lawyers for the Saudi royal accused the thirty-year-old Kenyan, who has not been named, of lying in an attempt to obtain a visa to stay in the USA.

8 October. A Saudi court sentences a well-known cleric convicted of raping his five-year-old daughter and torturing her to death to eight years in prison and 800 lashes. The court also orders the cleric to pay his ex-wife, the girl's mother, one million riyals ($270,000) in 'blood money'. A second wife, accused of taking part in the crime, is sentenced to ten months in prison and 150 lashes.

18 October. Angry by the failure of the international community to end the war in Syria and act on other Middle East issues, Saudi Arabia says it will not take up its seat on the UN Security Council.

22 October. A source says that Saudi Arabia's intelligence chief revealed that the kingdom will make a 'major shift' in relations with the United States in protest at its perceived inaction over the Syria war and its overtures to Iran.

24 October. Saudi women are warned that the government will take measures against activists who go ahead with a planned campaign to defy a ban on women drivers in the kingdom.

26 October. Saudi activists say more than sixty women claimed to have answered their call to get behind the wheel in a rare show of defiance against a ban on female driving. At least sixteen Saudi women received fines for defying the ban.

27 October. Saudi police detain Tariq al-Mubarak, a columnist who supported ending Saudi Arabia's ban on women driving.

3 November. A Kuwaiti newspaper reports that a Kuwaiti woman has been arrested in Saudi Arabia for trying to drive her father to hospital.

12 December. Saudi Arabia's Grand Mufti, the highest religious authority in the birthplace of Islam, condemns suicide bombings as grave crimes, reiterating his stance in unusually strong language in the Saudi-owned *Al Hayat* newspaper.

20 December. Saudi Arabia beheads a drug trafficker. So far in 2013, seventy-seven people have been executed, according to an AFP count.

22 December. Saudi Arabia's official news agency says King Abdullah has appointed his son, Prince Mishaal, as the new governor of Mecca.

2014   *20 February.* Rights groups criticize an agreement between Indonesia and Saudi Arabia aimed at giving Indonesian maids more protection in the kingdom, with one saying 'justice is still far away'.

A new anti-terrorism law is introduced which critics claim will further stifle peaceful dissent in the kingdom.

16 March. The local *Okaz* daily reports that organizers at the Riyadh International Book Fair have confiscated 'more than 10,000 copies of 420 books' during the exhibition, which began on 4 March. Organizers had announced ahead of the event that any book deemed 'against Islam' or 'undermining security' in the kingdom would be confiscated.

The Saudi government designates Islamic groups as terror organizations. The government bans any support or funding for these groups, which are the Islamic

State (ISIS), the Muslim Brotherhood and the al-Nusra Front.

8 April. Saudi Arabia's Shura Council recommends that a long-standing ban on sports in girls' state schools, which was relaxed in private schools in 2013, be ended altogether.

September. Saudi Arabia (along with other Arab states) joins with the United States in air strikes against the Islamic State's sanctuaries in Syria.

2015   *23 January.* King Abdullah bin al-Sa'ud dies. He was the sixth king to rule. King Salman ascends the throne as the seventh king of Saudi Arabia.

March. Saudi Arabia attacks Houthi rebels in neighbouring Yemen. Other Arab states join them in air strikes.

April. King Salman donates more than $30 billion to his people.

King Salman creates a potential crisis in the kingdom when he breaks with King Abdullah's plan to move away from the Sudairi clan (King Abdullah had appointed a half-brother – and youngest son of the first king – as Crown Prince). King Salman quickly reverses these appointments, pushing out the Crown Prince and moving to the third generation (the grandsons of the first

king), appointing Interior Minister
Mohammed bin Naif as the new Crown
Prince. The king then appoints his
own son, Muhammad bin Salman, as
Deputy Crown Prince. With this
unexpected move, King Salman moves
the crown closer to the next generation
of al-Sa'ud and specifically to the
Sudairis, as both his nephew and son
are descendants of the Sudairi side
of the family.

May. Two suicide bomb attacks on
Shi'ite mosques in the Eastern Province
kill at least twenty-five people, claimed
by the Saudi branch of Islamic Group, a
Sunni extremist group.

Saudi Arabia's King Salman announces
that he will not attend the summit
meeting called by President Obama. The
deputy Crown Prince, Muhammad bin
Salman, will represent Saudi Arabia
instead. This decision signals a huge shift
in the relationship between the United
States and Saudi Arabia.

King Salman and other leaders in the
Gulf Cooperation Council countries go
public with their displeasure at President
Obama's Middle East policies.

The government of Saudi Arabia
advertises job openings for executioners

for beheadings and limb amputations in public squares in the country.

The coalition led by Saudi Arabia resumes air strikes against the Houthi rebels in Yemen shortly after the five-day ceasefire ends. This renewed bombing threatens the ongoing relief efforts in Yemen.

Eighty people in Yemen are killed in one day from air strikes by the Saudi-led coalition against Houthi rebels.

The World Health Organization reports that approximately 2,000 Yemenis have died in the conflict since March. Millions of civilians are in urgent need of medical care for war-related injuries or other medical issues.

June. The Saudi royal family announces that it is building a theme park attraction in the old capital of Diriyah. The park will feature museums and restaurants.

The Saudi Arabian military coalition fighting against the Houthi rebels in Yemen kills more than fifty people. Reports claim that most of the dead are civilians.

The conflict with Yemen escalates. Houthi rebels fire a Scud missile into Saudi Arabia. Saudi Arabia shoots it down.

Despite the Saudi-led bombing campaign, Houthi rebels have taken the capital city of Yemen's Jawf Province, further consolidating their control over the country.

Saudi Arabia's Supreme Court upholds the verdict against Raif Badawi, who was previously found guilty of insulting Islam. Its Foreign Ministry rejects all criticism of the conviction and sentence of ten years and 1,000 lashes for the liberal blogger. Badawi is lauded worldwide for his bravery in the face of government harassment, arrest, imprisonment and torture by lashing.

July. Prince Saud al-Faisal bin Faisal bin Abdul Aziz al-Sa'ud dies at age seventy-five. The prince served as Saudi Arabia's foreign minister for four decades. He was a highly educated and sophisticated man who was respected worldwide.

Reports say that 3,000 Yemenis have died in the past three months of fighting.

Prince al-Waleed bin Talal of Saudi Arabia says he will donate his entire $32 billion fortune to help eradicate disease, empower women and for relief for disasters.

September. Hundreds of pilgrims die in a stampede near Mecca during the annual hajj pilgrimage.

November. Women run for office in municipal elections for the first time in Saudi Arabian history. Twenty women are elected to office.

2016   *January.* Shia cleric Nimr al-Nimr is executed by the Saudi government. There are Shia protests in Iran, Iraq and Lebanon. Saudi Arabia breaks off diplomatic relations with Iran.

April. The Egyptian government causes unrest in their country when they announce they are giving two Red Sea islands to Saudi Arabia.

The Saudi government approves a plan for reforms to diversify the economy away from oil.

June. The United Nations releases a report that accuses the Saudi-led coalition fighting Houthi rebels in Yemen of killing and injuring hundreds of children.

2017   *February.* For the first time, women are named as chief executives on the Saudi Stock Exchange and also at a major bank in the kingdom.

June. Tensions grow in the Middle East when Saudi Arabia leads an air, land and sea blockade by Arab countries against Qatar. This action is in an attempt to force Qatar to distance itself from Iran.

Saudi King Salman bin Abdul Aziz has replaced his nephew Mohammed bin Naif as Crown Prince and installed his own son, Prince Muhammad bin Salman, in the position, setting him up to be the next in line to the throne.

September. The ban on women driving in Saudi Arabia is formally lifted. Saudi women are set to start driving in June 2018.

August–October. Saudi Arabia increases the bombing of Houthi rebel-held territory in Yemen. In response, Houthi rebels carry out rocket attacks into Saudi Arabia.

November. The heir to the Saudi throne, Crown Prince Muhammad bin Salman, conducts a surprising purge of the kingdom's political and business leadership, saying that the move is to end corruption in the kingdom.

2018   *March.* With the war in Yemen ongoing, a missile is launched by Yemen's Houthi rebels over Riyadh. The missile is intercepted, although fragments from the missile kill one man.

April. The ban on public cinema in Saudi Arabia is lifted.

Saudi Arabian Crown Prince Muhammad bin Salman visits the United

States for three weeks, courting business tycoons and Hollywood moguls, striking multi-million-dollar business deals in defence and entertainment. After his trip to the United States, the Crown Prince makes similar visits to France, the United Kingdom and Egypt.

June. Women in Saudi Arabia are set to drive automobiles for the first time in Saudi history, however, there are age restrictions and time limits on when women can drive.

After the government announcement that women in Saudi Arabia will be able to drive, the Saudi authorities suddenly arrest more than a dozen prominent women's rights activists. The women are accused of making contacts with foreign enemies of the kingdom. The women are held without trial and it is reported by their families that they are beaten and tortured during detention.

24 June. Driving licences are issued to women for the first time in Saudi history. Images of delighted Saudi female drivers are flashed across the world through social media.

28 September. Self-exiled Saudi journalist Jamal Khashoggi, who writes critical opinion pieces about King Salman and his son Crown Prince Mohammad for the *Washington Post*, goes to the Saudi Consulate in Istanbul to request a permission document to marry Turkish fiancée Hatice Cengiz. The Consulate staff advises him to return for the documents.

2 October. Khashoggi returns to the Saudi Consulate in Istanbul with his fiancée, who waits outside the Consulate. Khashoggi fails to return. The Consulate staff claim that he left through a back entrance.

7 October. Turkish government officials report that Khashoggi was murdered inside the Consulate, but the Saudi officials deny the allegation. There is an international outcry over the disappearance and rumoured murder of Khashoggi.

19 October. A Saudi official is interviewed by ABC News regarding the Khashoggi mystery. The official admits that Khashoggi is dead after being accidentally killed when he was placed in a chokehold while in the Saudi Consulate in Istanbul.

4 December. The CIA Direction (Haspel) briefs senior US senators on the

Khashoggi murder. After the briefing, several senators report that it was Saudi Crown Prince Mohammad bin Salman who ordered the brutal murder.

2019   *January*. The UN formally investigates the execution of Khashoggi but most are disappointed, saying that the investigation falls short of expectations.

Qatar and Saudi Arabia remain locked in a political dispute without any end in sight.

Saudi teenager Rahaf Mohammed Al-Qunun escapes from Saudi Arabia through Thailand to Canada, saying that her family would kill her if she were returned.

31 January. The Saudi Arabian government ends the purge of wealthy and/or royal citizens who had been kept confined in the Riyadh Ritz-Carlton. Most are freed when they hand over the bulk of their wealth, but some refuse and are going to be put on trial.

February. The Saudi Arabian government replaces the Crown Prince's brother who was serving as Ambassador to Washington and in his place names a female ambassador, Princess Reema bin Bandar bin Sultan bin al-Saud. Princess Reema is the daughter of former

Ambassador to the United States,
Prince Bandar bin Sultan bin Abdul Aziz
bin al-Saud.

A Saudi-led assault in Yemen is blocked
by land mines which mainly kills Yemen
civilians.

The US House of Representatives votes
to stop aid for Saudi Arabia's war in
Yemen.

2 March. Saudi Arabia announces that
it is moving towards the trials of
women's rights activists in the
kingdom. If convicted, some of the
charges bring a death sentence.

7 March. Members of the UN Human
Rights Council rebukes Saudi Arabia for
human rights abuses.

Appendix Three

Syria Timeline (2011–18)

2011   *March*. Protesters in Deraa, Syria,
demand the release of political prisoners.
Syrian President Bashir Assad's security
forces shoot and kill the protesters. The
protest prompts violent demonstrations
that spread across the entire country.

President Assad broadcasts peacemaking
measures, freeing dozens of political
prisoners, discharging government and
finally lifting a forty-eight-year-old state
of emergency.

May. Ongoing anti-regime protests
continue in Homs, Deraa, Banyas and
some suburbs of Damascus. Syrian tanks
try to crush protesters. The United States
and the European Union tighten
sanctions.

President Assad announces amnesty for
political prisoners.

July. After mass demonstrations in the province of Hama, President Assad fires the governor. When protests continue, Syrian troops go in to restore order and many Syrian civilians are killed.

October. The Syrian National Council announces that it has formed a communal group of internal and exiled opposition activists to seek peace.

November. The Arab League suspends Syria and imposes sanctions.

The uprising against the Assad government is now recognized as a full-scale civil war.

December. Bombs outside security buildings in Damascus kill forty-four. These blasts are the first of many to come in the capital of Syria.

2012   *February.* The Syrian government increases the bombardment of Homs.

March. The United Nations Security Council endorses a non-binding peace agreement drafted by the UN envoy Kofi Annan.

May. Australia, France, the United Kingdom, Italy, Germany, Canada and Spain all expel senior Syrian diplomats in protest after more than a hundred civilians are killed in Houla, near Homs.

July. The Free Syria Army kills three security chiefs in Damascus. They also seize the city of Aleppo.

August. Syrian Prime Minister Riad Hijab defects.

President Obama warns Syria that if they use chemical weapons the United States will consider intervention in the ongoing war.

October. There is a huge fire in Aleppo that destroys that city's historical market.

December. The United Kingdom, the United States, France, Turkey and the Gulf States formally recognize the opposition National Coalition as legitimate representatives of the Syrian people.

2013   *January.* Syria claims that Israeli jets have attacked a military research centre near Damascus.

February. International donors pledge $1.5 billion (£950 million) to help Syrian civilians affected by the conflict.

March. After Syrian rebels seize control of Raqqa, the city is bombed by Syrian government military planes.

The Syrian government denies all allegations of chemical weapons use.

June. The Syrian government, joined by the Lebanese Hezbollah forces, recaptures the strategically important city of Qusair, located between Homs and the Lebanese border.

October. Syrian President Assad surprises the world when he agrees for international inspectors to start destroying Syria's chemical weapons as earlier agreed between the United States and Russia.

December. Great Britain and the United States break off 'non-lethal' support for Syrian rebels in northern Syria after it is learned that Islamist rebels have seized bases of the Western-backed Free Syrian Army.

2014   *January/February*. When Syrian authorities refuse to discuss the option of a transitional government, the United Nations peace talks in Geneva collapse.

March. The Syrian Government Army and Hezbollah forces recapture Yabroud, which is the last rebel stronghold near the Lebanese border.

May. Hundreds of rebels fighting the Syrian government/military are removed from their last stronghold in the city of Homs. This disappointing withdrawal ends three years of resistance in the city.

June. The United Nations announces that all of Syria's chemical weapons have been destroyed or removed.

The Islamic State of Iraq and Syria militants announce that they have formed a 'caliphate' that stretches from the Syrian city of Aleppo to the eastern Iraqi province of Diyala.

August. After the Islamic State captures the Tabqa airbase, which is near the northern city of Raqqa, ISIS now controls all of Raqqa province.

September. Five Arab countries join the United States in launching air strikes against ISIS, located near Raqqa and Aleppo.

2015   *January.* After a four-month battle, Kurdish fighters defeat the Islamic State, pushing them from the city of Kobane, which is located on the Turkish border.

May. Fighters of the Islamic State seize the ancient city of Palmyra in central Syria and proclaim they will destroy the pre-Islamic World Heritage site.

June. Kurdish fighters intensify the battle against Islamic State in a region between the Turkish border and Raqqa.

September. Russia bombs the Syrian rebels who are fighting against the Assad regime. The Russian government claims to be attacking Islamic State, but the opposition groups fighting the government declare this to be inaccurate.

October. The United States deploys a small force of Special Operations to the Kurdish-controlled territory in northern Syria in order to assist Kurdish forces who are fighting ISIS in that region.

December. Rebels fighting Assad evacuate the city of Homs. For the first time in four years, the Syrian government resumes control of the besieged city.

2016   *February.* A temporary ceasefire between the Assad government and the revolutionary rebels is called so that relief organizations can assist beleaguered Syrian civilians.

March. The Islamic State and the Assad government forces are in a battle over the city of Palmyra. Government forces, with the assistance of the Russians, win the battle and resume command (in December the Islamic State will retake the city).

Russia begins withdrawing forces from Syria, and the Syrian government announces to Western media that the Russian military campaign in their country will be ending.

August. Turkey enters the fray when its government sends forces into Syria to assist rebel groups battling Islamic State militants, as well as some Kurdish-led rebels.

September. Innocent Syrian civilians, including children, are killed during airstrikes in the country. Russia and the United States accuse each other of violating the ceasefire which came into effect three days prior to the murderous airstrikes.

The United States lead a coalition strike near the Deir Ezzor Airport, but there are sixty-two Syrian soldiers killed in the 'friendly fire' incident.

The UN halts air operations in Syria after a Syrian Arab Red Crescent aid convoy is bombed.

The ancient city of Aleppo is targeted, with 200 airstrikes from the Assad regime.

December. Syrian government troops, assisted by Russia and Iran, recapture the city of Aleppo. With the fall of Aleppo, the largest city in Syria, the rebels lose their last major city after four years of control.

2017   *January.* A ceasefire between non-Islamic rebels fighting Assad's forces and the government is enforced by Turkey, Iran and Russia.

April. Syrian civilians are killed in a suspected chemical attack in the rebel-controlled village of Khan Sheikhoun. The Russians and the Syrians make an attempt to blame the rebels for the chemical attack, but activists say no, it was the Syrian government. In response to the alleged chemical attack, the United States bombs a Syrian government airbase (where warplanes are based) with sixty-nine Tomahawk cruise missiles.

May. The United States arms the YPG Kurdish Popular Protection Units, who fight among the Syrian Democratic Forces which are fighting the Assad government.

June. The United States shoots down a Syrian fighter jet after the pilot bombs the Syrian Democratic Forces fighting against the Assad regime.

July. Putin and Trump reach an agreement to curb the violence in south-west Syria.

October. The Islamic State Group loses Raqqa, the village serving as their capital in Syria.

The UN and international chemical weapons inspectors find that the Assad regime is responsible for the April Sarin attack that killed more than eighty people. Despite the evidence, Syria denies the attack and denies having chemical weapons.

December. Putin visits Syria and announces that the mission is accomplished regarding their battle against the Islamic State.

2018   *January.* The government of Turkey attacks northern Syria in an effort to eject Kurdish rebels that control the area.

February. The Syrian government launches a massive military assault on Eastern Ghouta, which is the last rebel-held enclave near to Damascus.

The UN Security Council approves a thirty-day ceasefire in Syria, but the ceasefire is disorganized and does not really help the civilians in that country.

Within a few minutes of the 'humanitarian pause' ordered by Putin, Syrian activists report being shelled and attacked by artillery fire by Assad forces.

March. UNICEF announces that in only the first two months of 2018, 342 children have been killed and 803 injured.

April. Eastern Ghouta claims to have been struck by chemical attacks in

Douma. The United States, France and Britain quickly carry out retaliatory strikes on Syrian government targets.

It is reported that helicopters have dropped barrel bombs filled with toxic gas on a rebel-held town in Eastern Ghouta. WHO announces that as many as 500 civilians are victims of the brutal attack.

France, the United Kingdom and the United States launch punishing airstrikes against the Syrian government for the attack on Eastern Ghouta.

1 May. The US government announces that they will lead operations to liberate the final ISIS strongholds in Syria.

3 May. The United States government freezes all funding for the White Helmets, the volunteer group who work tirelessly to save civilian lives.

16 May. The Syrian Arab Army announces that rebel territory in the North (Homs and South Hama) is under their control.

21 May. Syrian government forces regain full territorial control over the countryside and suburbs of Damascus after the ISIL fighters and their families flee the area.

1 June. The US-led coalition conducts air raids that leave sixteen Syrian civilians dead, including women and children.

22 June. The Syrian government launches an offensive in the southern province of Daraa.

6 July. The Syrian Army is backed by Russian forces who help them to capture the Nasib Border Crossing which is on the border of Jordan.

31 July. The Royal Jordanian Army enters the fray when they attack Islamic State militants who appear on their border.

July. Syrian government forces recapture most of the south of the country up to the borders with Jordan.

1 August. A new coalition is announced by the Northern Syrian FSA factions. This comes after rebel factions in Southern Syria have collapsed.

6 August. The Syrian government forces launch an offensive against the Islamic State of Iraq.

September–December. During this three-month period, the Kurdish-led SDF forces launch a highly successful offensive that reduces the Islamic State previously held territory to a small enclave near the Iraqi border.

2019   *January*. US President Trump announces plans to withdraw US troops from Syria, but there is an outcry from American allies.

President Trump warns Turkey not to attack the US Kurdish allies which are headquartered in Northern Syria.

March. Syrian Civil War enters ninth year of conflict with no end in sight as helpless civilians continue to suffer and die.

Appendix Four

Prophet Mohammed

The historian Bernard Lewis has written about the magnitude of Prophet Mohammed's accomplishments. 'He had achieved a great deal. To the pagan peoples of western Arabia, he had brought a new religion, which, with its monotheism and its ethical doctrines, stood on an incomparably higher level than the paganism it replaced and in the following centuries was to become the guide for many millions of believers. But he had done more than that: he had established a community and a well-organized armed state, the power and prestige of which made it a dominant factor in Arabia.'

570   Prophet Mohammed is born in Mecca, Saudi Arabia. His father had died prior to his birth. His full name is Abu al-Qasim Mohammed bin Abd Allah bin Abd al-Muttalib bin Hashim bin Abd Manaf bin Qusai bin Kilab, meaning to praise or to glorify.

575	His mother dies and his paternal grandfather and uncle raise him.
595	He marries an older woman, who is a wealthy widow. Her name is Kadijah. They have six children. He has another son with a later wife, Maria al-Qibtiyya. All of the Prophet's children, other than a daughter, Fatimah, die before him. None of his sons ever reaches adulthood. His lineage continues through his daughter, Fatimah.
610	Prophet Mohammed receives the first revelation from God during the month of Ramadan.
613	Prophet Mohammed takes his message to the public. These messages would later become the Koran, Islam's sacred scripture.
622	Prophet Mohammed emigrates with his followers from Mecca to Medina.
624–627	The time of the three major battles with the Meccans, including the Battle of Badr, which is a victory. There is then the Battle of Uhud, which ends in defeat. Finally in 627, there is the Battle of the Trench, which is a victory.
629	Prophet Mohammed orders the first raid into Christian lands at Muta. This effort results in defeat.

630	Prophet Mohammed conquers Mecca.
631	Prophet Mohammed consolidates most of the Arabia lands under Islam.
632	Prophet Mohammed returns to Mecca to perform a pilgrimage.
	Prophet Mohammed dies in Medina after a brief illness. He is buried in the Mosque of Medina.

Appendix Five

The Necessary Steps to Perform the Islamic Daily Prayers

Muslims bow down to Allah in scheduled prayers five times a day. A Muslim should pray with a clean body after performing the correct ablutions. A prayer rug is not required, but most Muslims use one. Most Muslims actually carry a prayer rug with them when they travel.

Proper Procedure for Islamic Daily Prayers

After cleansing yourself of dirt and impurities, perform the follow steps:

> Stand, raise your hands up in the air and say *Allah Akbar* (God is most great).
> While still standing, fold your hands over the chest and recite the first chapter of the Koran. It is best to recite in the Arabic language, if possible.

Raise your hands up again and say *Allah Akbar* once more. Bow, then recite three times, 'Glory be to my Lord Almighty'.

Rise to a standing position while reciting, 'God hears those who call upon Him; Our Lord, praise be to You.'

Raise your hands up, saying *Allah Akbar* once more. Prostrate yourself on the ground, reciting three times, 'Glory be to my Lord, the Most High.'

Rise to a sitting position and recite *Allah Akbar*. Prostrate yourself again in the same manner.

Rise to a standing position and say *Allah Akbar*. This concludes one unit of prayer.

Repeat the exact same steps for the second unit of prayer.

After two complete units of prayer, remain sitting after the prostration and recite the first part of the Tashahhud in Arabic.

If the prayer is to be longer than these two units, you now stand up and begin again to complete the prayer, sitting again after all units have been completed.

Recite the second part of the Tashahhud in Arabic.

Turn to the right and say *'Assalamu alaikum wa rahmatullah'* (Peace be upon you and God's blessings).

Turn to the left and repeat the greeting.

This concludes the formal prayer.

All About Jean Sasson

Jean Sasson is a voracious reader. Almost as soon as she knew the alphabet she read everything she could – even at family meals her mind was in a book.

Jean grew up in a small town in Alabama. By the beginning of her teens she had read every book in the school library. At fourteen she started her book collection when she bought *The Rise and Fall of the Third Reich* by William Shirer – an unusual choice for a young girl from the Deep South. She wanted a good read and she wanted value for money, so she searched the shop and bought the book with the most pages.

At school Mrs Sam Jackson, her beloved literature teacher, soon noticed Jean's preoccupation and took it upon herself to make weekly trips to a nearby college library to exchange a selection of books to satisfy Jean's reading needs.

And today? When not absorbed in writing or the business of being a celebrated author, she reads and reads, maybe a book a day – literary success has enabled her to buy many books, no longer selected by the number of pages.

Her literary tastes are widely varied and she has a long list of favourites. Heading that list is Sir Winston

Churchill, a prolific writer and the leader of Britain in the dark years of the Second World War. Other historic figures, such as Napoleon Bonaparte and T. E. Lawrence ('Lawrence of Arabia') satisfy her two literary loves – history and travel.

The works of Gertrude Bell, Freya Stark and Sir Richard Burton opened her mind's eye to the fascinations and mysteries of the Middle East ... and those first musings led to her writing success.

No longer content to simply read about this magical part of the world, Jean, armed with hospital administrative skills in addition to her literary thirst, sought and found the ideal opportunity to gain first-hand experience of a closed and mysterious land, the Kingdom of Saudi Arabia.

In 1978, she was selected to work at the most prestigious royal hospital in the Middle East, the King Faisal Specialist Hospital and Research Centre in the Saudi capital, Riyadh. There, her talents blossomed. She became the administrative coordinator of medical affairs and personal assistant to the hospital medical and executive director, Dr Nizar Feteih. Through him she was introduced to various Saudi royals, including King Khalid and his Crown Prince Fahd, who succeeded as king on Khalid's death in 1982. In 1983, a close friendship between Jean and another royal, Princess Sultana, was forged and years later, based on that friendship, Jean was able to write her widely acclaimed *Princess Trilogy*.

Jean worked for four years at the King Faisal Hospital and during that time met the man she was to marry, Peter Sasson, an international man who came from an unusual background. Peter Sasson was a British citizen born in Egypt to a British/Italian father and Yugoslav mother. Although the couple later divorced, they remained devoted friends until Peter's death in 2014.

Jean lived in Saudi Arabia for twelve years. During that time, she dedicated herself to activities that would form the bedrock of her career as a writer when she returned to America. She met and made friends with Arab women from the Middle East before leaving Riyadh in 1992.

She was a freelance writer in war-torn Lebanon and in Kuwait before and after the First Gulf War. After living and travelling in the Middle East for so many years, she felt a special affection for the people of the region. After Saddam Hussein's army invaded the country of Kuwait, Jean became concerned about the fate of the innocent Kuwaitis who were victims of the invaders. Her concern drove her to contact the Kuwaiti Ambassador to the United States, Sheik Saud Nasir al-Sabah, requesting his advice on travelling to areas housing Kuwaiti refugees.

Armed with a letter of introduction from the Kuwaiti Ambassador, Jean returned to Riyadh, Saudi Arabia, where she conducted interviews with Kuwaitis. While in Riyadh, Kuwait's Minister of Information invited her to fly to the Saudi mountain village Taif, where the Kuwaiti royals had formed a government-in-exile. There, she interviewed the Emir and the Crown Prince of Kuwait, among other high-ranking officials of that country.

After leaving Saudi Arabia, Jean travelled to Cairo, Egypt, and then to London, meeting many dozens of Kuwaiti citizens living in exile. Jean used the invaluable material she gathered about Kuwaitis on the day of the Iraqi invasion to write her bestselling book, *The Rape of Kuwait*.

The book sold over a million copies in one month, proving to the world that ordinary people truly cared about the small country and its people. In fact, Jean was the first and only author to write about the innocent Kuwaitis who were caught in the cruel grip of the Iraqi invasion.

Her devotion to the cause won her an invitation to return there on a government-sponsored 'Freedom Flight'. Staying a month in ravaged Kuwait, she joined in the joyful celebrations of their hard-won freedom, even as she mourned with those who had lost loved ones. Never forgetting what she had seen, over the years she continued her writings and concern for those who were still missing, lost to the Iraqi prison system, despite the many efforts made by the royals, as well as ordinary citizens, to gain their freedom.

Her affection for the people of the Middle East continued, taking her to unusual stories that other writers and journalists missed. In 1998, she requested an invitation from Saddam Hussein to visit Iraq. Although she was the author of the book that had greatly displeased him (*The Rape of Kuwait*), she received a personal invite from the Iraqi dictator. Travelling to Iraq alone and without protection, she saw for herself the privations being suffered by those most vulnerable: the women and children. Her bestselling book *Mayada, Daughter of Iraq* was a result of that trip.

After her writing career was launched, with customary zeal Jean set off once again. With just her notes, computer and memories she shut herself in her house in Atlanta, Georgia, and wrote book after book. One of the most successful projects was the *Princess Trilogy*, a series of books about her friend, Princess Sultana al-Sa'ud, and named as one of the most important works written in the past eight hundred years by a woman.

Jean's books have won a number of awards. The Mohammed bin Rashid Al Maktoum Foundation, an organization in Dubai which promotes and recognizes cross-cultural understanding, chose Jean's critically acclaimed *Ester's Child* as a book that best promotes world peace.

With a solid background of first-hand experience and years of travel, research and writing, Jean Sasson has become a Middle Eastern expert. She has made many appearances on national and international television programmes, as well as having been featured in many international newspaper and magazine articles. She has a huge following of readers from countries all over the world, which is confirmed by the number of her readers and her enormous social media following.

Soon Jean will write her memoir of spending so many years living and visiting in the Middle East. This long-awaited book will reveal her many personal and compelling adventures in Saudi Arabia, Lebanon, Kuwait and Iraq.